Latin American Voices

Integrative Psychology and Humanities

Series Editor
Giuseppina Marsico, University of Salerno, Fisciano, Italy

Editorial Board Member
Alicia Barreiro, Universidad de Buenos Aires, Argentina
Antônio Virgílio Bastos, Universidade Federal da Bahia, Brazil
Angela Uchoa Branco, Universidade de Brasília, Brazil
Felix Cova-Solar, Universidad de Concepción, Chile
Maria Virginia Dazzani, Universidade Federal da Bahia, Brazil
Gabriela Di Gesú, Universidad de Buenos Aires, Argentina
Ana Maria Jacó-Vilela, Universidade do Estado do Rio de Janeiro, Brazil
María Noel Lapoujade, Universidad Nacional Autónoma de México, Mexico
Maria Lyra, Universidade Federal de Pernambuco, Brazil
María Elisa Molina-Pavez, Universidad del Desarrollo, Santiago, Chile
Susanne Normann, University of Oslo, Norway
Julio Cesar Ossa, Universidad de San Buenaventura, Cali, Colombia
Gilberto Pérez-Campos, Universidad Nacional Autónoma de México, Mexico
Lilian Patricia Rodríguez-Burgos, Universidad de La Sabana, Bogotá, Colombia
Mónica Roncancio-Moreno, Universidad Pontificia Bolivariana, Colombia
Lívia Mathias Simão, Universidade de São Paulo, Brazil
Luca Tateo, Aalborg University, Denmark
Jaan Valsiner, Aalborg University, Denmark
Floor van Alphen, Universidad Autonoma de Madrid, Spain

In the last decades, Latin America has been a productive and fertile ground for the advancement of theoretical and empirical elaborations within psychology, social and human sciences. Yet, these contributions have had a hard time to be internationally recognized in its original contribution and in its transformative heuristic power. Latin American Voices – Integrative Psychology and Humanities intends to fill this gap by offering an international forum of scholarly interchanges that deal with psychological and socio-cultural processes from a cultural psychological perspective.

The book series seeks to be a solid theoretically-based, though still empirical, arena of interdisciplinary and international debate, as well as a worldwide scientific platform for communicating key ideas of methodology and different theoretical approaches to relevant issues in psychology and humanities. It will publish books from researchers working in Latin America in the different fields of psychology at interplay with other social and human sciences. Proposals dealing with new perspectives, innovative ideas and new topics of interdisciplinary kind are especially welcomed.

Both solicited and unsolicited proposals are considered for publication in this series. All proposals and manuscripts submitted to the Series will undergo at least two rounds of external peer review.

More information about this series at http://www.springer.com/series/16145

Danilo Silva Guimarães

Dialogical Multiplication
Principles for an Indigenous Psychology

 Springer

Danilo Silva Guimarães
Institute of Psychology
University of São Paulo
São Paulo, São Paulo, Brazil

ISSN 2524-5805   ISSN 2524-5813 (electronic)
Latin American Voices
ISBN 978-3-030-26701-8   ISBN 978-3-030-26702-5 (eBook)
https://doi.org/10.1007/978-3-030-26702-5

© Springer Nature Switzerland AG 2020
This work is subject to copyright. All rights are reserved by the Publisher, whether the whole or part of the material is concerned, specifically the rights of translation, reprinting, reuse of illustrations, recitation, broadcasting, reproduction on microfilms or in any other physical way, and transmission or information storage and retrieval, electronic adaptation, computer software, or by similar or dissimilar methodology now known or hereafter developed.
The use of general descriptive names, registered names, trademarks, service marks, etc. in this publication does not imply, even in the absence of a specific statement, that such names are exempt from the relevant protective laws and regulations and therefore free for general use.
The publisher, the authors, and the editors are safe to assume that the advice and information in this book are believed to be true and accurate at the date of publication. Neither the publisher nor the authors or the editors give a warranty, express or implied, with respect to the material contained herein or for any errors or omissions that may have been made. The publisher remains neutral with regard to jurisdictional claims in published maps and institutional affiliations.

This Springer imprint is published by the registered company Springer Nature Switzerland AG
The registered company address is: Gewerbestrasse 11, 6330 Cham, Switzerland

In memory of Dindinha (Joana Ferreira Silva) and her mother, who, even in times of oppression and forced silence, kept alive the seeds of my indigenous ancestral roots.

Preface of the Series Editor

Accessing Otherness: Unity via Multiplicity

While writing this preface, I had the opportunity to share one of the most interesting intellectual experiences I have lately had. I have organized and chaired a panel session called *Anthropophagic Psychology: dialogue between Latin America and Europe,* at the International Conference of Theoretical Psychology 2019 in Denmark. It has been a quite provocative and breakthrough event that left the audience somehow both "disquieted" (Simão 2003) and intrigued.

Danilo Silva Guimarães was one of the panelists. He has discussed the principles of an indigenous psychology in light of the innovative notion of Dialogical Multiplication.

His speech has been a short essay of the complex theoretical and methodological framework he now proposes in *Dialogical multiplication: principles for an indigenous psychology.*

In this volume, Guimarães begins by arguing that the received knowledge, and the current epistemological reflection, has sought strategies to construct a subject able to represent the world apart from any cultural mediation. Then, he moves on to a critical reflection about psychology as a discipline that faces the limits of the modern project, that is constructing an universal epistemic subject while running the risk of producing epistemic injustice (Silva Filho and Tateo 2019).

To become a general science, psychology needs to understand how other indigenous perspectives participate to the process of knowledge construction about the topics approached, instead of imposing cultural values - present in all theories and methodologies - without reflecting about the ethnic-cultural perspective expressed in those theories.

Dialogical multiplication: principles for an indigenous psychology tries to answer the question of how we can overcome the deadlock of hegemonic, colonizing mainstream as opposed to a self-marginalizing "counter-culture".

The theoretical innovation proposed by Guimarães is that of building a conceptual account of unity via multiplicity - from the perspective of cultural psychology -

where the inclusive separation (Valsiner,1987) of the Self and the Other is the starting point, .

According to the author:

> *Considering that the purpose of cultural psychology is to produce general psychological theory on the cultural mediation of the relations between self, others and the world I argue that, to achieve this, cultural psychology needs to understand how indigenous perspectives participate in the process of knowledge construction, transforming psychological concepts and practices. This would prevent psychologists from imposing cultural values embedded in their theories and methodologies. Whether the psychologist is involved in research or practice in an interethnic field, they must consider their ethnic-cultural belonging and the consequences of their approach to other people* (Guimarães, this volume, p.7).

The analysis of the ethnopsychological perspective represents a continuation of the book *Ethnopsychology: pieces from the Mexican research gallery* by Rolando Diaz-Loving (2019), which inaugurated the new Springer Book Series *Latin American Voices – Integrative Psychology and Humanities*.

These first two volumes nicely address, in fact, one of the hot topics in contemporary psychology. These "voices of Latin America" illuminate the core issue of the cultural interchanges and knowledge production in the globalized world (Schliewe et al. 2018).

We may agree with Valsiner (forthcoming) who claims that:

> *[...] all psychology is indigenous. This means that all psychology as it has emerged as science is embedded in its historical societal context—emerging in Europe at the end of the 16th century, slowly finding its way to the elaborated interest in it in 18th century Europe, and became turned into a "science" in the 20th century. In parallel to the usual focus in the social sciences to what happened in Europe, there were developments in China and India that served the basis for what by our time is labeled "indigenous" versions of psychology* (Valsiner, forthcoming, p.X).

Guimarães' principle of dialogical multiplication brings before the reader the questions of the I-Other relations (Simão 2012) and the perspective epistemology.

Dialogical multiplication: principles for an indigenous psychology greatly contributes to these challenging issues with a theoretical proposal in which taking a particular perspective is understood as form of knowledge building. This contribution helps moving perspectivism from the position of an epistemological stance (Bruner 1996) to that of an empirical investigation about knowledge construction. So that perspectivism becomes both a philosophical credo, that enables a specific type of scientific research, and an empirical psychology that focuses on the negotiation of points of view.

Aalborg, Denmark Giuseppina Marsico
August 2019

References

Bruner, J.S. (1996). Frames for thinking: ways of making meaning. In: D.-R. Olson, & N. Torrance (Eds.), *Modes of thought: Exploration in culture and cognition* (pp. 93–105). New York: Cambridge University Press.

Diaz-Loving, R. (2019). *Ethnopsychology: pieces from the Mexican research gallery*, São Paulo: Latin American Voices, 1.

Schliewe, S., Chaudhary N. & Marsico, G., (Eds). (2018). *Cultural Psychology of Intervention in the Globalized World.* Charlotte: Information Age Publishing.

Silva Filho, W. & Tateo, L. (2019). *Thinking about Oneself: The Place of Reflection in Philosophy and Psychology.* New York: Springer.

Simão, L. M. (2003). Beside Rupture – Disquiet; Beyond the Other – Alterity. *Culture & Psychology, 9(4)*, 449–459.

Simão, L. M. (2012). The Other in the Self: A triadic unit. In: Valsiner J. (Ed.). *The Oxford handbook of culture and psychology* (pp. 403–420). New York: Oxford University Press.

Valsiner, J. (1987). *Culture and the development of children's action.* Wiley: Chichester.

Valsiner., J. (forthcoming). Culture & Psychology: 25 years of building a new science. *Culture & Psychology.*

Author's Preface

This work is the result of epistemological and ethical reflections concerning the interface between psychology and indigenous peoples. The present considerations stem from the work performed by psychologists with people from culturally diverse communities, who must deal with the said consequences. A cultural shock is produced when different cultural traditions meet, bringing along certain consequences. Cultural shock is a type of disquieting experience that may result from the psychologist's immersion in a foreign *ethos*. The *ethos* is a means of shaping people's perception and representation of themselves and their worlds, including socially shared as well as secretive experiences. Therefore, people that share a common *ethos* form an ethnic group. Psychology emerged as a modern science during the Renaissance, founded on values and principles from ancient Greek and Latin philosophy and from Jewish and Christian traditions identified, for instance, in the humanist philosophies. The cultural melting pot that constituted the *ethos* of the emerging modern European societies was also confronted with real and imaginary images of other peoples from recently explored lands worldwide. Modern epistemology proposed a novel conceptual entity, a "subject/object" immune to cultural "contaminants." It was an attempt to represent the world free from cultural mediation, which required rejecting traditional knowledge, but adopting certain mythological and religious assumptions. Psychology, as a discipline, faces the limits of the epistemic subject inherited from the modern project; the indigenous psychologies face the same limits even more dramatically. Considering that the purpose of cultural psychology is to produce general psychological theory on the cultural mediation of the relations between self, others, and the world, I argue that, to achieve this, cultural psychology needs to understand how indigenous perspectives participate in the process of knowledge construction, transforming psychological concepts and practices. This would prevent psychologists from imposing cultural values embedded in their theories and methodologies. Whether the psychologist is involved in research or practice in an interethnic field, they must consider their ethnic-cultural belonging and the consequences of their approach to other people.

The first part of this book is based on the experience of the Amerindian Support Network (Institute of Psychology, USP, Brazil), a service that provides psychological care for indigenous communities. The discussion focuses on the theoretical-practical implications of the notion of dialogical multiplication, given that our work in the Amerindian Network is coauthored by indigenous peoples. This discussion goes beyond the historical-philosophical debate over the constitution of the psychological space, centered in the tension between the epistemic subject and the empirical subject and in the relation between the public and private spheres. To do so, we proceed by (1) including cultural traditions foreign to the field of modern psychology, (2) re-signifying the notion of self as a territory for the cultivation of the person by the culture, and (3) establishing ritual participation as a means of controlling *equivocation* in the *transduction* of the meanings that emerge in the interethnic relation, notions that will be approached in detail in the book.

These ethnopsychological considerations emerged to the work my research group since 2008, stimulating a cross-disciplinary talk between a semiotic-cultural constructivist psychology and the anthropological theory of Amerindian perspectivism. The semiotic-cultural constructivism in psychology is a meta-theoretical perspective that addresses meaning construction and the role of human cultural experience in knowledge construction. Science and the arts, as other spheres of human symbolic action, are framed as specific ways of creating meaning from personal and culturally meaningful experiences. Amerindian perspectivism, in anthropology, addresses how the American Indians perceive the world and relate with it. The data used in these investigations was based on the native discourse, the conceptions of selected informants who were considered community leaders, specialists in different branches of native knowledge. Sociohistorical psychology and hermeneutics had a central role in the anthropological choices of ethnological strategies and informed our views.

The second part of the book includes contributions of an invited cultural psychologist from Denmark (Professor Mogens Jensen, University of Aalborg) and indigenous psychologists from New Zealand (Professors Shiloh Groot, Linda Waimarie Nikora, and Kara Areta Beckford, the University of Auckland, and Professors Pita King and Darrin Hodgetts, Massey University). They discuss some of the reflections addressed in the first part, relating them to their own academic projects.

São Paulo, Brazil   Danilo Silva Guimarães

Acknowledgments

I would like to thank the following people, without whom, this book would not have been possible:

Professor Lívia Mathias Simão, for her presence throughout my academic trajectory, supervising my initial research and remaining an important interlocutor, supporting my activities as a professor.

Professor Jaan Valsiner, for his trust, joy, support, and generosity in sharing ideas and projects, for enabling conversation between researchers, and for contributing to the dissemination of knowledge worldwide.

My graduate students, Djalma, Suara, Marcel, Kleber, Eloisa, Hercules, Sirlene, Douglas, Flaviana, and Daniel, for collaborating, from the standpoint of their particular research interests, in the development of important reflections for this book.

My undergraduate students, who participated in the different stages of the activities that resulted in this book, both in research and community service projects.

The employees at the Institute of Psychology of USP, for their care and support to our activities in the university, including lectures, research, and community services.

The partners in the indigenous movement, who sustain an important care network in historically marginalized communities in Brazil.

The *Xeramõi* and *Xejaryi kuery*, Laurindo, Sebastião, José Fernandes, and Virgínia, for defending, protecting, and strengthening their communities and for welcoming me in moments of great difficulty.

The *xeirun kuery* I made in the indigenous communities, Roberto, Priscila, Geremias, Patricia, Sonia, Anderson, Jurandir, David, Frank, Marcão, Ceará, Silvio, Elisa, Miqueias, Julio, Lucia, Neusa, Vladimir, Jefferson, Mariano, Gilson, Dida, Alisio, William, Edinaldo, and Emerson, among others.

My family, especially my parents, Vitor and Eliene.

Our ancestors.

Nhanderu Ete Nhandesy Ete, aguyjevete.

This work is supported by FAPESP (grant number 18/13145-0).

Contents

1	**Introduction**...	1
	An Interdisciplinary Border Between Cultural Psychology and Americanist Anthropology	7
	References...	10
2	**First Principle: Alterity, Ethics and Differentiation**	13
	Psychological Issues at the Border Between Indigenous Peoples and Colonizers..	15
	Alterity and Ethical Issues Involving Indigenous Concepts of Psychological Interest	20
	Guided Trajectories of Differentiation and Dedifferentiation.........	26
	Concrete and Conceptual Resistance	29
	A Process of Differentiation and Dedifferentiation in Education....	30
	Travelling in an Interethnic Arena	36
	References...	42
3	**Second Principle: Dedifferentiation, Personal Interaction and Sharing**...	47
	Misunderstandings as Signs of Disjunction in Perspectives..........	52
	Distinct Concepts of Nature	54
	Recursive Temporality	58
	Intercultural Parallelism	60
	Limited Perceptions and Imagination...........................	62
	Mutual Affective Transformations	66
	References...	68
4	**Third Principle: Dynamics of Involvement and Self-Transformation**	71
	Affective Body: A Territory for Self Cultivation	73
	Tuning Bodies..	79
	Resembling the Other	85
	Talking About Affective Experiences	88

	Steps of Tuning in the Interethnic Relation	93
	The Experience of Undergraduate Students in the Amerindian Support Network	98
	References	101
5	**Fourth Principle: Towards a General Psychology**	105
	Psychology is a Self-Contradictory Field	108
	The Researcher's Tradition and its Limits for Knowledge Construction	112
	The Multiplicity of Selves in Contexts of Varying Social Complexity	115
	Multiplying Psychologies and the Conditions for an Unstable Dialogue	123
	References	126
6	**The Infinite Process of Dialogical Multiplication: Considerations for Psychological Research and Professional Practice**	129
	References	132

Commentary 1: Developing Psychology From the Diversity of Living Conditions ... 135

Commentary 2: Pōwhiri: Rituals of Encounter, Recognition and Engagement: A Commentary on 'Dialogical Multiplication: Principles for an Indigenous Psychogy' ... 151

Index ... 161

Chapter 1
Introduction

In November 2017, we invited *Mbya Guarani Xeramõi'i*[1]Timóteo da Silva Verá Tupã Popygua to a conference in the House of Indigenous Cultures,[2] at the Institute of Psychology of the University of São Paulo. His lecture took place in the context of the project "Contemporary indigenous topics in intercultural meetings", which included the exhibition of indigenous documentaries and aimed to stimulate debate in the House. Timóteo had just published a book on Guarani narratives of the creation of the world (Tupã Popygua 2017a) and we were interested in understanding his worldview and ideas concerning the Guarani notion of *Yvyrupa*.[3] We recorded his speech, which started with a song in the Guarani language and proceeded in Portuguese:

> I would like to first thank this group, because there is a dichotomy between knowledge and wisdom. Wisdom has many colors, and when these colors collide, a great universe is formed. Our knowledge, the Guarani knowledge, is largely based on the *Yvyrupa* of the earth. It is about nature, because *Nhanderu*, God, created the earth and gave this knowledge to the Guarani people, and why? So that this knowledge could be passed from generation to generation, and in this universe of knowledge the most important thing we have is love... because love, it is... it is structural, beyond knowledge... and this we learn from our

---

[1] *Xeramõi'i* is the term used by the *Mbya Guarani* to designate their male elders and shamans. The *Mbya Guarani*, live across a large territory that includes the south coast of Brazil, the Atlantic forest, the Brazilian countryside and other countries, such as Argentina, Paraguay and Bolivia.

[2] The House of Indigenous Cultures is a traditional *Mbya Guarani Opy*, built by a group of *Mbya* Indians in the Institute of Psychology (University of São Paulo, Brazil), as the result of a collaboration between our academic service, the Amerindian Support Network, and the *Jaraguá* community. The *Opy* is a typical house for community meetings, where activities range from informal talks to ceremonies. In the later, they dance, sing and have the *Japyxakaa*, the ceremonial speeches that inform relevant community decisions.

[3] *Yvyrupa* is an utterance in the Guarani language used to designate the structure that sustains the terrestrial world. Its meaning is related to the way Guarani people freely occupied the territory prior to the arrival of the white people, before municipal, state and federal borders were created, leading to the present segregation of their people in islands of indigenous territories (source: http://www.yvyrupa.org.br, accessed in 2017).

© Springer Nature Switzerland AG 2020
D. S. Guimarães, *Dialogical Multiplication*, Latin American Voices,
https://doi.org/10.1007/978-3-030-26702-5_1

Xeramõi and our *Xejary'i*, who pass it on to us. My grandfather, who was called Chico, he passed away in 2009, at 130, and when I was about 6, I'm not sure, he told us this story, this narrative, about this knowledge… as time passed and I grew up, children are very… a child is just a child, and the elders told us these stories, this narrative, about this knowledge… hearing this as a child… at the time I didn't care at all… but as I grow older, I realize the world is, in fact, as my grandfather would tell me, in the *Yvyrupa* world. I learned to master this perception and I learned Portuguese, listening to people speaking, here and there…so I learned… I reached the conclusion that the language the *Xeramõi*, my grandfather, spoke, the human language, is founded on the human word; and I turned my attention to this, that when he spoke about this language and also about the spirit, the spirit is called *Nhe'e*. My grandfather said that the world, this knowledge, is like a necklace… and the necklace is formed by placing each little bead…and making a necklace tying both ends together (he gesticulates closing the necklace). Then it becomes a necklace you can wear. Our knowledge is also like this, when we are born, we learn little by little so we can make this necklace, each one of us with our own knowledge. I would like to talk a little about our struggle, and then I would like to talk a little about the book and about how I gained knowledge about the culture, because knowledge… there is a limit to human knowledge, if we think about the academic world, and the Guarani knowledge, there is much ignorance, so this is why there is a dichotomy in knowledge. (Tupã Popygua 2017b)

This lecture's excerpt summarizes what I intend to present in this book as a set of principles for an Indigenous psychology. It is a reflection about the ethnic-cultural nature of knowledge, the possibilities and limits of dialogue between distinct forms of knowledge. It proposes the existence of a dichotomy in knowledge, a basic ignorance or unfamiliarity between distinct ethnic-culturally situated forms of knowledge and a human impossibility to know everything, to access all points of views. Timóteo argues that knowledge is gradually acquired and constructed in the course of life. Like handcrafting a necklace, creating knowledge depends on the person's active role of joining the pieces in an aesthetically organized way. Knowledge is furthermore supposed to be useful, not just a pure representation intended for contemplation; it affects the world we live in. There is something beyond knowledge that structures it, an affection that moves us in its direction. The *Xeramõi* called it love. Love emerges from the transgenerational care between people in a community, enabling the construction of intimacy in a shared language through which the spiritual-subjective life is evinced.

After meeting Guarani people and their communities, and in the position of psychologist and professor at the University, I proposed, in 2012, the Amerindian Support Network as an academic project. The Amerindian Network works in collaboration with community leaders. Since its beginning, our activities consisted in organizing a series of meetings with people from indigenous communities, aiming to identify psychosocial vulnerabilities to find possible strategies to overcome some of the negative impacts of the colonial and post-colonial societies. The students under my supervision and I make regular visits to the communities, in which we participate in and collaborate with ongoing community projects based on self-ethnic affirmation.

The meaning of ethnic self-affirmation I discuss here is expressed in the following excerpt is from the Manaus Letter for an integrated indigenous healthcare ("*Carta de Manaus, por uma saúde integral aos povos indígenas*"), which was written during the Fourth Brazilian Congress of Mental Health (Manaus, September 4–7, 2014) and signed by more than a hundred professionals, indigenous peoples, and associations:

> We note that the psychosocial vulnerabilities affecting the Amerindian peoples are largely due to their marginalization, to the conflicts involved in the struggle for land, their state of invisibility, the prejudices they must face and the lack of recognition of the Amerindian identities in the contemporaneous world. There is no future for the Amerindian peoples if they cannot maintain their habits and sustainable practices in their territories. These habits and practices should be the guidelines for the full exercise of the peoples' capacity to manage educational processes, promote healthcare and nourishment, organize their economy, create knowledge and make their own choices according to their intentions for the future generations.
>
> Having consulted the Amerindian peoples here present, we emphasize the need to enforce the laws about the respect to the Amerindian cultural diversity, since the reality is far from this. (ABRASME 2014, s. p.)

Therefore, ethnic self-affirmation is the struggle to overcome prejudices and affirm Amerindian identities in real-life situations, opening perspectives for future generations to exist and resist as indigenous peoples.

Beginning its activities as a university extension project,[4] the Network was formally recognized as a community service headquartered at the Institute of Psychology of the University of São Paulo (IPUSP). Gradually, Amerindian communities in regions near the city of São Paulo and in the State coast started to request our partnership in different projects. We became involved in these new projects and invited them to interact with the academic community at the University, promoting forums to discuss topics of their interest. At this stage, however, we noticed repeated complaints about the inadequacy of the buildings and auditoriums of the University for conveying the indigenous messages. This encouraged us to consider the possibility of a more adequate setting for this interethnic dialogue. Together with indigenous leaders, we developed the project for a House of Indigenous Cultures in the campus of the University of São Paulo, at the Institute of Psychology.

After we obtained all the necessary approvals at the institutional level of the University, a group of Guarani people from the *Jaraguá* Indigenous Land, located in the northwest region of the city of São Paulo, came to build the house. The House of Amerindian Cultures is relevant to the interethnic dialogical collaboration, since it is the first time the indigenous community in Brazil introduces a permanent traditional house inside a University campus to promote a more equitable dialogue with the academic community. Instead of promoting the usual academic aim to describe and explain the other, the indigenous people are co-managers of the cultural activities planned in this setting, such as cultural events, expositions, conversations, and so on. By visiting the communities and meeting the leaders at the university, we guide our activities in co-authorship with indigenous peoples.

---

[4] According to the University of São Paulo's regulations, university extention is the process that articulates higher education and research to enable a transformative interaction between the university and society.

Our team adopts a feed-forward approach, in which the experience provides the opportunity to develop new conceptual explorations that help us overcome the obstacles that come up in our work. This process depends on the cultivation of trust between psychologists, students, and communities. Then, knowledge is constructed through an unconventional methodology in psychology. It includes being together with people in the indigenous communities without research concerns. Besides studying anthropological and ethnographic material, employing abstract philosophical ideas, theoretical and methodological propositions from psychology, it also involves, furthermore, reflecting on the fundamental references for the psychological work with the communities. Back to the speech of the *Xeramoi*, we are putting together the pieces of knowledge from different traditions to build a useful necklace that attends to our needs in the concrete work with the communities.

In this path, we needed to adopt general principles beyond scientific knowledge and method. They concern our commitment to respecting the diversity of interpretations about human existence and the search for a way to promote a conversation with such diversity. Thus, we prioritize theoretical and methodological references that help promote the human potentials for creativity, for multiplying the possibilities of understanding and for talking about ourselves.

Science and the arts, as other spheres of human symbolic action, are cultural constructs stemming from meaningful personal and social experiences. I assume culture as a fundamental dimension of human experience. It offers symbolic resources for thinking about personal actions and aspirations, thus creating points of view, i.e., relatively singular ways of being and of acting, either reflectively or not. The points of view that evolve from different cultural traditions establish the horizons that define limits for people to inhabit and reflect about the world. Furthermore, the conceptions that emerge from each culturally grounded point of view are not easily interchangeable, given that they belong to diversely built language systems, where each term is "culture-laden".

The ideas discussed in this book pertain to the line of emerging indigenous psychologies. They problematize the adequacy of philosophical concepts and scientific categories inherited from the colonizer's culture, which dominate the field of psychology, to understand meaningful personal and social experiences lived in distinct cultural traditions. The *ethos* of each cultural tradition is the basis for the different indigenous psychologies. I sustain it is possible to avoid an interminable epistemological confrontation and irrational relativism in the field of psychology by including the notion of ethics in our debate. Ethics is a polyssemic term, derived from the Greek *ethos*. We may employ this notion to address the possibilities of coexistence and dialogue among people from different cultural traditions. In a world where each person is partially informed about others, ethics enables us to approach the issue of alterity, the incommensurability of the others and our responsibility in relation to their existence. When faced with alterity, part of the psychologists employs epistemological approaches and conceptual devices to better define the world and dispute it in relation to other concepts and practices based on distinct traditions (epistemological, cultural, indigenous, etc.). Despite this tendency, psychologists can choose

1 Introduction

to respect the diversity of interpretations about human existence and find ways to dialogue with it.

The indigenous qualifier indicates a category that emerges in a tensional border formed also by the colonialist. It lacks a fixed and essential content; it is, rather, a relational category. Belonging to it involves resisting the foreigner's attempt of hegemonic control and proliferating consistent divergence, alternative habits and sustainable practices anchored in native traditions. I am considering tradition in the Gadamerian sense, connected to the notion of *Bildung*, the process of self-transformation through involvement with the strangeness of the other (cf. Gadamer 1960/2008; Simão 2010).

In the field of the semiotic-cultural constructivism in psychology, Simão (2005, 2010) approaches the notion of *Bildung* from the point of view of Gadamer's philosophical hermeneutics (1960/2008). Simão emphasizes its complexity as a process of construction and transformation of the person. "*Bildung* is to *form one*self *and become*, by means of a hermeneutic relation with a given content" (Simão 2010, p. 2017). This goes beyond acquiring precise information about something; it implies the person's transformation through their involvement with the communicative experience with the world and the other. To be personally involved, one must allow the strangeness of the experience of communicating with others in the world to affect one's own prejudices and preconceptions (cf. Simão 2010).

Knowledge construction operates with the contents of personal experience, since it originates from the experience of real persons living in the world. Understanding personal experience, however, depends on establishing the links between all the new contents that emerge and their processual roots, i.e. the macro, meso, and micro genesis of sense and meaning construction.

I differentiate knowing the content from understanding the process with the words of Yanomami shaman Davi Kopenawa, who distinguishes knowledge and wisdom:

> White folks are crafty, they have many machines and lots of commodities, but they have no wisdom. They no longer think of their ancestors, of what they were when they were created. In the beginning, they were like us, but they forgot all their old words. Later, they crossed the water and came in our direction. Now, they keep saying they discovered this land. I only understood this when I learned their language (Kopenawa 1998, p. 21).

From Kopenawa's sayings (1998), I understand that the white people's characteristic craftiness comes from their technical-scientific knowledge. It enables them to, among other things, use machines to explore and extract natural resources from the Yanomami lands to produce their commercial goods. Kopenawa (1998) contrasts an affective-cognitive disposition that wreaks havoc in a world shared by many cultures with the notion of wisdom. The later involves ancestrality as a determinant aspect behind a person's actions and decision-making. By drawing attention to the importance of ancestrality for understanding past and present situations, the indigenous psychology focuses on the process – the origin and course of events – rather than only on the results of human interventions in a given context.

Besides that, "the Amerindian *Bildung* happens to the body more than in the spirit: there is no spiritual change which is not bodily transformation, a redefinition of its affects and capacities" (Viveiros de Castro 2002/2006, p. 390). To understand the other's perspective and intentionality, one must understand how the affective body is formed and achieves an aesthetically organized shape.

Cultivating the body as a *cluster of affections and capabilities* (cf. Viveiros de Castro 1998) enables the construction of socially shared realities. Guimarães and Simão (2017), considering the Amerindian perspectivism, argue that creating differences and similarities between the bodies provides the means for a mutual adjustment in perspectives. Producing and maintaining similar bodies enables establishing correlations between points of view. Along individual life courses, the task of affective organization involves careful attention to the relation between beings and substances that may transform the body. Furthermore, wisdom is transmitted in an objective manner through bodily transformations. It requires the ability to identify and manage the transformative power of relations, given the susceptibility of the sensitive bodies. Wisdom is thus related to the ability of "seeing each *event* as being in reality an *action*, an expression of internal states or intentional predicates of some agent" (Viveiros de Castro 2002/2006, p. 488).

Viveiros de Castro (2002/2006) proposes a distinction between the idea of knowledge in the indigenous world and in modern science. While for modern science explaining implies reducing the intentionality of what is known, to the Amerindian, it implies the exact opposite, "that is, defining the object of knowledge as subject of knowing" (Viveiros de Castro 2002/2006, p. 488). Each of these models for knowledge construction, which mark basic cultural choices, has its gains and losses. They each promote advances and impose limitations in different directions. Later on in this book, we will see that in the field of dialogical epistemology a path similar to the indigenous one is taken, since the phenomena in question cannot be perceived or studied as a passive object.

Subjectivizing or objectivizing is a central issue in the construction of psychology as a field of knowledge. The point of greatest tension lies in the opposition between objectivist materialism and spiritualist subjectivism. This opposition contributes to the dispersion of the field of psychology and hinders the efforts to unify it (cf. Vygotski 1927/1991). The following pages will also present a discussion on how the indigenous psychologies coming into being included in the scientific field can amplify the dispersion in the field of psychology, which is already characterized by inconclusive efforts of unification. As distinct psychologies dispute the prerogative to unify the field under a single epistemological perspective related to their particular theories and method, they usually assume a colonialist posture. In their attempt to enhance the likeness between distinct cultural systems, they reduce the other to supposedly translatable categories, creating patterns and homogenizing knowledge. I propose diversely to focus on what happens in the interethnic, intercultural communicative borders: the processes of I-other differentiation and dedifferentiation, the tensions in the paths of creating knowledge and wisdom while coexisting with others.

Linked to our work with the Indigenous communities, our debates guide us in a continued review of the notion of dialogical multiplication. This notion was first proposed in 2008 (Guimarães and Simão 2008), aiming to organize a set of propositions in the field of the semiotic-cultural constructivism in psychology (cf. Simão 2010). To reach this notion, we mobilized ideas from the philosophy of language of Bakhtin and the philosophy of alterity of Lévinas. I used the preliminary organization of this reflection to compare and evaluate the possibility of articulations with Amerindian perspectivism in anthropology (Viveiros de Castro 1996, 2006; Lima 1996). The resulting theoretical construct has been the basis for our approach to the indigenous communities and to the constitution of the Amerindian Support Network since 2012. The community work, in turn, guided a continued debate that improved the notion of dialogical multiplication, adding unpredicted nuances and complexities to it.

In sum, when I refer to an indigenous psychology, I refer to one that addresses the multiplication of our dialogical potential. This indigenous psychology aims to promote increasing diversity in social life and expand the possibilities of human experience, while committing to the ethical implications of cultural innovations. It does not advocate a normative perspective, with rules or penalties for violations. Rather, it is aware that each choice in the psychological field has consequences to our ways of life, particularly to our coexistence with others' points of view, which we may either acknowledge or attempt to silence. Therefore, our purpose is to understand how to elaborate theoretical and methodological tools to make ethically based decisions together with the others in the psychological field.

I am sure that many of the ideas discussed in this book are still preliminary, the first steps in a long path with infinite possibilities.

An Interdisciplinary Border Between Cultural Psychology and Americanist Anthropology

Working together with indigenous persons, trying to construct mutual understandings and develop projects to engage psychologists, students from the university, and *Mbya Guarani* is a challenging task that requires careful thought at the epistemological, ontological, and ethical levels of the science of psychology.

The notion of dialogical multiplication is a theoretical result of an effort to articulate two research traditions, psychology and anthropology. Both are concerned with the dialogue between perspectives, which involves cultural differences, alterity, and the unknown aspects of the other in a relation (cf. Guimarães 2011, 2016). The semiotic-cultural constructivism in psychology is a meta-theoretical perspective that understands science "as one particular kind among other cultural constructions in the human search for meaningful I-Other-World relationships" (Simão 2015b, p. xi). According to this framework, knowledge construction is a specific type of symbolic action that transforms people and knowledge in human exchanges over time. This tradition has been systematized in the works of Brazilian psychologist Lívia Mathias Simão (2005, 2010, 2015a), who based her ideas on Boesch, Valsiner and Marková. Semiotic-cultural constructivism also articulates contributions from Lewin, Vygotsky, James and Baldwin, in the field of psychology, with Gadamerian hermeneutics, Bakhtinian dialogism, and the phenomenology of Bergson, Merleau-Ponty and Lévinas.

Dialogical multiplication is, then, a theoretical system in the field of semiotic-cultural constructivism that focuses on alterity relationships, showing the diversification of objects referred in the dialogical situation, whose meanings are never completely translated between the different cultural traditions (cf. Guimarães 2011, 2013, and 2016). Moreover, the notion of dialogical multiplication belongs to the territory of ecological epistemologies.

The second research tradition focused here, Amerindian perspectivism, was developed by the Brazilian anthropologist Eduardo Viveiros de Castro (1996, 2004, 2006) and has had a substantial impact on general anthropology over the last three decades. This tradition refers to how the American Indians construct the world and relate to it. The identities of the persons brought into relation are deeply determined by the alterities to which they relate, as each person is positioned in a vast network that articulates all beings and assemblages of multiple natures and only allow the subject to know one's own identity when contrasted to the alter with which it relates (cf. Nigro and Guimarães 2016).

While articulating these two research traditions, I focused on the issue of the dialogue between perspectives, in which cultural differences, alterities and the unknown aspects of the other in a relation are dimensions that lead to the emergence of disquieting experiences. Disquieting experiences are "amorphous zones of meaning and ambiguous situations [...] that touch the person affectively and pre-reflexively" (Simão 2016, p. 20). These experiences create an instability that moves the person to reflect and create solutions in order to diminish the precipitated tension. Reflecting on the issue of perspectives in semiotic-cultural constructivism and perspectives in Amerindian perspectivism may be said to constitute a disquieting experience to those who are supposed to build scientific knowledge based on a naturalistic worldview, because

> [...] the intersubjective asymmetry [...] if observed at the contact between an indigenous and non-indigenous, is radical: while we distinguish one nature of many cultures, for the indigenous there is a cultural form that varies little, a type of relationship with multiple natures or supernatures (Nigro and Guimarães 2016, p. 252).

The notion of dialogical multiplication emerged as a possibility to understand the borders between psychology and anthropology, thereby unfolding a path for exchanges between them. These disciplines are concerned with issues that originated in phenomenology and hermeneutics and, more broadly, socio-historical psychology. Nevertheless, articulating the notion of perspective in semiotic-cultural constructivism and Amerindian perspectivism is challenging, due in part to a deeply rooted dichotomy between materialism and idealism in the field of behavioral sciences. The phenomenological sociology of Berger and Luckmann (1966/1991) provides the epistemological support to discuss this dichotomy in terms of the social construction of subjective and objective realities. The debate surrounding ecological epistemology, in the field of anthropology, resonates with this particular sociology. Steil and Carvalho (2014) have discussed this convergence, problematizing the social-constructivist approaches. These anthropologists define ecological epistemologies as:

> [...] a territory of the theoretical-philosophical contemporary debate that includes authors from different disciplinary origins and theoretical choices, who share the effort to overcome modern dualities such as nature and culture, subject and society, body and mind, inventiveness and nature, subject and object (Steil and Carvalho 2014, p. 164).

The "radical program of "social constructivism" has never completely left behind "residual" notions such as objectivity, body and substance" (Steil and Carvalho 2014, p. 165). The proponents of the ecological epistemologies attempt to overcome these categories through "a reformulation of historical materialism, highlighting blind spots that, although present in the analyzes, were ignored due to the ascribed immateriality of thought in the modern Western tradition" (p. 165). Ecological epistemology in cultural psychology guides my understanding that culture is neither identification with sociohistorical origins, nor the proliferation of new products (artifacts, knowledge, and so on). Culture is experienced as an embodied, dynamic and meaningful memory, passed on through narratives of personal trajectories. Such memories are impregnated in the *ethos*, in the rites and myths of communities, cultural and ethnic groups, who dwell in the land in meaningful manners. The way in which the land is organized guide human action and memories; they become settings for remembering.

The term ethnicity (from Greek *ethnikos*) was originally used to refer to foreigners, heathen peoples, expressing an opposition between 'us' and 'the others'. The notion of disquieting experience employed in this work leads us to a different approach in the field of ethnicity, bringing our attention to the cultural shock in the encounter between different cultural traditions, considering that an ethnic people share a common *ethos*. Being regularly present in the communities and open to the other's culture can lead the psychologist, for instance, to learn the other's sings. This type of availability improves the psychologist's understanding and awareness of their own culture and language (cf. Wagner 1981/2010). The cultural shock that results from the psychologist's immersion in a foreign *ethos* promotes disquieting experiences. The etymology of the word ethics goes back to the Greek *ethos*, used to designate human ways of being and relating. It is currently discussed as a means of shaping people's perception and representation of themselves and their worlds, including socially shared as well as secretive experiences. (cf. Figueiredo 1996/2013).

Psychology derives from the *ethos* of a specific tradition. It is relevant to take into account that ethnocentrism is a basic characteristic of every society in the world (cf. Lévi-Strauss 1952, 1965/1984; Viveiros de Castro 2002/2006). Therefore, terms, conceptions and practices developed in the psychological tradition present limitations to its aimed universality as a science. From an indigenous perspective, we ask ourselves if it is possible to integrate the cultural diversity in a general theorizing effort that is effectively open and inclusive.

Dialogical multiplication concerns the multiple possibilities of symbolically elaborating experience, provided by the different cultural fields (cf. Guimarães 2016, 2018). Different cultures guide human action and thought by means of embodied affective exchanges, some of them elaborated into verbal and/or other meaningful signs (cf. Guimarães and Cravo 2015). Cultural mediation through embodied exchanges and through other semiotic devices, such as narratives, is present in all human life. These verbal and non-verbal resources interact with each other.

From these considerations, a primarily ethical issue emerges, with epistemological implications. The cultural melting pot that constituted the complex *ethos* of modern European societies is confronted with real and imaginary images of other peoples in the explored lands worldwide. Therefore, it is not possible to define psychology as pertaining to a specific ethnic group. As a tool for human reflexivity, psychology emerged in the context of intense and conflictive interethnic relationships. Its reflexivity expanded with the interethnic and intercultural experiences reported by travelers (cf. Jahoda 1982); different cultural traditions participated in the upbringing of the newborn psychological science of the nineteenth century. However, the participation of these other cultural traditions was and still is subjected to asymmetries in which hegemonic notions continue to silence emerging voices.

Acknowledgement This work is supported by FAPESP (grant number 18/13145-0).

References

ABRASME [Associação Brasileira de Saúde Mental] (2014) Carta de Manaus por uma saúde integral aos povos indígenas. *4° Congresso Brasileiro de Sáude Mental*. Retrieved June 15, 2019, from http://www.congresso2014.abrasme.org.br/informativo/view?ID_INFORMATIVO=127&impressao.

Berger, P. B., & Luckmann, T. (1991). *The social construction of reality: A treatise in the sociology of knowledge*. London: Penguin books. (Original text published in 1966).

Figueiredo, L. C. M. (2013). *Revisitando as psicologias: da epistemologia à ética das práticas e discursos psicológicos* (p. 183). Petrópolis: Vozes. (Trabalho original publicado em 1996).

Gadamer, H-G. (Meurer trad). (2008). *Verdade e Método I: Traços fundamentais de uma hermenêutica filosófica*. São Paulo: Vozes. (Trabalho original publicado em 1960).

Guimarães, D. S. (2011). Amerindian anthropology and cultural psychology: Crossing boundaries and meeting Otherness' worlds. *Culture & Psychology, 12*(2), 139–157.

Guimarães, D. S. (2013). Self and dialogical multiplication. *Interacções, 9*, 214–242.

Guimarães, D. S. (2016). *Amerindian paths: Guiding dialogues with psychology* (p. 366). Charlotte: Information Age Publishing.

Guimarães, D. S. (2018) Affectivation: A cut across the semiotic hierarchy of feelings. In: Cornejo, C.; Marsico, G. & Valsiner, J. (Orgs.). *I Activate You To Affect Me I* (pp. 203–223). Charlotte: Information Age Publishing.

Guimarães and Simão (2008) The notion of perspective in the semiotic-cultural constructivism and the Amerindian perspectivism. Paper presented at *The Fifth International Conference on the Dialogical Self*, Cambridge, UK.

References

Guimarães, D. S. & Cravo, A. M. (2015). Understanding others without a word: Articulating the shared circuits model with semiotic-cultural constructivist psychology. In: Beckstead, Z. (org.). *Cultural psychology of recursive processes* (pp. 143–160). Charlotte: IAP – Information Age Publishing.

Guimarães, D. S. & Simão, L. M. (2017) Mythological constrains to the construction of subjectified bodies. In: Han, M. (org.) *The Subjectified and Subjectifying Mind* (pp. 3–21). Charlotte: Information Age Publication.

Jahoda, G. (1982). *Psychology and anthropology: A psychological perspective* (p. 270). New York: Academic Press Inc..

Kopenawa, D. (1998). Descobrindo os brancos. In Ricardo, C. A. (Ed.) (2000). *Povos indígenas no Brasil: 1996/2000* (pp. 20–23). São Paulo: Instituto Socioambiental.

Lévi-Strauss, C. (1952). *Race and history*. Paris: UNESCO.

Lévi-Strauss, C. (1965/1984) *Tristes tropiques*. Paris: Plon.

Lima, T. S. (1996). O dois e seu múltiplo: reflexões sobre o perspectivismo em uma cosmologia Tupi. *Mana, 2*(2), 21–47.

Nigro, K. F. & Guimarães, D. S. (2016) Obscuring cannibalism in civilization: Amerindian psychology in Reading Today's sociocultural phenomena. In: Valsiner, J.; Marsico, G.; Chaudhary, N.; Sato, T.; Dazzani, V. (Orgs.). *Psychology as the Science of Human Being*. The Yokohama manifesto (pp. 245–263). Basel: Springer International Publishing.

Simão, L. M. (2005). Bildung, culture and self; a possible dialogue with Gadamer, Boesch and Valsiner? *Theory & Psychology, 15*(4), 549–574.

Simão, L. M. (2010) *Ensaios Dialógicos: compartilhamento e diferença nas relações eu outro*. São Paulo: HUCITEC (286p.).

Simão (2015a) "The contemporary perspective of semiotic cultural constructivism: For an hermeneutical reflexivity in psychology". In Marsico Ruggieri and Salvatore (orgs.) *Reflexivity and Psychology* (pp. 65–85) Charlotte: Information Age Publishing.

Simão, L. M. (2015b) Time-not always the same. In: Simão, L. M.; Guimarães, D. S. Valsiner, J. (Orgs.) *Temporality, culture in the flow of human experience* (pp. xi-xiv). Charlotte, Estados Unidos: Information Age Publishing.

Simão, L. M. (2016). Culture as a moving symbolic border. *Integrative Psychological & Behavioral Science, 50*(1), 14–28.

Steil, C. A., & Carvalho, I. C. M. (2014). Epistemologias ecológicas: delimitando um conceito. *Mana, 20*(1), 163–183.

Tupã Popygua, T. S. V. (2017a). *A terra uma só* (p. 78). São Paulo: Hedra.

Tupã Popygua, T. S. V. (2017b) *A terra uma só*. Conference presented at the *House of indigenous cultures*, Institute of Psychology, University of São Paulo, November 9, 2017. Retrieved June 23, 2019 at https://drive.google.com/open?id=1zgPtajkNnVhqjyIHPDSZHF8RMGF96lqN.

Viveiros de Castro, E. B. (1996). Os pronomes cosmológicos e o perspectivismo ameríndio. *Mana, 2*(2), 115–144.

Viveiros de Castro, E. B. (1998). Cosmological Deixis and the Amerindian perspectivism. *The Journal of the Royal Anthropological Institute, 4*(3), 469–488.

Viveiros de Castro, E. B. (2004). Perspectival anthropology and the method of controlled equivocation. *Tipití: Journal of the Society for the Anthropology of Lowland South America, 2*(1), 1–22.

Viveiros de Castro, E. B. (2006). *A inconstância da alma selvagem e outros ensaios de antropologia (2ª Ed.)*. São Paulo: Cosac Naify. (Original publicado em 2002).

Vygotski, L. S. (1927/1991) El Significado Histórico de la crisis em Psicología [the historical meaning of the crisis in psychology: A methodological investigation. (van der veer, R. translator)]. Em Vygotsky (1991) *Obras escogidas I: problemas teóricos y metodológicos de la Psicología* (pp. 257–407). Madrid: A. Machado Libros, S. A.

Wagner, R. (2010). *A invenção da cultura* (p. 253). São Paulo: Cosac Naify. Original published in 1981.

Chapter 2
First Principle: Alterity, Ethics and Differentiation

The term "indigenous" is of Latin origin. It refers to that which is native to the land, generated in its own land. Despite its widespread use to refer to non-European populations in remote regions who were there before colonization, the term formerly encompassed any autochthonous group native to a land or country that was later colonized. That said, I assume that any group of people are indigenous in relation to their original territory and cease to be when they assume a colonialist relation with their surroundings.

This chapter focuses on indigenous psychology as a field of knowledge that emerges in a tensional border between the science of psychology, historically exported to the colonized portions of the world, and the knowledge produced in indigenous contexts. Indigenous psychologies are counterparts of the colonial process, a resistance movement of the quasi-colonized peoples to affirm their own understandings of psychological descriptions, theorizations and methods. The understanding that a relational process produces multiple perspectives and meanings about human experiences is the ground for the emergence of indigenous psychologies. They arise at the resilient and resistant border of differentiation from colonized perspectives, where the colonization of peoples, territories and knowledge still advance.

Indigenous psychology is at the vanguard of the defensive edge against colonialism. It converges with an ethical horizon, committed to the attention and care to the communities. It also relates with historically threatened and silenced sociocultural perspectives. Listening carefully to the indigenous ideas concerning the relation with the colonizers is, then, relevant to the construction of an indigenous psychology. The following excerpt is part of Ailton Krenak's narrative. Krenak is an important indigenous leader who, among other things, fought to introduce indigenous peoples protection laws of in the Brazilian Federal Constitution. He talks about the indigenous perspectives on the encounter with the colonizers:

> How has the history of the contact between White peoples and the old peoples from here been happening in this part of the planet? How has our relationship been during these last 500 years? Is the timing and the understanding of this contact different for each one of our

> tribes? In each one of the old narratives there were already prophecies concerning the arrival of the white man. Some of these narratives are two, three, four thousand years old and already talked about the arrival of this other brother. This other brother was always seen as someone who left us and we didn't know where he was anymore. He went far away and lived for many generations separated from us. He learned another technology, created new languages and learned to organize his life in ways that are different from ours. And in the old narratives he appeared as someone who was coming back home, but didn't know what he thought anymore, nor what he was looking for. And although he was always announced as our visitor, someone who was coming home, who was coming back again, we didn't know anymore exactly what he wanted. And this was preserved in all these narratives, always reminding us about the prophecy or the threat of the white man's arrival, which was, at the same time, the promise of a bond, a reconnection to our old brother.
>
> Both in the old texts, the documented narratives, and in the speeches of our relatives in the tribes today, whenever the elders speak they start their talk reminding us, whether in my people's language, in which we call the white man Kraí, or in the language of our relatives, like the Yanomami, who call the white man Nape. And the Kraí and the Nape always appear in our narratives as taking their opposition claim around the world, not only here in the Americas, but in the whole world. They show the difference and the founding aspects of each one of our traditions' identities, of our cultures, pointing out the need, for each one of us, to acknowledge the difference, the original difference, that each people, each tradition and culture is heir to. Only when we achieve an understanding of these differences not as flaws or oppositions, but as differences in the nature of each culture and each people, only then will we be able to advance a little in recognizing the other and establishing a more authentic coexistence. (Krenak 1998, p. 43).

It took until 1988 for the Federal Constitution of Brazil to determine that the indigenous peoples "[...] shall have their social organization, customs, languages, creeds and traditions recognized, as well as their original rights to the lands they traditionally occupy, it being incumbent upon the Union to demarcate them, protect and ensure respect for all of their property." (Brasil 2012, p. 130) The Brazilian Federal State has since then committed to "protect the expressions of popular, Indian and Afro-Brazilian cultures, as well as those of other groups participating in the national civilization process." (Brasil 2012, p. 124)

Krenak (1998) refers to a set of indigenous narratives about the colonizer, emphasizing the need to acknowledge common grounds and differences. The common grounds are expressed through the notion of 'brotherhood' between the indigenous and the white people: the latter would be brothers who left a long time ago. However, the differences are also and even more emphasized, due to the long period of separation between these peoples, which creates a gap in the possibility of understanding the intentions, feelings and thoughts of the other.

The diversity of indigenous narratives about the origins of the white people[1] shows the multiplicity of forms the differentiation between the indigenous peoples and the colonizers, and among the indigenous peoples themselves, assumes. On one hand, the lack of contact creates difference, distrust and misunderstandings in the relationship. On the other hand, there is an expectation regarding the return of the long lost relative. Such encounter is evaluated as potentially good, if people are able to acknowledge their differences, provided that the cultural shock brings

---

[1] For a first contact with the diversity of these narratives see https://pib.socioambiental.org

opportunities for respectful coexistence and mutual admiration of each one's singular ways of being.

We approach here Wagner's understanding of cultural shock (1981/2010), which involves a feeling of inadequacy in a situation that escapes the person's control. In the light of the new culture, the foreigner becomes visible, as in any situation where we are lead to live in a new environment, even in a social sphere familiar to us (for example, when we enter a new educational or work institution). In these contexts, we experience a type of anxiety or sadness that leads us to close ourselves or make exaggerated attempts to create bonds. This situation demands, in turn, making use of communicative skills to ensure some stability in the relation with others. Cultural shock, therefore, demands a self-dislocation, a personal transformation, to the extent that the usual references are destabilized or lost. In situations where we find ourselves in a subculture of our own culture, this process is less radical than in the case of intercultural and interethnic relations.

Psychological Issues at the Border Between Indigenous Peoples and Colonizers

The encounters involving ethnic and cultural diversity, which began in the historical period known as the European Renaissance, produced significant psychosocial impacts on the European tradition. Specific forms of unease, confusion, and dispersion entered the picture, concerning: (1) the redefinition of territorial frontiers and of the limits imposed by the traditional social order; (2) the fear arising from the possible consequences of an interethnic and intercultural mix; (3) the complexity and diversity of the ways of life found at the alterity frontier (cf. Figueiredo 1992/2007a). The cultural shock caused by the encounter of European traditions with autochthonous peoples from other parts of the world also made new cultural combinations and previously inexistent paths for individual and collective choices possible. The different cultures/ethnicities contributed with their specificities to the emergence of novel ideas concerning human nature and the universality or relativity of the ways of organizing life, of transmitting values, and of explaining and understanding people and the world.

The dissolution of feudalism and of established limits, the diversification and increase in complexity of the ways of life, the encounter with new beings, all opened those societies to an expansion of the horizons of knowledge. Advances in science in general and in psychology in particular also brought much unease, confusion, dispersion, and fear in relation to the blurring frontiers where the European tradition met alterity, brought in the form of strange peoples and beings, different and unknown to them.

Figueiredo (1992/2007a) highlights that the issues that gave birth to psychology as a modern Science are closely connected to the encounter of the European world with internal and external alterities:

> The limits of Western Christian civilization (the limits of Christianity) itself were being questioned. The closest external enemies were the Ottoman Turks, [but] although [some] retraction of Cristianity [due to expansion of the Ottoman Empire] was being compensated by the expansion towards Africa, Asia, and the Americas, these new frontiers had innumerous threats. These ranged from real and imaginary dangers involving the great navigations to the contact with radically different alterities, realities therefore unpredictable and potentially hostile. (Figueiredo 1992/2007a, pp. 36)

In a range of situations, the fear of the frontier and of frontier beings produces intense emotional responses. This is caused by exposure to the variety of things and people, "when this [variety] is prone to escape control and produce mixtures and combinations that profoundly threaten the world stability and order." (Figueiredo 1992/2007a, pp. 36). The dissolution of the internal European borders and the encounter with the external borders produced hybrids and ethnic, linguistic, and religious transformations in the habits, customs and rites of daily life. The relatively stable feudal life in a relatively small territory with small communities was, little by little, destructured by the variety of previously unknown life forms. The population and the familiar languages were transfigured by the presence of foreigners, of new dialects and accents. The rigid social order started being questioned, the clear distinction between center and periphery became blurred, as did the traditional assumptions of regularity and order in the social life. In place of a clear and complete world, with durable personal and collective identities, the experience of disorder.

The European Renaissance is a complex historical phenomenon that produced deep economical, sociocultural, and political transformations. It is worth noting, however, that from this moment on, European and other peoples worldwide underwent intense changes in their ways of life, whether we consider the growing interaction between feuds in Europe or the individuals who engaged in intercontinental nautical explorations. Todorov (1982/2011) even suggests that the encounter with the Amerindians is the most remarkable one in European history, given the radical feeling of strangeness it produced. This encounter founded the new identity of the European peoples, giving rise to the modern age and to a planet-level understanding of the world. At the same time, other peoples around the world were forced to acknowledge the forced influence of the European traditions in their sociocultural organization of the world.

Such complex sociocultural circumstances produced different strategies in the attempt to reorganize the world from the chaos. Throughout the following centuries after the great navigations, sociocultural transformations were an object of investigation in the European intellectual life: the religious reform; the search for consistent philosophical systems in which rational deductions were central in the organization of phenomena; the growing empirical studies from Galilei to Newton, to Francis Bacon's empiricism, and so on. In this context, returning to ideas found in the powerful narratives of the Greek-Roman and Judeo-Christian traditions, as well as to classical philosophy, gained strength. Novel solutions, based on central cosmological concepts of the European tradition, emerged to fill in the gaps and suppress the uncertainties of an unbalanced natural and social world (cf. Cassirer 1994). When new ideas and solutions are being developed, previously stabilized concepts are reelaborated (cf. Gadamer 1960/2008 e Simão 2010) to fill in the gaps of the ruptures caused by new life experiences. Thus, the experience of alterity potentializes the meeting with oneself, in a process that implies transformation.

Alterity, a philosophical notion that points to the dimensions of oneself, of others and of things that cannot be assimilated (cf. Lévinas 1993), has its psychological counterpart in what Simão (cf. 2003, 2004, 2010, 2015) calls a disquieting experience that "gives rise to amorphous zones of meaning and ambiguous situations for the self" (Simão 2015, p. 7). Disquieting experiences "belong to the phenomenological order of feelings regarding subjective experiences that touch the person affectively and pre-reflexively. As such, they are lived in the first person" (Simão 2015, p. 7). These experiences create instability and tension, confounding or even disorganizing the person's expectations about their ability to understand themselves or their relationships with the others in the life world. Therefore, to adapt cognitively as well as affectively, the person is guided to feel, think and act in new directions; in such a way, the person may come to integrate the feelings produced by the disquieting experience into their personal cognitive-affective base, which, in turn, will also change (cf. Simão 2015).

The other's alterity cannot be immediately apprehended; it is mediated by trace elements. These trace elements are aspects of the communicative experience that enable the construction of some margin of understanding of the other. The other's alterity remains, however, as a permanently strange dimension. This is an important aspect to take into consideration in the relationship with the other, since they experience their connection to certain people and aspects of the world in a way different from the I. This means there is always a dissonance between the other and the I, even though everything we learn in the world carries, in its roots, an alterity-driven action. To the philosopher of alterity, Lévinas (1954/1987):

> The world of perception manifests a face: things affect us as possessed by the other. [...] Things qua things derive their first independence from the fact that they do not belong to me; and they do not belong to me because I am in relationship with those men from whom they come. (pp. 28–29).

Therefore, the other's alterity is never fully accessible or comprehensible through predefined forms of communication or cultural manifestations. To establish a relation of alterity, it is necessary to make oneself available and open to be with the other beyond stereotyped encounters and to overcome prejudiced views about them. Doing so depends on the ability to handle the unknown, that is, an affective condition to not feel threatened by the other's independence in relation to what we do know of them. Handling the other's openness to different meanings implies a continued effort to deconstruct and reconstruct provisory regularities that may hold, even if temporarily, the relation.

Elaborating the alterity relation, in turn, involves articulating sensitive experiences, intuitive perceptions, fantasy, and sensuality. These dimensions are present when knowledge is being created about things that escape a previous understanding of any given phenomenon. A person's symbolic elaborations of alterity are guided by culture in match-and-mismatch; they can be linked to established niches such as academic, philosophical, scientific or artistic production, as well as surpass them.

Fictionalized assumptions about the other have had an important role in Western societies since antiquity; in ancient times, they were particularly useful to ideologically protect some commercial routes. The Phoenician narratives about monsters and humanoid beings worked as *barriers* against the commercial initiatives of different peoples in Mesopotamia. Boesch (1991) developed the notion of semiotic barrier when he discussed the obstacles between an action and its intended goals. He proposes the notion of barrier to refer to difficult areas for passage, which may require intervention from specific actions. When the barrier is crossed, however, the person's actions may resume their former rhythm. In contrast to this idea, Boesch (1991) discussed the notion of frontier as the mark that separates two distinct action fields. It requires a specific type of effort from the person to adjust the shape and direction of their actions (p 113). Both a barrier and a frontier may be either easy or difficult to overcome. However, once the barrier is passed, the person's actions tend to return to their previous state, but once a frontier is crossed, the action field is transformed, which leads to personal transformation. The notions of barrier and frontier are useful to distinguish an indigenous psychology from a psychology on indigenous peoples. The later finds difficulty to overcome some methodological barriers to create data on this population or produce effective interventions using pre-existent psychological perspectives. An indigenous psychology, as opposed to that, involves crossing frontiers and thus transforming psychology itself. This subject will be resumed in the following chapters.

Concerning the encounter between Europeans and Amerindians, Melo Franco (1937/2000) discussed the presence, in the European narratives, of beings such as mermaids and cyclops, at the same time fantastic and terrifying, as a sort of customs for naïve sailors. They avoided the places where these creatures supposedly lived, which freed the routes from competition for the Phoenicians, who knew those dangers did not exist. Fictitious ideas about foreigners overflowed during the entire classic antiquity, providing fantastic images that satisfied the ignorance certain social groups had of distant lands and their inhabitants.

In these cases, in which experience is strongly marked by fantasy, there is still no space for the unknown in relationships. In such situations, the disquieting experience of the lack of order is substituted by comforting images of a supposed knowledge, even if it is wrong. When the Europeans reached the lands now called the Americas, what surprised them the most was not the singularities or beauty of the landscape, but the rupture in their expectations of finding supernatural creatures. Instead, they were amazed to find inhabitants similar to themselves. Jahoda (1999) discusses the European's surprise in finding more similarities than differences with the people they met in the new continents. The discrepancy between their expectations and the actual and unfamiliar situation they found produced controversy and attempts to lodge the experience according to their preconceptions:

> [...] When it comes to European encounters with hitherto unknown peoples, there were always multiple ways in which they could be potentially categorized according to familiar templates. The kind of image of the Others that came to be constructed, on the basis of real

or alleged 'facts' about them, will have been dependent on the prior background of ideas and values of the perceivers; and if these varied, so did the result of assimilation to the 'familiar'. It is only after images have become culturally conventionalized that more uniformity can be expected. (Jahoda 1999, p. 11)

Representations of native inhabitants from diverse parts of the world pervaded the European intellectual circles and gave support to the racist scientific theories on the nineteenth century. Philosophers, artists and scientists built their knowledge and took it as true, often without much consideration. They were convinced that their hierarchy of human societies and cultures was justified (Jahoda 1999). This knowledge was founded on ancient preconceptions and prejudices, which taint to this day the Western tradition's approach to foreigners.[2] Immersed in the ritualistic and mythical texture of their societies of origin, these preconceptions and prejudices have been passed on for centuries, constituting the affective-emotional grounds of a specific cultural field. These affective grounds leave their traces in artistic, philosophical and scientific constructions, the *Naturwissenschaft* and *Geisteswissenschaft*. Their vestiges are as stones embedded in the towers of academic and common sense knowledge.

The history of psychology offers a considerable number of examples of preconceptions and prejudices from European tradition in knowledge construction. Modern psychology was born largely from the interest that took over Europe, since the end of the eighteenth century, in finding fundamental laws of psychological development (Jahoda 1982). This interest has its landmark in the foundation of the Society of Observers of Man, in Paris, 1799. The Society gathered zoologists, philosophers, naturalists, and psychiatrists, in a time when these sciences were still not entirely separated fields of knowledge.

Valsiner (2000) discussed the issue of the European ethnocentrism in Wundt's work. It can be found in the different theories in psychology throughout the twentieth century, especially until World War II. From this moment on, the Humanities turned their attention more consistently to the subjacent sociocultural and psychological determinants that motivated the holocaust's acceptance by a significant part of the population, despite the uncritical acceptance of mass murders not being a particularity of this historical moment.

The European ethnocentrism of the nineteenth century was marked by the fascination that took over the Europeans in relation to the ways of life of "natural people" (indigenous people, for example), in contrast to their own ways of life, which they affirmed to be the ways of "the person who has culture" (Valsiner 2000, p. 284).

---

[2] The term "Western" here is used here in the same sense as Kawaguchi e Guimarães (2018) discuss it:

We adopt the word "Western" to generally refer to the peoples of European culture, which includes all countries in the Americas. Mostly, "Western" here appears in opposition to "indigenous peoples of Americas." We could else use "white," "modern," "Humans"—in the absolutely ironic sense attributed by Danowski and Viveiros de Castro (2014)—"non-indigenous," "Jewish-Christian," or "Eurocentric" as well as "Western," that is our choice, once it is still the more comprehensive expression and the most used in the literature consulted throughout the research. At times, however, we use "Eurocentric," in order to emphasize specifically the hegemonic character of Western culture (cf. Quijano, 2000, on neocolonialism and its influences in science).

The former were seen as less developed than the later. Valsiner (2000) points out that the nineteenth century European psychologies clearly projected this distinction in their views of the primitive man. Wundt and other psychologists in the twentieth century incorporated the consensual view that the distinction between nature and culture applied to the European distinction "us – them" (Valsiner 2000; p. 284).

Considering the classic authors in psychology, it is evident that culture, although meaning different things for each one of them, is a central issue for the majority. Examples are abundant. They can be found in Wundt's "folk psychology" (*Völkerpsychologie*); in human ethological studies, focused on the relation between the individual and their social and material environment; in Freud's views on the different cultures and peoples and in his use of sociological and ethnographical texts in psychoanalytical theory; in the attempts to generalize Piaget's hypotheses on cognitive development; in Vygotsky's attempts to demonstrate the importance of sociocultural aspects in the structuring of human language and thought, among others.

By observing concrete phenomena from a specific sociocultural perspective, developing theory and methodology to understand them, and employing this knowledge in the field of modern science, psychology actively transforms the culture. The psychologist's cultural and epistemological positions guide how he or she apprehends and elaborates the meanings of the experience with others, co-determining the possibilities and limits for framing research problems. Thus, there are ethical implications in knowledge construction. Psychological references may determine the scientific validity of cultural concepts about the nature of man and influence our understanding of the impacts of certain ways of life for the development of individuals and societies. These concepts frequently contrast with the indigenous ones.

Alterity and Ethical Issues Involving Indigenous Concepts of Psychological Interest

The image of the cultural shock between the Amerindian and the colonizer shows some of the meanings the relation of alterity can assume in the heterogeneous field where the indigenous psychologies are emerging. Meeting others and seeing they do not coincide with the preconceptions we had of them leads us to ethical considerations. The person who experiences this difference must decide whether to acknowledge it or identify it as an error, which a supposedly correct image will aid in correcting.

In their fight for justice and rights, the indigenous peoples face the State and the colonialist society and defend the need for reparation for historical wrongs. Considering this, the Amerindian Support Network promotes dialogue keeping in mind an ethical dimension that involves the acknowledgement of the ethnical-cultural diversities. The ethical dimension implies giving space for the living expression of alterity, in verbal and non-verbal language, reassuring the other that their singularity is not interchangeable (Lévinas 2004, 1980), and accounting for the unaccountability of others' utterances. This depends on the effort to build a world where the other may participate with their own dimension that is foreign to the field of the I.

Lévinas' philosophical contributions (cf. 1980, 1993, 2004) are related to the field of social relations. He states that the Western philosophical discourse has historically aimed to shed light on existence under a unified concept: whether placing man as a part of an existence that involves them or as the one who determines existence. A totalizing logic understands the multiplicity as a degradation of the original unity, so that every divergence would tend to find its community of belonging, which was previously lost. In this horizon, the essence of things themselves would be expressed.

On a different perspective, Lévinas (1980) provides philosophical foundations for social multiplicity by affirming the essential absence of a common ground on which intersubjective relations occur. The principle of the absence of a privileged ground where subjectivities may situate themselves is called the "essential anarchy of multiplicity" (Lévinas 1980, p. 274). To the philosopher, the alterity of the other presents itself to the I in an anarchical dimension, of a multiplicity without totality, irreconcilable with and inadequate for conceptualizations. The presentification of a being that is external to the I happens when the other motivates the desire of the I, who then opens itself to the other's alterity. In a world marked by diversity, given that the presence of alterity is inevitable, susceptibility to the other does not depend solely on the will of the I, since the other precedes the constitution of the I. Susceptibility is foundational to individuality, establishing a frontier between the interiority of the I and of the other. Subjectivity, therefore, does not emerge as a clean slate. On the contrary, it is preceded by a susceptibility and a desire in relation to that which exceeds it.

In Lévinas's philosophy, the I's interiority emerges as a personal knowledge from the original susceptibility of the instinctive system that is prior to the determination by the other (Lévinas 2004). When relating to exteriority as a source of knowledge, the person may impose a certain distance from the other to constitute something personal while at the same time relating to the other. Therefore, instead of an internal system that shocks with exteriority in a match-and-mismatch relation, the thinking being relates with exteriority through suffering and thought, establishing a frontier that postpones the impact of the shock.

The cultural shock that creates cultures is similar to the cultural shock that emerges from the susceptibility of psychologists to the native's ways of life and ideas. This shock produces a frontier region; the field where indigenous psychologies emerge. Wagner (1981/2010) argues that culture is a mediational term used to describe others as the Western traditions describe themselves. Different phenomena in human life and thought are referred to in terms of our notion of culture, implying necessarily a process of creative invention in the act of studying another people. In the course of this translation, the person who builds knowledge creates, at the same time, ambiguity in the concepts from their own tradition, as part of the effort to precisely determine the concepts of other peoples. However, in assuming the other's culture has a fixed identity, the researcher reduces it to systems that are incapable of reinventing themselves creatively, thus naturalizing culture (cf. Wagner 1981/2010).

When we propose the indigenous psychologies, we open a field for reflection that tends to reduce the tension caused by the impact of foreign concepts. At the same time, the susceptibility to the other implies a responsibility: on the one hand, we are inevitably susceptible, that is, incapable of avoiding the other. On the other hand, we may answer to this susceptibility in a singular way, building personal elaborations that produce effects in the social field. The social field is always in dynamic transformation, and personal elaborations have an effect on the relations with others; moreover, some of these relations may be continued or interrupted.

The ethical answer is to relate to the other without excluding their inapprehensible aspects, in a dynamics of implication and reserve (cf. Figueiredo 2007b). The other maintains their inassimilable excess, which Lévinas (1993) relates to the idea of infinity. The *other* causes ethical considerations in the I's consciousness, "which disorganizes the good consciousness of the coincidence of the Self with itself" (p.62). The openness to the other, according to Lévinas (1993), can be experienced in the most ordinary social situations. The author calls the fundamental motivation that orients the meaning of this experience *desire for infinity*. The relation with alterity implies spontaneity, an unequivocal sincerity, and a critical posture, since the I is questioned by the other with whom the I intends to establish an ethically grounded, decolonized relation.

Creating knowledge on psychology demands constructing and reconstructing views about the other, in an effort that involves exercising power over an objective reality, which the knower may relate to as if it were his property. When we aim to understand the world, we find that human activity has pre-established goals, which require imagination, planning, and postponing short-term action. To accommodate alterity in our understanding of the world, we must reorganize our cultural systems as our subjective sphere. We assign meanings to the other, therefore, according to our desire to include alterity. The will to welcome the elements of the other that exceed ourselves is present when the encounter brings us a sense of responsibility.

As creative beings, humans build meaning from experience. They actively construct the reality in which they live in, selecting elements to build new settings. In society, however, a will beyond individuals' takes part in meaning construction, determining its outcomes in unpredictable manners. Those who speak out have the chance to dispute meanings and defend their particular views. This point-of-view battlefield may involve violence in relational contexts. This violence may present itself as a refusal to consider the other as a subject, but rather considering them as an object. This is the case with psychology, when it is impervious to the indigenous perspectives. The result is the objectification of these peoples, relegated to universal categories or generalized identities. In this type of knowledge construction, there is no space for singular, active subjects, whose existence exceeds any given generalization. The indigenous psychologies, conversely, resist the colonizing drive of modern science by constantly problematizing its categories and methods, pointing out divergent roads and thus differentiating themselves from the foreign perspective and pre-defined modes of understanding.

Furthermore, an indigenous psychology can be understood as "oeuvre" in the philosophical sense. To Lévinas (1993), a cultural oeuvre emerges as the result of an attempt to preserve the other. To the author, an oeuvre is the product of human will; it is carried out through human freedom and is unconditionally directed towards an other. An oeuvre expresses a specific relation between the I and the other, conveying desire and implying the emergence of novelty. The notion of oeuvre adopted by Lévinas (1993, 1980) is broad and indicates any human expression with meaning. Cultural oeuvres organize disquieting experiences in which a person meets alterity, thus enabling them to embrace the other. The meaning of an oeuvre is connected to the maintenance of hospitality, through which it is possible to continue in contact with the other.

Aside from philosophical considerations, there are some sociocultural and psychological ones. I consider our service in the Amerindian Support Network (IPUSP) is an opportunity to establish alterity relations in the contact with Amerindian peoples, showing the way for creating relations based on hospitality. To do so, we must acknowledge the continued abuse these peoples have faced during centuries, having witnessed the permanent threats to their lands and cultural subsistence. This legacy of suffering that continues to this day allows us to understand the little trust indigenous peoples show in relation to State institutions. Its vestiges can be seen in subjectivation processes:

> My grandmother, Francisca Nunes Maciel, died without identifying herself as an indigenous person. She is the result of a policy that forced the indigenous identities into invisibility, adopted by the State from the 17th to the 19th century. The State deliberately used indigenous work force, their knowledge, their traditional rivalry to pacify other ethnic groups, their geographical knowledge to occupy territories and, at last, their extermination, when they would not subject to pacification. They did this until they reached their final goal, the generalized indigenous person who could then be introduced into the national society. (Maciel 2014, p. 10).

The indigenous people's distrust in relation to the State evolved into a distrust in relation to scientific practices and discourses, including psychological ones. The violence they face is concrete and symbolic, when their singular indigenous ways are not acknowledged or accepted. Violence often shows itself in ambiguous manners, not always easily identifiable.

The image of indigenous peoples as something from the past or highly exotic and distant from life in dominant society and its decisions contributes to widen the gap between cultures and peoples. This perpetuates the violence indigenous peoples face in the contemporary world. I understand this process as the crystallization of semiotic walls that obstruct expressions of alterity. Situated in the past or in distant and inaccessible lands, the indigenous peoples pose no threats and in still no fear; there is no risk that they may cause disquieting experiences that disorganize the status quo. Many opportunities for mutual learning are lost this way; a positive interaction could lead, among other things, to new manners of handling current socio-environmental issues.

When people visit a foreign culture, they initially come across a noise-zone. There is a difference in rhythm between the cultures that may be understood as one

24   2 First Principle: Alterity, Ethics and Differentiation

of the elements that produce a certain dissonance between cultures. However, if the foreigner is willing to actually *land*, *be* in a community, and effectively exchange experiences, this person might go through an adaptation process. They must first calm their breathing, observe and perceive the other, the local culture's peculiarities and thus settle into the community's rhythm, opening opportunities for future partnerships. Alterity experiences require, therefore, procedures to find the rhythm and reduce the background noise to create effective dialogue. These procedures may take hours or even days, and frequently "nothing happens", because the rhythms could not come in synch (Guimarães and Nash in preparation).

The solid lines in Fig. 2.1, below, form a sine wave. The semi-circle formed by a dotted line, where the arrows tend to infinity, marks the central chaotic region where the voices in different 'cultural tunes' meet and may find some consonance. This space forms a type of 'arena', or 'stage' for encounters.

In 'cultural tunes' A and B, the sources of vibration are two distinct bodies: sources of information that vary in relation to one another. This can be two lines of thought, or, as previously described, two different cultures. These different stimuli, or signals, travel towards the central chaotic area, which receives the many interactions in different rhythms, represented in Fig. 2.1 by the dotted lines inside the semicircle. This is the space where noisy affective exchanges happen between the different interacting cultures. It also indicates the different cultural tunings during a life period. Here, rhythms are different, but may find harmony. The noisy area emerges due to a relevant order of I-other-world elements that coordinates the rhythmic characteristics of life in a given culture. This means there is a distinct temporality between the cultures in relation. This difference in semiotic and rhythmic organizations of life courses makes the tense central area also a place that is fertile in communication opportunities, beyond the noisy background.

Inside the chaotic area where the background noise is found, Guimarães and Nash (in preparation) also situate the *semiotic walls* (SW), indicating that some paths for rhythmic consonance are blocked. In the search for consonance, however, some anomic hybridisms coexist without interacting. In common sense, we say

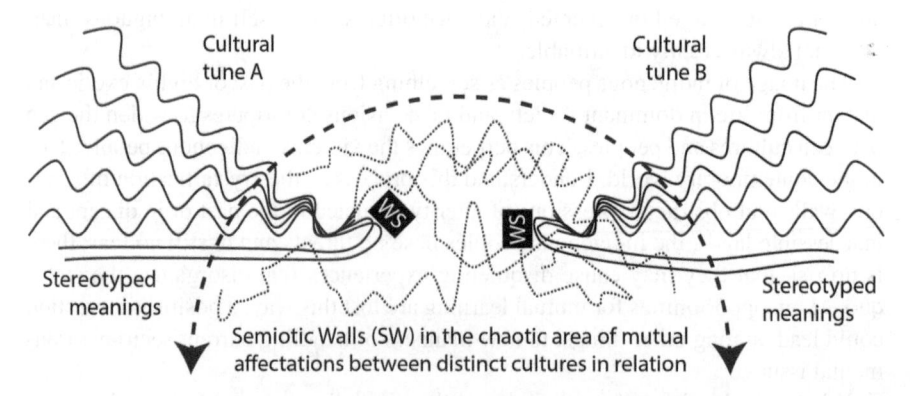

Fig. 2.1 Processes of rhythmic consonance in the encounter between different 'cultural tunes' (Source: Adapted from Guimarães 2016, p. 321)

DIALOGUES TO BREAK DOWN SYMBOLIC STEREOTYPES / SYMBOLIC WALLS
"CULTURAL RESISTENCE"

"there is no dialogue". This happens when there is a refusal to find paths to regulate both sides' principles and cultures and thus make a life encounter possible, even if some noise remains. This is the semiotic process marked in Fig. 2.1 as *stereotyped meanings*. In this situation, there is no possibility for sharing rhythmic-affective experiences with the other. Those involved are hardened, unavailable for meaningful transformations as a result of the relation. They remain in their path of meaning construction, distanced from the rest and uncoordinated with other's points of view.

Interpersonal exchanges are not always possible in social situations. The *other's* subjectivity is never completely accessible or comprehensible by means of fragmented expressions. Semiotic walls (Guimarães 2016a) are built between the I and the other when meanings are crystallized and the other is not open to negotiating the signs involved in the relation. When these walls are rigid, rhythmic consonance does not happen during communication. This means the person, or culture, does not have available alternatives to rebuild their rhythmic basis in the relation with the other.

When the semiotic walls are permeable, however, they may have a role in the process of understanding alterity, in the articulation of temporary meanings about the other. *Understanding* the other creates a barrier in the tuning process, which can be more or less rigid, since *understanding is imprisoning the other* in the cognitive categories of a given culture, while opening oneself to alterity presupposes entering a tuning process, temporarily bracketing pre-established ideas to create new meanings.

The attempt at an interethnic dialogue is not to create intersubjective sharing between interlocutors through verbatim translations of meanings. Translating indigenous languages is a difficult and sometimes impossible task, similar to translating poetry. Achatz and Guimarães (2018) follow the debate concerning the notion of *transduction*, discussed by Faleiros (2014) and Viveiros de Castro (2004). To Faleiros (2014), the impossibility of translating certain poems from one language to another requires the translator to experience the poem in their body to, then, build a new text that does not have the same literal meaning, but communicates the sensible experience established in relation to the poem. Transduction comes from the Latin transductione, 'to conduct by certain means'. Biologically, the term generally refers to the reproductive process in which a foreign DNA is transferred from one cell to another through a virus. Here, the term refers to a process in which the "experience" of the poem crosses one's body, providing other routes of textual comprehension so that translated words may gain meaning through feeling.

To Viveiros de Castro (2004), transduction is the process where the difference between terms is the condition for meaningful communication. The I and the other connect precisely because of the difference, because their discourses do not express the same thing. The interethnic relation continuously produces difference in meanings, even when the same language is used in dialogue. Equal words do not necessarily have equal referents (as in the case of the word territory, after discussed here). Transduction concerns, therefore, the production of difference. It assumes that equivocations are inherent to dialogue, but may be controlled when we abandon the expectation of explaining the other. In this way, the meaning of the terms employed in the dialogue can be ressignified, step by step, as the relation with the other develops.

Guided Trajectories of Differentiation and Dedifferentiation

European knowledge about Amerindian peoples was built through comparisons with other societies, which were equally reified as scientific study objects, such as the African, Asian, and Oceanian societies. Numerous parallels were drawn between the indigenous peoples and Western folklore. Influenced by Marco Polo's literature, Christopher Columbus was hoping to find the Chinese Empire to propagate the Christian faith. He also believed, as was typical in his time, in "[…] Cyclopes and mermaids, Amazons and men with tails, and his belief, as strong as in Saint Peter, therefore lead him to find them" (Todorov 1982/2011, p. 21).

Columbus also thought he would reach Paradise, leading him and his crew in search of destinations that could confirm this belief. His diaries, meticulously studied by Todorov (1982/2011), present a clear example of how imagination and perception are integrated in an active cognitive assimilation of reality. It also shows that this process has significant personal, collective and social implications. Todorov (1982/2011) understood the relation between Columbus and the original peoples from the lands he visited as a communicational deadlock. What Columbus "understood", then, was merely a summary of Marco Polo's and Pierre d'Ailly's books (p. 44). To Gândavo[3] and other historical characters of the time, as Columbus, the natives were devoid of anything significant: "Physically naked, the natives were also, in the eyes of Columbus, devoid of any cultural property; they were characterized, in a certain sense, by the absence of customs, rites, religion" (Todorov 1982/2011, pp. 48–49).

The religious psychology of the sixteenth century, in turn, suspected the indigenous people had no soul. The Spanish sent forth inquiry Commissions to verify the issue, which sparked off intense debate in the first half of the sixteenth century (Lévi-Strauss 1952). At the time, instead of naturalistic research procedures, the debate surrounding indigenous peoples was oriented by moral judgment (e.g., the Valladolid case, 1550–1551, in Todorov 1982/2011). The controversy continued even after it was decided that the indigenous peoples could assimilate the catholic faith, as reported in the papal bull of Pope Paul III, issued on June 2nd, 1537.

Modern psychology developed in a scientific environment where indigenous peoples were thought to be at a less developed mental stage. This is due to the assumption that they lived in primitive conditions, prior to "a series of intermediate

---

[3] Pêro de Magalhães Gândavo (Braga, c. 1540 — c. 1580) was a portuguese historian and chronist. He authored the "History of the Province of Santa Cruz, popularly known as Brazil", in which we find a widely disseminated view on the indigenous peoples:

> One language only is spoken throughout the coast side […]. It lacks three letters, one should know. One will not find F, or L, or R, a remarkable thing, since for this reason there is no Faith, no Law, no Reign: and in this way they live, in a disorderly fashion, having besides this no count, weight or measure (Gândavo 1576, fl. 33) [Originally "A língua de que usam toda pela costa é uma […]. Carece de três letras, convém a saber, não se acha nela f, nem l, nem R, cousa digna de espanto, porque assi não têm Fé, nem Lei, nem Rei: e desta maneira vivem desordenadamente sem terem além disto conta, nem peso, nem medido"]

steps in the direction of more advanced civilizations" (Wundt 1916, p. 14). It is noteworthy that the criteria for determining a society's primitive status were the absence of a National State with military organization and of a national religion (as opposed to the natural religions). The latter should be employed to converting non-believers, morally guided by universalizing principles. In the twentieth century, in turn, the indigenous cosmologies were confused with folklore, eventually to be overcome by scientific narratives and arguments. Education assumed the role of universalizing the Western naturalistic perspective as the correct image of the world.

Attention was focused on what was lacking in indigenous peoples: a specific type of faith, material goods, scholarly education, respect for the State and laws, etc. These supposedly objective comparisons, oriented by values extrinsic to these peoples, functioned as moral imperatives. These moral imperatives produced crystallized preconceptions and prejudices that to this day influence psychologists.

Amerindian societies built notably fluid cultural dynamics, with modes of relations that even the anthropological tradition has difficulty in understanding since the nineteenth century (cf. Overing Kaplan 1977). When indigenous peoples were compared to other peoples worldwide, ethnologists also guided their descriptions in terms of absences: absence of a State, of structured kinship bonds, of elaborated architecture, of material conditions for cultural development, etc. (Seeger 1980).

These ideas fueled colonialist projects. When, eventually, the indigenous peoples did not conform to the colonizer's interests, such stereotyped ideas justified resorting to violence against them. From the objectification and attempt to homogenize people and cultures to the conspicuous populational decrease that took place from the fifteenth century to the twentieth century, the frontier between indigenous traditions and the values and practices of the naturalist tradition was marked by intense suffering. For instance, social diversity in Brazil was reduced from around 1000 different ethnic groups with unique customs and languages to around 305 ethnic groups, speaking 246 different languages today. Armed conflict, epidemics, initiatives to disorganize cultures and communities, and assimilationist policies are among some of the reasons for the Amerindian genocide and ethnocide.

During the last two decades, Brazilian demographic censuses have registered a considerable increase in the indigenous population. Concomitantly, various studies (Grubits and Guimarães 2007; Souza et al. 2010; Aureliano and Machado Jr. 2012) show an increase in mental illness diagnoses, substance abuse, domestic violence, and an increase in suicide rates in communities destabilized by violent interethnic interaction. These phenomena have been observed since the early years of the invasion (Todorov 1982/2011), providing evidence that the intercultural frontier is not a comfortable zone to be in. As we build an indigenous psychology, we face a significant challenge for these communities: how to dialogue with psychology in general, in which Western, Eurocentric values and ideas are prevalent, and at the same time resist the constant equivocations produced in relation to the indigenous traditions?

Indigenous psychology is, therefore, an arena for strengthening the continuous fight for the recognition of ethnic identities and alterities, in which people participate with their particular strategies. A current type of resistance can be seen in the partnerships and bidirectional support in dialogues with the academic community to revert the condition of naturalized study objects and, instead, create a position where indigenous views are recognized as valuable and sophisticated knowledge that has been built over millennia.

The self-critique movement in Americanist anthropology that began in the 1970's lead to innovative conceptual propositions, directly connected to methodological changes in knowledge construction. The subject of knowledge construction, previously an external observer, was then transported to a position inside the studied culture so that an insider point-of-view could be developed. Thus, the focus was in the categories, ideas and concepts each culture develops to understand the challenges they face in their experience horizon; the paths they choose and solutions they create to handle problems they consider relevant. This investigative practice in anthropology is intrinsically connected to ethical concerns distinct from the moral imperatives that oriented the approaches from the previous centuries, and has political and epistemological consequences. It changed the status of indigenous knowledge, collaborating in a considerable manner to grant it a position of equity. From a methodological point of view, the research that emerged from this new paradigm is an attempt to create understandings based on informants' views. The informants are chosen for their perceived role as leaders, as specialists in different branches of native knowledge (cf. Viveiros de Castro 1987). Socio-historic psychology and hermeneutics had a central role in this shift in anthropology, influencing some of the strategies and ideas generated from ethnographic studies. The first studies in this field were considered a type of ethnopsychology.

It is important to note that Americanist anthropology was fueled by strategies established in the field of socio-historic psychology, as Carneiro da Cunha attests:

> Seeing [...] the person as an object of anthropological study is justified, despite seeming heretic, when there is an attempt to create an ethnopsychology, that is, an attempt to apprehend the categories a specific society uses to elaborate their notion of person. To do so, there was much more to learn from what is known as "historical psychology" than from anthropologists whose orthodoxy lead to well delimited territories. (Carneiro da Cunha 1978, p. 1)

To overcome the difficulties imposed by moral imperatives extrinsic to the studied culture, the psychologist, listening to the indigenous communication, must be willing to experience negativity (cf. Simão 2010) in relation to the theoretical-methodological preconceptions they carry from their years of academic life. This depends on their affective condition to bear the cultural shock as evidence that something in the other exceeds the possibility of apprehension by the I. This is because the symbolic resources (Zittoun 2006) used to understand alterity are always linked to a particular cultural field (Boesch 1991, 2007) in which alterity does not entirely fit. To create the ability to experience negativity in interethnic dialogue, the psychologist must manage their affective (symbolic, aesthetic, bodily) availability to feel safe enough during the vulnerable construction of the relation.

Concrete and Conceptual Resistance

In the second semester of 2014, the Indigenous Network team attended to indigenous leaders' demands for more visibility concerning their fight for the right to their land. To handle this demand, we proposed, collaboratively, to conduct discussion forums about the indigenous presence in the city of São Paulo. We held a total of six meetings, up to May 2015, five of which took place at the Institute of Psychology (USP). The forums were open to participation by the academic community and to the public. With each edition, new guests were invited besides the Guarani lecturers and other indigenous leaders living in the urban context. The audiovisual recordings were made available in the internet by the IPTV-USP service (Internet Protocol Television of the University of São Paulo[4]), with the indigenous guests' consent.

The forums were important to raise awareness about the activities of the Indigenous Network, the issues of the communities and the ideas of the leaders. While the Network's first 2 years were focused on visiting the communities, the idea now was to enable visits from indigenous people to the academic community. In this way, we intended to broaden the understanding of the University's potential for partnership construction and collaborative projects.

Some of the forums speeches were transcribed and led to two publications. The first one is based on a speech titled "Indigenous health and education: oral tradition, culture and public policies", by Guarani educator Pedro Macena (2014). The publication was written by the indigenous educator and me, and focused *Mbya Guarani* views on education (Macena and Guimarães 2016). This was my first experience coauthoring a publication with an indigenous person. The second publication was result of an undergraduate science apprenticeship, in which Achatz and Guimarães (2018) conducted a dialogical analysis of the transcribed speeches from the forums as well as of some speeches from indigenous persons delivered at the meetings organized by the Regional Council of Psychology of São Paulo (CRPSP) in previous years. These meetings promoted debate on the manner psychologists related to indigenous people and identified some recurring tensions in this process.

Bellow, I discuss in more detail the results of these two productions, since they organize some of the tensions the Indigenous Network handled during its four initial years and present the issue of alterity, differentiation trajectories and ethics in our paths for constructing an indigenous psychology.

---

[4]The recordings can be accessed in the following links:
  1) http://iptv.usp.br/portal/video.action?idItem=24382;
  2) http://iptv.usp.br/portal/video.action?idItem=24518;
  3) http://iptv.usp.br/portal/video.action?idItem=27891;
  4) http://iptv.usp.br/portal/video.action?idItem=27891;
  5) http://iptv.usp.br/portal/video.action?idItem=28849

A Process of Differentiation and Dedifferentiation in Education

Pedro Macena's speech, delivered in the third edition of the Forum *The Indigenous Presence in the City of São Paulo*, organized by the *Amerindian Support Network* of the *Institute of Psychology of USP*, on October 09, 2014, was an important guided in the construction of an indigenous psychology. Currently one of the *Xeramõi'i* of the Indigenous Land of Jaraguá, São Paulo/SP, he was at the time a Guarani Mbya Educator at the Center of Indigenous Education and Culture (CECI) of Jaraguá.

The CECIs are a product of demands made by Mbya Guarani leaders of the city of São Paulo to strengthen their ethnic-cultural roots through a project of differentiated education, focused on children from 0 to 6 years old. The negotiations for creating the CECIs began in 2000, involving the three villages in São Paulo, Tenondé Porã, Krukutu and Jaraguá (cf. Macena 2014). The perception that their traditional territory had receded, which presented an obstacle to the culture's survival, to the maintenance of their language, to traditional nurturing, health, wisdom and knowledge, was central to unite the leaders from the three communities to defend the project of the CECI.

Concerning the specificities of their education, the Mbya Guarani consider the relation with their surroundings, with their community and other beings in the environment, to be central:

> [...] this is the Guarani traditional education, with enough space, where children have the freedom to learn [...] Observe the space, all this helps a lot in childhood education. [In the old days] we didn't need this type of space [a building for the school], this physical space, which is determinant for children's learning. We didn't need that, but now we do. So because today we need it, we have the CECI, which Marta[5] built from our project (Macena 2014).

During the construction of the CECI, however, a series of misunderstandings had to be solved between the community and the government organizations concerning the distinct concepts of education. Macena (2014) reports much discussion with the City Bureau of Education, because the municipal technicians and teachers did not initially have an adequate understanding of the meaning of a differentiated education.

> [...] to us, the Guarani people, a differentiated education means respecting people despite the language they speak. For example, I speak Guarani, so my language, the way I live in my community, must be respected in its difference. You must respect the way I raise my children in the community [...] When you see and understand, you have to respect, because we are not all the same, we are different. [...] I am Guarani, I have my culture, my language, and my way of teaching the children at home, what will I teach them? I will speak to them in Guarani, I will teach them in Guarani, they will have to learn the Guarani language because this is our people, our culture. So, if I speak Guarani here, will any of you understand it? No. So this is the difference, I want to be respected as I am. So, when it comes to differentiated education, it is valuing each of our cultures, the way we are, this has to be respected. You can't talk about equal rights the way they do in the meetings. [...] I am

---

[5] Marta Suplicy was mayor of São Paulo from 2001 to 2004. During her mandate, the CECIs were built.

Guarani, I have my culture, my people, my village, where I live, where I learn, my everyday life, I live it differently. Different in a way that I feel at home where I live [...] no one is there to interfere in my day-to-day life, because that is my territory [...] (Macena 2014).

Macena and Guimarães (2016) point out that a differentiated education should focus on the respect to the cultural and personal singularities of the teaching-learning relation. This depends on an intercultural and interethnic equity condition that may hold asymmetries, in which differences can be acknowledged and valued without creating hierarchy, that is, without a culturally based knowledge overrunning the other. This is the case, for example, when the Eurocentric model of formal schooling overrides the Guarani Mbya form of transmitting knowledge and its contents. The demanded equity for a differentiated education presupposes a rejection of eclectic attitudes, since they eliminate the differences between traditional and scientific knowledge, as well as a rejection of dogmatic attitudes, which assume one form of knowledge is superior to the other. Instead, we propose the coexistence of different types of knowledge, as expressed by a young Guarani Mbya mother, in the documentary *Tenonderã: um Olhar para o futuro* (Tenonderã: a View on the future) (Ideti and Duwe 2010): "I think it is very important to value education. The *Juruá's* [non-indigenous peoples] and our own".

These considerations on the differentiated education have been important in our construction of a psychology that is also both indigenous and differentiated. In education as well as in psychology, understanding the processes of the construction of the person is central:

We speak in this sense: each one should respect the other's values. We pass this on to our children. When we speak of our territory, we are not talking only about the village in Jaraguá, but the whole territory we move through, that runs from the state of Paraná, São Paulo, Santa Catarina, Rio de Janeiro, Espírito Santo, it runs a long way. We speak of this, I tell the children like this, "This is our territory, wherever there are Guarani, it is our family", so the children learn to have a broader view, so they don't go saying "No, Jaraguá is my territory". If we don't pass this on, they won't understand, they won't imagine [...] This they have to learn, so when they grow up, they will pass it on to their children (Macena 2014).

Being able to move through a vast territory and be welcomed in different places makes encounters with different people and experiences possible. These encounters solidify the ability to be open to the other's alterity. One of the roles of the educator towards the smaller children, who are the majority at the CECI, is to make their circulation possible in a safe manner, so that each child may built in a singular manner the meaning of life in community:

Often, as educators [...] we are not there to teach, but to learn with the children as well, because we learn a lot from being with them, together. The physical space of the village helps a lot in the children's learning [...] In Jaraguá [...] we use the whole space of the village to do activities with them. Because the children must learn, they will learn from being together, observing [...]. From the moment they occupy that space, they are learning: [...] to walk [...] to listen to the sounds, and then to distinguish the sounds they hear, the sound of the birds, the hawk, the river, the trees... they register this in their minds, and store it in their minds. This is why the Guarani never had a writing system, because they store everything in their memory.

> [...]
> This is how we educators of the CECI work with our children, this is our education. We are not used to pencils and writing, to three or four hours a day confined to a room, because children can't learn that way [...] because all those walls around them don't help them learn [...] Because [the walls] keep out all the wind, the air, the noises from the birds, the songs from the trees [...]. The child is not registering anything in there and this is bad for the child's education: [...] "just this space here for me, all closed, I can't hear anything, just the teacher telling me what to do, to do this, to not do that". [This way] the children, when they're grown, won't have an open mind, they will have a closed mind, and this mind, [...] cannot develop children's learning [...]. What is done to children today, not just the Guarani, but the other children, in the state and city schools [...] is outrageous; I observe and think "how will children learn in a place like this?" But I don't say anything, I just observe, how will they learn like this?
>
> So the Guarani children are different, they have all the freedom, all the space of the village to explore [...] The Guarani children like to explore the space they have, and in exploring, they acquire knowledge. [To] develop wisdom, they explore everything in that space (Macena 2014).

The Mbya Guarani perspective is different from the classical educational model, systematized in the nineteenth century to prepare the labor force to work in factories in the recently industrialized western societies. In this context, little space was left for freedom and for people's individuality. Quite the opposite: young learners were demanded a sedentary discipline, in which their movement was controlled and they were required to obey hierarchically empowered adults: first, the teachers, and, later, the factory managers (cf. Patto 2008). In this way, education restricted creativity and the possibilities of handling social relations. Traditional Eurocentric schools became, then, spaces where experiences of prejudice and social violence were intensified, later to be continued in the adult life. At the same time, education contributed to form a consumer market by creating a target audience more dependent of heteronomous and directive discourse, whether stated by a supervisor or disseminated by the books and the media. Regulating the experience of temporality was also a part of this human mind and body-standardizing package: it was up to education to train children to accept the regular and uninterrupted rhythms of work (cf. Patto 2008).

While this Eurocentric education aims predominantly to form people for a profession and for the market, the differentiated education defended by the Mbya Guarani educators in CECI aims to form children for life, to value partnerships in knowledge exchanges between peers:

> [As children] grow up, all that they memorized during that time, they distribute it little by little, passing it on to others. They don't transmit what they memorized in a single day, in two or three days. [...] They teach the children little by little: this is why, in the Guarani tradition, we never tell children they have a limited time to learn, we never put pressure on them to learn. To me, children have all the time in the world to learn: there's no hurry. In CECI, as educators we never evaluate children, who learned less, who learned more. This doesn't exist in the Guarani education, especially when we're talking about early childhood education. If you evaluate children [...] it's as if you were dividing them. As the white people slang goes, it's like giving them the elbow. We have to understand is not about who learns more and who learns less, it's not how we should see it, because for the white people, the non-Indians, education has a meaning, it means money. When they start to learn, they

already start to think about money. Not the Guarani, they think of the people, the future, they start learning and as they learn it's to live their lives, to carry on their culture, towards their future. The actual future, because it's when they will be able to teach others, their family, their people (Macena 2014).

In the Mbya Guarani understanding, therefore, freeing the child from the teacher's guardianship, from confinement to a classroom and from the pressure of time and a heteronomous judgment is conducive to the development of integrity, making them capable of knowing their own limits and ambitions, as well as the limits and ambitions of others around them. Forming people with integrity, independent of extrinsic regulations despite being connected to their own collectives, promotes the development of responsibility and respect towards difference:

> Because often the *Juruá* uses educated to refer to that person who went to school, to a lawyer, a teacher, or others. They say like this "this guy is educated because he went to school", and many times we see that [this] education is not everything, [this] education doesn't form people. Education should let people live being respected, knowing how to be with others, this is the [true] education […]. The child learns in order to live, for the world, to be a person, to be a good person. And this is what we need in our country. [To] our children, in early childhood education, we always pass this knowledge and wisdom, so they can take it with them and pass it on to their children, and […] their grandchildren and so on. So our education is passed on from generation to generation, and valuing the culture is very important, because children, once they realize they belong to a people, they certainly will start to value it, […] identify themselves as part of that people, and respect other peoples with different cultures. (Macena 2014)

We realize that a differentiated education takes place at the frontier between a laic State education and the Guarani Mbya culture. It presupposes a refusal to a universalizing pattern that eliminates difference or assimilates it in a supposed "umbrella-shaped" pedagogical structure, in which cultural differences are superficially contemplated in an eclectic relativism. It also presupposes a refusal to dogmatism, and to cultural isolation. On the contrary, this type of education considers ethnic-cultural belonging central. A strengthened cultural belonging is able to embrace other cultures in an equitative dialogue. In the Guarani Mbya wisdom, when a child grows up as a well-formed adult in their culture, connected to a collective that gains power as it deepens its ethnic-cultural perspective, this adult is able to welcome alterity without feeling threatened. This eliminates the affective dispositions that could lead to disrespect between the different, mentioned above.

Introducing schools or other historically exotic institutions into the community, such as classic psychology, cannot be done blindly. Special consideration about the consequences to the dynamics of communitarian practices is critical. Neither it is possible to avoid a mediational work between the distinct forms of tuning the rhythms of life in the institutions and communities. The organization of children into traditional grade classrooms seems to illustrate the tensions that institutions can produce in community life.

> I will make a brief comment on the separation of the children we receive today at the CECI. As I said before, we don't separate children, and today there's this difficulty when [the children] are transferred from the unit [CECI] to a State school. When we transfer them, they have difficulty in understanding the reason for this division the State makes, of

the classrooms; so they have difficulty when there's this division; for example, in the State [school] there's first, second, third, fourth, fifth and [...] sixth grade. So the child begins to be separated, [...] they don't understand. Why this separation? [In the] Center of Indigenous Education and Culture, which is city administration, [...] there's no division, why does there have to be a division in the State school? So the child, I understand that when they grow up with this separation, they keep this prejudice, this discrimination [...] (Macena 2014).

The separation of schoolchildren mirrors the separation of social classes in society and leads to the ranking of knowledge and hierarchy in personal relations. This is distinct from the ways defended by the Guarani Mbya wisdom:

[...] to us it is important not to divide the children. [...] Division is not nice, in any culture [...]. When it comes to education, this is why today [...] it is so difficult to live together, in society, in a community, to understand one another, because children, they grow up divided already. [...] Out there the children are [often] divided in social classes, something we don't have in the village. In the village we are a family, there is no richer class or poorer class, or further, a middle class, they don't exist. In the village we are a family, a people, nobody is better than anybody else in the village, and out here, outside the village it is different, sometimes the rich kid, the one from the upper class, they don't let them play with the child of the poorer people [...]: "no, he doesn't belong to our class, you can't play because he's not from our class", and the child grows up with that in their mind, and the children are divided from a small age, and when they come to a certain age, they can't respect people, they start to discriminate, the prejudice starts. [...] The other day I was lecturing at the state school, and a kid raised their hand and said to me: "I don't want to study in the state school anymore!", then I said: "why? What's going on? Why don't you want to study? Studying is very good", and they told me "no, it's because, in the state school, we are divided, and lots of times, I'm in third grade, and a kid in fifth grade, a Guarani kid, came up to me and said "you're stupid, you didn't learn anything, I'm in fifth grade and I learned more than you, you're late"" (Macena 2014).

The social division endorsed by the State bureaucracy and uncritically reproduced by the school makes people vulnerable, subjected to a centralized power from which knowledge supposedly emanates. In this way, community bonds that affectively support social cohesion loose strength. Dividing children in school produces a fragmentation of social bonds and millenary values of the Amerindian tradition "this is not a part of the Guarani culture, [...] we are a people, a community, we are Guarani and we cannot be divided". The indivisibility of community cultural values permeates the processes of the construction of the person. Once internalized, they make the person capable to move about and relate with integrity in the multiple sociocultural spaces and contexts:

[...] Sometimes people leave and are not recognized as Indians anymore, but, in the Guarani view, the land is one only. We still don't have this division view, our view is not to divide, our view is that the land is one only in the whole world. For instance, the Indian who lives in Argentina, in Canada, in the United States, in our Guarani view, they are not a North-American Indian, an Argentinean Indian, a Bolivian Indian, no. It's the same Brazilian Indian, because the land is one only. In our knowledge, there is no division, the white people were the ones to divide everything, not the indigenous people, the whites divided: country, state; not satisfied, they divided cities, making it each time harder for the indigenous peoples to move about in their territory, because of this division (Macena 2014).

Since overcoming preconceptions depends on a cognitive-affective involvement with alterity, indigenous psychology collaborates in the construction of equitative dialogues in the interethnic context, towards strengthening cultural reflexivity founded on ethnic self-affirmation. This seems to us a condition for building respect to difference. With this in mind, São Paulo CECIs' educators have a hard task at hand:

> [...] as an educator, [...] my students are tiny, from 3 to 5 years old. You [have to be] very careful in this initial stage, [in] which they start to see the world. Being in a group, in the world and with other children is very important, isn't it? You have to be very careful [in] teaching these children, the teaching has to be gradual for them to understand very well what it is to be with people, how to be [in a] community, for them to have the notion they belong to the Guarani group, which is a community, a people, for them to understand this, so they can [...] value themselves and their people, and identify themselves as a people (Macena 2014).

The gradual process of learning and of constructing the person is bidirectional; it depends on the educator's experience and educational background, acquired through immersion in their own tradition. At the same time, it depends on whether the learner has enough freedom. The indigenous education aims to facilitate the child's path for exploring the world and their relations with the community. The next step is assisting them in amplifying their horizons to other communities, peoples and the world. The Mbya Guarani wisdom is not a type of knowledge that moves from abstractions to concrete life. On the contrary, it is strongly grounded in the elaboration of experience:

> [...] The child learns slowly and, even after we're grown, we still learn. We never stop learning, because, informed by our knowledge, we learn every day, with each step, on the run; with time, we learn, by looking around us. In this way the Guarani child learns to observe. That's why, as an educator, when I arrive at the CECI, the children don't stay close to me; they play around, they have the freedom to do what they want, so they learn with freedom. Why should they cling on to me to learn? Just because I am an educator, they have to stay right next to me for three, four hours? No, that's not how it is, they have to explore the space around them to learn and develop [...] (Macena 2014).

Interethnic dialogue can help guarantee the necessary freedom for learning in the indigenous education, considering that, despite being differentiated, this education must also reach the instituted goals of the educational public policies. A constructive dialogue can also lead to revisions of these goals, so that they may fulfill their ethical purpose of contributing to the emancipation of the population targeted by these policies:

> It's like this, I was saying the other day: nowadays I'm educated. Not in the state schools. I'm educated in my culture; the elders educated me to be a childhood educator in the village, but in the indigenous culture. In my village I am recognized by my people, I am an educator; I have the wisdom and knowledge to work with the Guarani children, with the little ones. It wasn't the State that appointed me, neither the State that educated me, because the State can't educate me in my own culture. My credentials as an educator belong to my people; it is the elders' incumbency. I was formed by them, I was appointed by them [...] (Macena 2014).

The State legitimating autonomous processes of education seems to be a good path for indigenous communities to face psychosocial vulnerabilities. With autonomy, they may find unique manners of facing colonial and post-colonial marginalization and conflict involving land rights, the invisibility of the peoples, prejudice and lack of acknowledgement of the indigenous identities in the contemporary world. In this sense, CECIs' educators have quite advanced arguments and proposals, developed through negotiations with government institutions:

> [...] Now that we have this freedom, we perform our activities according to our day-to-day life, according to our monthly calendar, because the activities change from month to month; for instance, in August, we have baptism with chimarrão,[6] first with the men, then with the women. All this is a part of the CECIs' activities. This activity is a part of the children's education; in that month, for example, all we talk about is the chimarrão baptism. What is its meaning? We have not only the Cultural Center, but also the House of Praying,[7] because to us knowledge, its basis, [...] is in the House of Praying. [...] When it comes to Guarani education, it has a lot to do with religion, because religion is important, for children to learn what education is. Because often we start from top to bottom, isn't it? And the Guarani like to learn bottom up, do you understand? This is why our education is in the right path, never the opposite, that's why our children learn from a small age, not only in the village, but in each family, with their parents, observing, and in this way they learn. This is how the Guarani child is. There are things we learn with practice, aren't there? (Macena 2014).

Precisely the things learned through practice are the hardest to explain; they can only be transmitted through customs and collective actions. Attention to this field of experience as the source of multiple, culturally guided paths for elaborating meanings is, therefore, central to the formation of the indigenous person.

Travelling in an Interethnic Arena

Achatz and Guimarães (2018) analyzed speeches from leaders of different ethnic groups living in the state of São Paulo: the *Mbya Guarani, Pankararu, Xavante, Baniwa, Tupi-Guarani, Terena* and *Krenak*. The speeches were delivered in events organized by the Regional Council of Psychology of the State of São Paulo and by the Amerindian Network (IPUSP). The CRPSP meetings were spaces for conversation between indigenous people, psychologists and other professionals that deal with the subject of indigenous peoples, especially from the fields of health, education, and social service, as well as the general academic community. Twenty-one indigenous people, from seven different ethnic groups, had their reports published (Conselho Regional de Psicologia da 6ª Região 2010). We conducted dialogical analysis of these reports, in an effort to show the referents of the semantic contents and the expressive aspects of the speeches (cf. Wertsch 1993; Guimarães 2016b).

---

[6]TN: Brazilian Yerba-Mate, a tradition drink consumed by South American indigenous populations, including the Guarani.
[7]A traditional Guarani house, used for ceremonial meetings.

The non-indigenous audience was, mostly, psychologists or people connected to psychology. The indigenous speeches addressed the possibilities of mutual understanding and partnership construction. People from different ethnic groups spoke, each one of them with their own complex cosmological and historical conceptions. In the context of the events, it was not possible to delve into the cultural specificities of the speakers. Dialogue thus takes place in a zone of mutual unknowns, from which the recognition of the other, although temporary and restricted, comes from being together.

Analyzing the leaders' speeches, and from our experience with some of them in regular meetings promoted by the Amerindian Support Network, we realized, as dialogue developed, that there were several levels of meanings in the relation between psychology and indigenous peoples. These meanings relate to the interlocutors' most cherished values and assumptions. We understand there is a disjunction in the psychologists' and the indigenous peoples' forms of living and attributing meaning to experience. They each depart from different cultural bases to understand personal and social experience. There is, however, some permeability in the forms of sensibility that enables the construction of a field for sharing, even if it is provisory. We understand the construction of shared experiences as a four-layered path: outlining difference, expressing feelings, creative possibilities and semantic rectifications.

The first layer is the most evident during the initial approaches between psychologists and indigenous leaders. It involves circumscribing positions, in which indigenous leaders speak to the psychologists sometimes as generic foreigners, sometimes questioning the specificity of their position as psychologists interacting with indigenous communities. The leaders also refer to themselves in a generic form, as indigenous persons, without claiming their ethnic specificity, and at the same time emphasize the heterogeneity of the indigenous peoples. We also noted, in the leaders' speeches, their perception that the psychologists did not know how to hear them properly, and that the proper form of listening results from being together and learning slowly from this. They are concerned the interaction with the psychologists might be just another failed attempt at an encounter, marked by violence, as they have already experienced in their relations with the Brazilian society. They call attention to the unsolved issue of how to create a careful dialogue to face the psychosocial vulnerabilities that result from these mismatched encounters. Regarding this subject, the following excerpt from Dora Pankararu's speech (2010) is significant:

> When I was talking to some of my relatives, at first we thought that this event would be a group of professionals evaluating us, studying us. What we think and hope in this moment is that this new work group is really interested in helping us find a path, a course of action, since a solution is more complicated. (Pankararu 2010, p. 41)

Dora *Pankararu* points out two problematic attitudes related to psychology. The first concerns the interest in studying or psychologically evaluating people. The second concerns a problem-solving attitude without due consideration of the situation's complexity. She also asks for partnerships to find paths together, which in turn demands that psychologists persist in being together and understand that this takes time. Psychologists are asked to show a positive disposition to trail a path together and to be self-critic in relation to the references they use, which may be foreign, and strange, to the indigenous peoples. Trailing a path together requires developing trust, from which an understanding may be reached and solutions for conflicts created, together. Trust, however, depends on the willingness to handle ambivalent emotions that emerge in the relation. Only then it is possible to reestablish the dialogue, each time it is shaken by memories of a conflictive past with the surrounding society and mistrust rearises. This involves an affective investment and an acknowledgement of the different meanings the other may assume in a relation. Acknowledging prejudices and preconceptions in a context where there is space for the other's alterity makes it possible to manage new ideas and resignify the relation.

The second layer in partnership construction regards the possibility of expressing feelings related to traumatic experiences. This is possible once the psychologist's ability to listen and embrace the community's and individuals' psychosocial vulnerabilities is recognized. At first, the psychologist is seen as a generic foreigner who is willing to witness the impacts caused by their own cultural tradition over the indigenous populations; the psychologist is seen, from the start, as a spokesperson of the Eurocentric point of view. We observe the leaders express anger, fear, pain and concern, and denounce the attitudes of the white man in relation to their peoples and other living beings in their territories. Each utterance is followed by personal stories of suffering, calling psychologists to reflect about the psychological impacts of colonization, leaving the question open as to how these impacts could be reverted. The psychologists are called forth to break down prejudices resulting from coarse generalizations and idealizations, and to respect the other as an interlocutor.

Tension emerges when the leaders highlight their cultural and ethnic specificities, for this same specificity is often seen in a derogatory manner, causing suffering. Eunice Marins expresses this in her speech:

> I live in a community in the Jaraguá Peak, which is 15 min by car from the center of the city of São Paulo. So, as we are living in the middle of the white community, we feel a bit shy, a bit caged. When you walk on the street, people stare at you as if you were an animal, as something different. When they come in the village to visit the Amerindian People (…) they are surprised: 'wow, this little child is running all naked in the village!' It is as if it was something extraordinary, and I think it is very bad for us to feel that we are something different. (Marins 2010, p. 57)

Eunice speaks of looking different in the eyes of the other and that this hurts. She speaks of being perceived in a sub-human condition that excludes her humanity. In relation to this type of differentiation, the indigenous peoples point out the need for a dedifferentiation. It should not be contradictory with other types of differentiation, seen for example in their demands for a differentiated healthcare and education. This is not a fixed differentiation, as an ethnic identity taken as the marker of difference would be. Differentiation and dedifferentiation are part of a process of singularization in which people and communities can explore and express themselves in an active and creative manner.

Differentiation and dedifferentiation paths coexist in the indigenous discourse and express a form of elaborating the suffering generated by the impossibility of living a satisfactory life in their territories of belonging (cf. Achatz and Guimarães 2018; Sousa et al. in preparation). Numerous leaders criticize the situation their communities are in, in demarcated lands, often reduced in size, where they feel confined. There is a parallel between this and the feeling that their cultures are cooped up in reduced identities, which are fixed in time and tied to stereotypes and stigmas. Assuming that culture is homogeneous and that people are bound to sociocultural settings tends to produce mismatched encounters and suffering in the dialogue with the indigenous peoples:

> We have to hear most of the public opinion chastising Amerindian People; we hear it a lot. Sometimes we have to remain silent, to avoid feeling indifferent. This hurts our people and our children feel it too. (Lulu Darã 2010, p. 70)

We note that the treatment given to indigenous peoples in Brazil has historically removed their condition of active subjects, creators of knowledge and interlocutors whose point of view is worthy of attention. This frequently caused forced silence and sometimes silence as a resistance strategy or even as an option when the interlocutor is notably unable to understand them (cf. Guimarães 2016b). Because of the various forms of silencing, prejudiced views about indigenous peoples, impermeable to revisions, remained for a long time unquestioned.

Concerning this second layer of dialogue, in which feelings become more visible, Achatz and Guimarães (2018) conclude it is of utmost importance to understand historical, political, and cultural aspects that permeate the leaders' positions. However, these elements must be taken into account together with the heterogeneous positions each individual has and the personal meanings attributed to them. From the singularity of the cultures that cannot be fixed in static identities, we pass to the singularity of the individuals in the culture, their multiple forms of feeling and giving meaning to life experiences in the community.

A third and deeper layer in dialogue involves the opportunities of acting together, given the differences marked in the two previously described layers. This layer concerns an insurmountable asymmetry in the alterity relation, articulated with the creative possibilities of reinventing the present. The willingness to create with the other is also a willingness to transform oneself, to handle the dimensions of experience that are not yet confined to pre-established determinations. This layer in dialogue leads us to reflect also about the consequences of creation in the context of alterity relations.

From the leaders' speeches, we noted that creating paths together is only possible when the interlocutors feel respected. Some equivocations in communication stand in the way of sharing. This is seen, for instance, when what the other supposedly lacks is substituted by an identity between the I and the other. This is the typical procedure of assistentialist practices, whether implemented by the State, by private institutions or by people who come to the communities: they diagnose a problem and try to solve it from a perspective that is exogenous to the communities. This ends up being another violent practice, even if it is presented in the form of charity.

Assistentialism, as an uncritical assistance to the indigenous populations, tends to depreciate communities' autonomy to create solutions for what they judge to be their problems. They reduce the communities' issues to economic factors, placing indigenous people in the scope of class conflicts, as citizens whose access to means of production and capital is restricted and who are for this reason subject to systematic violence and lack fundamental rights. Indigenous leaders, however, call attention to the insufficiency of the universalizing public policies, designed for a generic and abstract citizen without allowing the participation of the communities. Brazilian public policies guidelines determine that the communities be heard in relation to education and healthcare, taking into account their cultural specificities and including them in the implementation process. Despite this, the non-indigenous healthcare and education professionals' educational background limits their possibilities of understanding the community. They are, most of the times, formed at the universities to think that some types of knowledge are above others. This precludes these professionals from being able to listen to the communities' specificities. Achatz and Guimarães (2018) point out that creating projects and communitarian actions with the indigenous communities depends on the due consideration the heterogeneity of the indigenous peoples, since healthcare, education, forms of social organization and so on are not equally conceived and practiced.

Dialogue can further develop when an affective ground is formed between the interlocutors and they are able to dislocate themselves, forming a forth layer in interaction, as discussed by Achatz and Guimarães (2018). In this layer, it is possible to encounter the cosmological foundations of the indigenous thoughts and practices. These foundations were briefly presented in the meeting organized by the CRP and in the forums. While apprehending a different thought system is not entirely possible and a language barrier is often imposed, some hints of this dimension are exposed in translations, explanations of fragments of rites and myths. In these brief accounts, people may open themselves, gradually, to experience an imbalance, a certain creative disorganization of their ways of experiencing and acting in the world. At this stage, the semantic rectifications in the dialogue become clearer, bringing new meanings to the dialogical relation.

An example of these semantic rectifications is found in the meanings of the term "to fight" to the indigenous leaders. On the one hand, it is connected to the lack of choice, since they are continuously challenged by the State, companies, churches, etc. On the other hand, fighting also strengthens them, because the more and the better you fight, the more you reinforce your relations with the past, the present and the future, conferring a deeper meaning to political actions. In their accounts of their fights, the leaders return to narratives where they are not victims of the colonizers, but "warriors", political agents that transform history. Victimization is, further, a perspective where Europe is in the moving center of history. This is precisely the point of view that is reverted in the leaders' narratives. Yet another sense to fight lies in the maintenance of the territory. The leaders emphasize that the meaning of the fight for the land is, to them, very different from what the white people understand as "land", "territory", "environment" or "religion". To them, the semantic field of "land" involves temporality, ancestrality, children, the multiplicity of living beings, and "spirituality".

Each term that appears in dialogue demands new rectifications. This is the case with the notion of spirituality, as well as the notion of God, employed often by some of the leaders. These words make reference to personal and collective experiences distinct from those present in normal academic life in Brazil. Spirituality, psychologically related to the opposition between transcendence and immanence, is a term the indigenous leaders often employ to refer to a certain type of relation to their territory, their ancestors, their memories and dreams. It is also connected to the relations between generations, the subjectivity intrinsic to each being and the care each person should have when relating to the beings in their unique character.

In this sense, we analyze some of the speeches:

> First of all, I don't know if what's missing today is respect or value to each people, because we, the Guarani, my formation I started when I was thirteen and the Guarani spirituality made me a leader and a *cacique*.[8] We, the Guarani, have always taken into account spirituality because this is what makes and keeps us Guarani, we believe in this very much. (Mariano, R. S. 2010, p. 44)

Spirituality also appears as something particular for each person, profoundly intimate and of great value to the communities, as seen in the following excerpt:

> This is why the spiritual part is so important to us. We carry it in our hearts, and people at my age, we already pass on to others how important the spiritual part is. (Cândido Lima 2010, p. 79)

Being valuable and intimate, spirituality is also an aspect of experience that indigenous peoples try to protect in encounters with whom they still do not trust (cf. Achatz and Guimarães 2018). They also consider this the aspect most complex and difficult to understand to those who do not share cosmological foundations. Even inside the communities, certain parts of knowledge are preserved and accessible only to those who become wise elders:

> Nowadays I don't do my prayers here, in public, because it's something sacred to us. So we made songs for the children to sing, because, honestly, I don't like to pray in public, because this part of our culture is sacred to us, to me in particular, I don't know if it's always going to be like this. But it's very important to us, this part, I don't even know how to explain it, because we have our children in the villages and we pass on to them what was passed on to us. I spent time with many people older than I am, and so we remember how important our culture is, most of all spirituality, in the village. (Cândido Lima 2010, p. 79)

Spiritually involves furthermore a relation with temporality based on respect to each person's rhythm of approaching the meanings of life trajectories; this knowledge cannot be acquired in its entirety, but in parts, in each person's path, followed with their own bodies: it is a personal experience.

> It's really hard to talk about the spiritual part, because we have feelings, we are dealing with our ancestors, who were very strong, and today we are searching for this slowly. You can't

---

[8] Term used to refer to one type of leader of the community. This is a specific position in the community, whereas others can also be leaders.

just rush and dig it all at once, the emotion is too strong, when it's over we can't handle it, you understand? So our search is slow, first the indigenous culture set on the ground, then the language and then Nhanderu, like she said, Nhanderu is God, he will bring the rest to us, so this is our objective. (Marcolino, C. 2010, p. 81)

The meaning of spirituality, of 'fighting', 'land', and 'territory' can only be communicated in the indigenous people's own temporality. Besides this, there must be an adequate environment for communication. The forums about the indigenous presence in São Paulo presented limitations to dialogue. They relate not only to linguistic barriers, since, for some of the speakers Portuguese was not the first language, but also to the university facilities, the architecture and the format of the event, in an auditorium. In these occasions, we had a small glimpse of how the communities conceived the abovementioned terms and others employed in the dialogue.

The recurring complaints about the inadequacy of the buildings and auditoriums for the transmission of indigenous messages encouraged us to develop a project to create more adequate settings for such interethnic dialogue. One of the strategies we thought of was to build an Amerindian house inside the Institute of Psychology of the University of São Paulo. Together with indigenous leaders, we proposed a project to build the House.

While preparing documents for the project's formal submission, I remembered a dialogue I had had years before with an indigenous elder in his community. He explained to me that their traditional houses were like a memory stick, because that is where they stored their memories. Everything that happens during rituals – the songs, dances, and speeches – constitutes embodied and narrated memories that impregnate the space and are kept alive by the people who preserve this space.

A group of Guarani from the Indigenous Land of *Jaraguá*, in the periphery of São Paulo, came to build the house after all approvals were obtained at the institutional level of the University. Instead of creating psychological intervention projects *for* Amerindian communities and people, we invited them for a shared intervention to transform *the University*: a small step in the process of transforming psychological knowledge, involving the academic community and addressing theoretical innovations.

Acknowledgement This work is supported by FAPESP (grant number 18/13145-0).

References

Achatz, R. W., & Guimarães, D. S. (2018). An invitation to travel in an interethnic arena: Listening carefully to Amerindian leaders' speeches. *Integrative Psychological and Behavioral Science, 52*(4), 595–613.
Aureliano, A. L. P., & Machado, E. V., Jr. (2012). Alcoolismo no contexto indígena brasileiro: mapeamento da bibliografia nacional. *Antropos, 4*(5), 40–72.
Boesch, E. E. (1991). *Symbolic action theory and cultural psychology*. Berlin.
Boesch, E. E. (2007). Culture – individual – culture: the cycle of knowledge. In W. J. Lonner & S. A. Hayes (Eds.), *Discovering cultural psychology: a profile and selected readinds of Ernest*

References

E. Boesch (pp. 201–212). Charlotte: Information Age Publishing. (Texto original publicado em 1992).

Brasil [Constituição (1988)]. (2012) *Constituição da República Federativa do Brasil:* texto constitucional promulgado em 5 de outubro de 1988, com as alterações adotadas pelas Emendas Constitucionais nos 1/1992 a 68/2011, pelo Decreto Legislativo n° 186/2008 e pelas Emendas Constitucionais de Revisão nos 1 a 6/1994. Brasília: Câmara dos Deputados, Edições Câmara, 2012.

Cândido Lima, J. (2010). Juraci Cândido de Lima. Conselho Regional de Psicologia da 6a Região (Ed), Psicologia e povos indígenas (pp. 78–79) São Paulo, SP: CRPSP.

Carneiro da Cunha, M. (1978). *Os mortos e os outros: uma análise do sistema funerário e da noção de pessoa entre os índios Krahó. [the deads and the others: An analysis of the mortuary system and the notion of person among the Krahó Indians].* São Paulo: Hucitec.

Cassirer, E. (1994). *A filosofia do iluminismo.* Campinas: Editora da UNICAMP. (Original published in 1932).

Conselho Regional de Psicologia da 6ª Região. (2010). *Psicologia e Povos Indígenas [psychology and indigenous peoples].* São Paulo: CRPSP.

Danowski, D., & Viveiros De Castro, E. (2014). *Há mundo por vir? Ensaio sobre os medos e os fins* [is there world for coming? Essay on the fears and the ends]. Desterro (Florianópolis), Brazil: Cultura e Barbárie, Instituto Socioambiental.

Faleiros, A. (2014). Tradução poética e xamanismo transversal: correspondências entre Llansol e Baudelaire. *Revista Brasileira de Literatura Comparada, 24,* 16–32.

Figueiredo, L. C. M. (2007a). A invenção do psicológico: quatro séculos de subjetivação 1500–1900. São Paulo: Escuta (184p.) (Trabalho original publicado em 1992).

Figueiredo, L. C. M. (2007b). A metapsicologia do cuidado. *Psyche, 11*(2), 13–30.

Gadamer, H-G. (Meurer trad. 2008). *Verdade e Método I*: Traços fundamentais de uma hermenêutica filosófica. São Paulo: Vozes. (Trabalho original publicado em 1960).

Gândavo, P. M. (1576). *Historia da prouincia Sa[n]cta Cruz a qui vulgarme[n]te chamamos Brasil* [History of Santa Cruz province that we usually call Brazil]. Lisboa: Antônio Gonçalves.

Grubits, S., & Guimarães, L. A. M. (2007). Alcoolismo e violência em etnias indígenas: uma visão crítica da situação brasileira. *Psicologia & Sociedade, 19*(1), 45–51.

Guimarães, D. S. (2016a). *Amerindian paths: Guiding dialogues with psychology* (p. 366p). Charlotte: Information Age Publishing.

Guimarães, D. S. (2016b). Descending and ascending trajectories of dialogical analysis: Seventh analytic interpretation on the short story "The Guerrillero". *Psicologia USP, 27*(2), 189–200.

Guimarães, D. S., & Nash, R. (in preparation). O que nos comunica o ritmo? Reflexões a partir do construtivismo semiótico-cultural em psicologia.

Ideti, & Duwe, E. (2010). *Tenonderã - Um olhar para o Futuro* [Documentário on-line]. In *São Paulo*. Recuperado de: Brazil. http://vimeo.com/20263900.

Jahoda, G. (1982). Psychology and anthropology: A psychological perspective. New York: Academic Press Inc. (270p.).

Jahoda, G. (1999). *The Images of Savages: Ancient roots of modern prejudice in Western culture* (p. 320). New York: Routledge.

Kawaguchi, D. R., & Guimarães, D. S. (2018). Is everybody human? The relationship between humanity and animality in Western and Amerindian myth narratives. *Culture & Psychology,* 1354067X1877905.

Krenak, A. (1998). O eterno retorno do encontro. In Ricardo, C. A. (Ed.) (2000). *Povos indígenas no Brasil: 1996/2000* (pp. 43–48). São Paulo: Instituto Socioambiental.

Lévinas (1954/1987). The Ego and the totality. In Levinas (1987) *Collected Philosophical Works of Immanuel Lévinas* (pp. 25–46). Dordrecht, NL: Martinus Nijhoff Publishers.

Lévinas, E. (1980). *Totalidade e Infinito.* Lisboa: Edições 70. (287 p.)

Lévinas, E. (1993). *O Humanismo do outro homem.* Petrópolis: Vozes.

Lévinas, E. (2004). O eu e a totalidade. In E. Lévinas (Ed.), *Entre Nós: Ensaios Sobre a Alteridade* (pp. 34–65). Petrópolis: Vozes.

Lévi-Strauss, C. (1952). *Race and history*. Paris: UNESCO.
Lulu Darã, A. (2010) Cacique Antonísio Lulu Darã. Conselho Regional de Psicologia da 6a Região (Ed), Psicologia e povos indígenas. (pp. 60–71) São Paulo: CRPSP.
Macena, P. L. (2014). *Saúde e educação indígenas: oralidade, cultura e políticas públicas*. Conference presented at the *3rd Fórum: A Presença Indígena em São Paulo*, Institute of Psychology, University of São Paulo, October 9, 2014. Retrieved Novemeber 3, 2015 at http://psicologiacultural.ip.usp.br/sites/default/files/Carta%20de%20Manaus.pdf.
Macena, P. L. & Guimarães, D. D. (2016) A Psicologia Cultural na fronteira com as concepções Mbya Guarani de educação. In Conselho Regional de Psicologia 6ª Região (Org.). *Na Fronteira da Psicologia com os Saberes Tradicionais: Práticas e Técnicas* (pp. p. 135–147). São Paulo: CRPSP.
Maciel, M. N. (2014). As histórias que ouvi da minha avó e o que aprendi com elas. *LEETRA Indígena*, 4(1), 10–16.
Marcolino, C. (2010). Cacique Claudino Marcolino. Conselho Regional de Psicologia da 6ª Região (Ed.) *Psicologia e povos indígenas* (pp. 80–81). São Paulo, SP: CRPSP.
Mariano, R. S. (2010) Cacique Renato da Silva Mariano. In Conselho Regional de Psicologia 6ª Região (Org.). Psicologia e Povos Indígenas (pp. 43–45). São Paulo: CRPSP.
Marins, E. (2010) Eunice Augusto Marins. In Conselho Regional de Psicologia 6ª Região (Org.). Psicologia e Povos Indígenas (pp. 57–59). São Paulo: CRPSP.
Melo Franco, A. A. (2000). *O índio brasileiro e a revolução francesa*: as origens brasileiras da teoria da bondade natural. Rio de Janeiro: Livraria José Olympio (Texto original publicado em 1937).
Overing Kaplan, J. (1977) "Comments (Symposium 'Social time and social space in lowland South American societies')". Actes du XLII Congrès International des Américanistes, vol. II, pp. 387–394.
Pankararu, D. (2010) Maria das Dores da Conceição Pereira do Prado (Dora Pankararu). Conselho Regional de Psicologia da 6ª Região (Ed), Psicologia e povos indígenas. (pp. 41–43) São Paulo, SP: CRPSP.
Patto, M. H. S. (2008) *A Produção Do Fracasso Escolar* [The production of scholar failure]. São Paulo: Casa do Psicólogo (Texto original publicado em 1990).
Quijano, A. (2000). *Colonialidad del poder, eurocentrismo y América Latina [Coloniality of power, eurocentrism and Latin America]*. Buenos Aires: Consejo Latinoamericano de Ciencias Sociales.
Seeger, A. (1980). *Os índios e nós: estudos sobre sociedades tribais brasileiras*. Rio de Janeiro: Editora Campus Ltda.
Simão, L. M. (2003). Beside rupture – Disquiet; beyond the other - Alterity. *Culture & Psychology*, 9(4), 449–459.
Simão, L. M. (2004) Alteridade no diálogo e construção do conhecimento. In: Martínez, A. M.; Simão, L. M. (Orgs.), *O outro no desenvolvimento humano:* diálogos para a pesquisa e a prática profissional em psicologia (pp. 29–39). São Paulo: Pioneira Thomson Learning.
Simão, L. M. (2010). *Ensaios Dialógicos: compartilhamento e diferença nas relações eu outro* (p. 286). São Paulo: HUCITEC.
Simão. (2015). The contemporary perspective of semiotic cultural constructivism: For an hermeneutical reflexivity in psychology. In *Marsico, Ruggieri and Salvatore (orgs.) Reflexivity and Psychology* (pp. 65–85). Charlotte, NC, Estados Unidos: Information Age Publishing.
Sousa, F. R.; Gonzalez, R. & Guimarães, D. S. (in preparation) Luta e resistência: dimensões para a promoção da saúde Mbya Guarani. (Manuscript in preparation). Universidade de São Paulo. São Paulo.
Souza, M. L. P., Deslandes, S. F., & Garnelo, L. (2010). Modos de Vida e modos de beber de jovens indígenas em um contexto de transformações [ways of life and ways of drinking among indigenous youth in a context of transformations]. *Ciência e Saúde coletiva*, 15(3), 709–716.
Todorov, T. (2011). *A conquista da América: a questão do outro*. São Paulo: Martins Fontes. (Texto original publicado em 1982.

Valsiner, J. (2000). *The social mind: Construction of the idea* (p. 504). Cambridge: Cambridge University press.
Viveiros de Castro, E. B. (1987). "Nimuendajú e os Guarani". Em Nimuendajú, C. (1987). *As lendas da criação e destruição do mundo como fundamentos da religião dos Apapocuva-Guarani* (pp. xvii-xxxviii). São Paulo, Hucitec.
Viveiros de Castro, E. B. (2004). Perspectival anthropology and the method of controlled equivocation. *Tipití: Journal of the Society for the Anthropology of Lowland South America, 2*(1), 1–22.
Wagner, R. (2010). *A invenção da cultura* (p. 253). São Paulo: Cosac Naify. Original published in 1981.
Wertsch, J. (1993). *Voices of the mind: A sociocultural approach to mediated action.* Cambridge: Harvard University Press.
Wundt, W. (1916). *Elements of folk psychology* (p. 533). London: George Allen and Unwin Ltd.
Zittoun, T. (2006). *Transitions: Development through symbolic resources.* Greenwich: Information Age Publishing.

Chapter 3
Second Principle: Dedifferentiation, Personal Interaction and Sharing

To approach a different cultural tradition, psychology must delve deeply into it, which in turn will produce changes in psychological concepts and methodologies themselves. Cross-cultural psychology and even cultural psychology usually work with concepts and methodologies that come from and are more adequate to the reality of WEIRD (Western, Educated, Industrialized, Rich and Democratic) societies (cf. Groot et al. 2011; Hwang 2015; Teo 2011). Much work is necessary if these psychologies expect to produce more extensive knowledge about human beings in different societies.

During our activities, numerous indigenous leaders have addressed the possibilities and limits to intercultural interaction in their speeches. Each utterance brings new nuances to this issue. In this chapter, I will develop considerations on these nuances, with special attention to the indigenous speeches directed to psychologists. Creating spaces for constructive dialogue has contributed to the Amerindian Network's understanding of indigenous people's demands and to finding solutions together. As we listen to them, we gain familiarity and, gradually, new paths are shown to us regarding possible partnerships and projects.

Understanding the disquieting experience that emerges in our intercultural experiences guides the construction of a temporary ground of meanings for significant exchanges in the relation with the other, i.e., the participants in the relation must necessarily build some regularity that will be the basis for establishing mutual trust.

The process of psychological knowledge construction in the Amerindian Network does not start from academic inquiries into the other's world. It begins in communities' concrete situations, which provide the basic foundations for reflections that may eventually result in relevant academic knowledge. In this way, we reorient the direction of knowledge construction, starting from participation in the communitarian social field to observation and selection of relevant aspects for consideration. This theoretical-methodological path has been characterized as *observant participation* (cf. Albert 2002; Bastien 2007), an inversion in relation to the well-established qualitative method known as participant observation.

In observant participation, participation precedes all else. It is centered in the affective constructions of the referents that guide co-authored projects. I understand that psychological knowledge production and all the ethical values it encompasses are subject to the affective basis that emerges in the relations. Understanding this affective basis is central to creating collaborative actions and to producing knowledge committed to the communities. In the scope of indigenous psychology, it is thus important to provide theoretical-methodological grounds for this trajectory.

I will establish these grounds through further analysis of some of the speeches of the indigenous leaders who were present in the CRPSP meetings. The analysis shed light on the cognitive-affective tuning process and the semiotic elaboration of alterity relations, as developed in a previous publication (cf. Guimarães 2018), revisited here. Other speeches from these same meetings were dialogically approached in the previous chapter, based on the work of Achatz and Guimarães (2018).

Before presenting the selected speeches, I will discuss theoretical-methodological dialogism in the Amerindian Network from the point of view of the Russian linguist and philosopher Mikhail Bakhtin, one the main references of the semiotic-cultural constructivism in psychology (cf. Simão 2010). Bakhtin is an influential author in literary theory and criticism, discourse analysis and semiotics. His main propositions state that linguistics should include extra-linguistic factors, such as the situation of the speech, the speaker's intentions, the relation of the speaker to the listener, and the historical moment (Holquist 2004). The author's understanding of linguistic processes is thus *trans-linguistic*, since it goes beyond the idea of language as a system. It is important to consider in more detail some of Bakhtin's propositions, since he was one of the first authors in dialogism to describe the I as "oriented according to the other's language and world" (Marková 2006b, p. 126). His work is in line with the purpose of the present investigations.

Bakhtin (1979/2015) understands the utterance as the real unit of discursive communication (p. 274), which should not be confused with the *sentence*, the language unit. The difference resides in the fact that, in the sentence, the word is assumed to be neutral, impartial, devoid of expressiveness, while in the utterance the word is connected to a communication's concrete circumstances, involving a context, the interlocutors, the addressivity, responsivity, and so on. In the sentence, the word is reduced to its linguistic aspects – the phonetic, syntactic, semantic, grammatical, lexical elements – while in the utterance, the word goes beyond this field and becomes extra-linguistic. It acquires characteristics of expressiveness, intention, intonation, etc.

The extra-verbal situation is composed of three factors: "(1) *the interlocutors' shared spatial horizon*, which can be seen by both, (2) the knowledge and understanding of the situation that is common to both interlocutors, (3) their shared evaluation of this situation, that is unanimous between them" (Achatz 2016, p. 17). Thus, the extra-verbal aspect of communication concerns the speakers' shared horizon, but it is not external to the utterance. The whole of signification is in part *perceived*, in the words used in dialogue, and in part *presumed*, in the shared horizon of the speakers; the connection to the speakers' social existence, given by the extra-verbal aspects of the utterance, is what makes it intelligible.

All genres of discourse involve utterances: from real dialogue, the simplest and most classical form of discursive communication, to more complex constructions, as scientific and artistic works, because "discourse can only truly exist in the form of concrete utterances, from determined speakers, the subjects of discourse" (Bakhtin 1979/2015, p. 274). The utterance has some structural particularities. One of them is that it is limited by the alternation of the speakers. This means that before a verbalization starts, there are others' utterances; and, after it is finished, there are others' responses or, yet, a silent but actively responsive understanding from the other, or even a responsive action based on this understanding. From the alternation of the speakers comes another particularity of the utterance: its specific conclusibility, which expresses the position of the speaker and evokes a possible answer. In this sense, "every concrete utterance is a link in a particular field's chain of discursive communication" (Bakhtin 1979/2015, p. 296), since the answers that follow an utterance are interconnected and interdependent. Other constitutive elements of the utterance are its direction towards someone, or addressivity, and its expressive aspect, related to the compositional choices in discourse, as style, the means, and so on.

The notion of extra-verbal situation, connected to the notion of utterance, concerns that which is shared in dialogue, but remits us also to its opposite, that which remains inaccessible to the other in the alterity relation, the other's singularity, their ipseity. The search to understand the place of alterity in the utterance led Leão and Guimarães (in preparation) to discuss the notion of polyphony, which, etymologically means "many sounds". In music, polyphony is a type of composition in which the different melodic vocal or instrumental lines are autonomous and are articulated according to the rules of the counterpoint. Polyphonic music contrasts with monophonic music, in which all the voices follow the same melodic line, in unison, as in Gregorian chants, or homophonic music, in which the voices have different melodic lines, but are rhythmically identical. Polyphony is a notion taken from music by Bahktin (1929/2013) to describe the network of tensions between the narrator and the characters in Dostoyevsky's novels.

Bakhtin (1929/2013) points out that the term polyphony is used in a metaphoric sense, since music and literature are very different, there being no more than a figurative analogy between them. In polyphony, the I does not make the other a mere object of their consciousness, but recognizes them as subjects with a conscience of their own, of equal value to the I's consciousness. The essence of polyphony consists in the fact that the voices remain relatively independent and autonomous, at the same time they combine. "The artistic will of polyphony is the will to combine many wills, the will to the event" (Bahktin 1929/2013, p. 23). In this sense, the notion of the counterpoint shows the relation between two or more relatively independent voices. The counterpoint originates and rules the polyphony.

Leão and Guimarães (in preparation) consider, yet, Bakhtin's (1929/2013) statement that "dialogical relations are extra-linguistic. However, they cannot be separated from the field of *discourse*, that is, the field of language as an integral and concrete phenomenon" (p. 209, italics by the author). According to him, "dialogical relations are absolutely impossible without logical and concrete-semantic relations, but they are irreducible to them and have their own specificities" (p. 210), so that to become dialogical, the logical and concrete-semiotic relations must be materialized, that is, they must pass to another field of existence, becoming discourse, an utterance produced by someone who occupies a particular position in life and a position of authorship in relation to the addressees of their speech.

In other words, the dialogical relations require at least two concrete utterances, made from distinct subjective positions. In the case of a single utterance from only one person, to constitute a dialogical relation, some distance from oneself must be identifiable, an internal reservation, limitation or deviation from authority. There may be likewise dialogical relations between styles of language, social dialects, images, sounds, etc.

Dialogicity is usually represented according to triadic diagrams, as elaborated by Moscovici (cf. 2000/2003) regarding the dialogical process of transformation of social representations, summarized by Marková (2003/2006a), explaining the alterego-object dynamics, and considered by Cornejo (2008) as the minimal dialogical situation.

In an alternative perspective, I understand that in the relations between distinct cultures what is presumed/shared between the I and the other has become overburdened. It is therefore necessary to bring into light the gaps, to understand the processes that happen in the borderland where the other is unknown. This carries the potential for elaborating novelties. In this case, there is no extra-verbal shared horizon, since the antecedent dimensions of the relation have not yet been tuned.

In the course of observant participation, meaningful affective experiences take place, making it possible to problematize perceptions and imagined scenarios that sustain prejudices and preconceptions about the other, while new cognitive-affective meanings are elaborated. The process of affective activation of the other, emphasized by indigenous people, depends on the willingness to participate in sensitive experiences that create extra-verbal sharing, even if temporarily. I defend that this sharing is the basis for possible semiotic elaborations in the direction of creating an indigenous psychology. In it, affective experiences cross the psychologist's semiotic process, supporting the resetting of previously established knowledge.

The first excerpt selected for this study comes from the transcribed speech of Mariano Fernando, at the time the *cacique* of the *Tekoa Rio Silveira* Mbya Guarani community, situated in the rural area of the city of Boracéia/SP:

> In the indigenous community of Rio Silveira, in Boracéia, we have a cleaning project, to promote hygiene. We already did this before. It is difficult to carry things in parallel, to manage both [cultures], because today there is no more organic food. It used to be yucca, corn, sweet potatoes, so the husks were useful, they were fertilizers, it was all organic. Today it's cans everywhere; you cannot throw them on the ground because they do not decompose the forest.
> [...]
> Outsiders don't understand how the indigenous politics works. So nowadays, we have to deal with indigenous politics, but together, in parallel with you.
> [...]
> You have to work with the entire situation, you have to work the parallels; the mind has to be in both places at the same time. It is not because we speak Portuguese very well that

we say: "I'm not an indigenous person anymore". This also has to do with people's minds, because people go to the city and they think "I'm a minority, I don't want to say I'm an indigenous person", they will think: "I don't want to say I'm Indian, because if I do I'll be disrespected". This affects the mind of the indigenous person. (Fernando, M. 2010, pp. 46–49).

The second excerpt selected comes from the transcribed speech of Julio César Pio, of the Terena people, then vice-*cacique* of the Ekeruá village, situated in the rural area of the city of Avaí/SP:

> I would also like to talk about the non-Indians who stay with us in the community, because of what Bianca said. […] Anyone can come and say, "Look, I'm also an Indian", but this is not as we see, is it. This is why *cacique* Anildo put it well, we must be careful with what we say, we have to pay close attention, and why?
>
> Because we have many young people in the community, and they can even marry an outsider. Then this young man comes and learns our language and says, "I'm also an indigenous person, I have my rights", but what about the indigenous feeling? Does he have the indigenous feeling? The white folk are a different feeling. So, we are indigenous, we can live in an apartment, in the city, abroad, but we are still indigenous. This is what I would like to say to you (Pio, J.C. 2010, p. 85).

The third excerpt selected for this study comes from the transcribed speech of Gerson Cecílio Damaceno, of the Krenak people, *cacique* of the Vanuíre community, situated in the rural area of the city of Arco-Íris/SP:

> […] In the Vanuíre community many have already been arrested for fishing in the Aguapéi River. They are prosecuted for this, I've seen Indians handcuffed. Honestly, it broke my heart to see this. As our relative just said, we need to have a strong spirit so we don't do anything stupid, because the worst thing is when the man or the woman does something stupid and then it's too late. I even saw a minor and an older boy, walking handcuffed in the street, because they had killed a capybara to feed their family.
>
> To fish in the Aguapeí River, we leave our village. There's no river in our village, nor woodlands, everything has been cut down, they left the land practically barren, there's nothing. Sometimes we want to fish, but we are afraid. Long ago, I was 13, 14 years old, so many people went fishing, and we were banned by gunmen. We went fishing and it was people running all over, and they were shooting us. And now we are inside our land with our hands tied.
>
> […]
>
> We have a cabin too, where every Monday is culture day, and every day we have two teachers, a Kaingang and a Krenak, teaching our children. All Indian children there speak two languages, Krenak and Kaingang. So, we are like this: we are living in a place where many people come and think everything is okay, but in our hearts we know: we know what we've been through and what we need (Damaceno, G. C. 2010, pp. 75–76).

I consider the speeches as utterances, that is, the meaning they express is not restricted to the relation between the speaker and the addressee. It includes the concrete, extra-verbal situation, in which the utterance answers to a discursive chain that precedes it and points to a horizon of future possibilities in the course of interactions that unfolds from what is being said.

The excerpts' analysis was based on the identification of the semantic contents' referents. We identified antinomies, to which the speaker attributed emotional value: the expressive aspect of the utterance (Wertsch 1993, p. 108). The contents of the excerpts are cognitive-affective elaborations concerning the life situations and thoughts of the speakers, narrated to the specific public of the CRPSP events. The psychologist/researcher who interacted with the speeches, materialized in the form of written reports, becomes also an interlocutor in a dialogical field and actively builds meaning relating to them. It is not, however, an arbitrary construction; it includes their reader's perspective, which adds another link to the dialogical chain that unfolds from the initial oral expressions, recorded from the events.

From this borderland, I highlighted six referents from the semantic contents of the speeches that I believe to be relevant for the present discussion. Misunderstandings as signs of disjunction in perspectives, distinct notions of nature, a recursive (cyclic and irreversible) notion of temporality, the notion of intercultural parallelism, limitations to the cognitive process that articulates perceptions, and imagined scenarios grounded on the affective dimensions subjacent to the dialogue.

Misunderstandings as Signs of Disjunction in Perspectives

In the excerpts, the speakers establish an antinomy between the observers who create meaning from an outside perspective (for instance, people who are not members of an indigenous community) and those who observe and create meaning from the inside (the indigenous view). The difference in perspective creates impasses in dialogue, misunderstandings and equivocations. As Mariano points out in his speech: "*outsiders don't understand how the indigenous politics works*", as well as Gerson: "*we are living in a place where many people come and think everything is okay, but in our hearts we know: we know what we've been through and what we need*".

Equivocation is recurrent in the encounters between the colonizers and the indigenous peoples. I have been discussing this subject during the last few years (cf. Guimarães 2011). An evidence of the high frequency of misunderstandings is in the plurality of names given to each indigenous group. They derive from the first contact with the foreigners, who wanted to identify the peoples to understand their differences, which lead, however, to a series of mistakes. Many such cases where noted already in the fifteenth century, when the Portuguese, French and natives were in conflict in the Brazilian coastline. For instance, the names the Portuguese Jesuits gave to their indigenous allies "varied from one chronicle to the other to an extent that little is known of their criteria for division of these peoples" (Sztutman 2005, p. 137). The Amerindians, in turn, seemed accustomed to the phenomenon of external naming and its unavoidable mistakes. This subject has been developed in many myths about the encounter with the white people, as the following:

> The first time a White man saw an Indian, he had no clothes on and was playing with a bat. […] The white man asked the Indian who he was and the Indian, not understanding Portuguese, answered in his language: I am killing [playing with] a bat. We call the bat kaxi. So the white man gave the name: "you and your tribe are the Kaxinawa (kaxi-nawa)" (Lindemberg Monte 1984, as cited in Lagrou 2007, p. 182).

The gap between the addressed question (who are you?) and the given answer shows an effort to satisfy the other's expectations (I am doing this). Concerning the excerpt from the Kaxinawa people, Lagrou (2007) affirms that if there were no communication problems, the foreigner would have called his interlocutor *hunikuin* (true human), which is the way Pano speakers call themselves. The ethnonym that identifies a group as a people is frequently a foreign designation. The foreign view is never neutral, as no view is, when people are in a position of observers who attribute qualities to an event. Therefore, nomenclature follows the impressions or apparent characteristics observed by the foreigner (cf. Guimarães 2011). Every group, in turn, identifies themselves with an expression that means "truly human beings" (cf. Lagrou 2007; Lima 1996, 1999; Viveiros de Castro 1996, 2002/2006). This type of ethnocentrism – attributing truth to themselves in relation to other beings – is, according to Lévi-Strauss (1965/1984), a basic characteristic of all cultures.

The interethnic field of meaning construction is marked by foreign views that interact. The difference between internal and external points of view in relation to a cultural field tends to produce equivocation in dialogue. To Viveiros de Castro (2004), equivocation is inherent to the process of a culture becoming intelligible to another. It founds and motivates the relation instead of stopping it from happening, pointing out a difference in perspectives. Translating efforts assume equivocations always exist, establishing a communication from difference "instead of silencing the Other by presuming univocality – an essential similarity – between what the other and we are saying" (Viveiros de Castro 2004, p. 10).

The dialogical process is, thus, multidirectional. Each participant in the dialogical situation creates meanings and expresses them through different symbolic resources (Zittoun 2006), attempting to control the amount of equivocation, even if, to a certain extent, it is inevitable. The interethnic relation is thus an arena for multiple meaning constructions. Deconstructions, reconstructions and adjustments constitute the cycle of novelty production in culture. As perspectives are negotiated in the heterogeneous cultural field, tensions arise. All participants involved are agents of transformation, situated in particular positions.

Misunderstandings are more frequent in interethnic dialogue when objective reality is questioned; often, the ontological status of one of the participant's presumed reality is not shared by the other. Concerning the adequacy of certain psychological theories and practices to different cultural fields, Berger and Luckmann (1966/1991) propose:

> Psychological theories may be empirically adequate or inadequate, by which we do not mean their adequacy in terms of the procedural canons of empirical science, but rather, as interpretative schemes applicable by the expert or the layman to empirical phenomena in everyday life. For example, a psychological theory positing demoniacal possession is unlikely to be adequate in interpreting the identity problems of middle-class, Jewish intellectuals in New York City. These people simply do not have an identity capable of producing phenomena that could be so interpreted. The demons, if such there are, seem to avoid them. On the other hand, psychoanalysis is unlikely to be adequate for the interpretation of identity problems in rural Haiti, while some sort of Voudun psychology might supply interpretative schemes with a high degree of empirical accuracy. The two psychologies

demonstrate their empirical adequacy by their applicability in therapy, but neither thereby demonstrates the ontological status of its categories. Neither the Voudun gods nor libidinal energy may exist outside the world defined in the respective social contexts. But in these contexts they do exist by virtue of social definition and are internalized as realities in the course of socialization. Rural Haitians are possessed and New York intellectuals are neurotic. Possession and neurosis are thus constituents of both objective and subjective reality in these contexts. This reality is empirically available in everyday life. The respective psychological theories are empirically adequate in precisely the same sense. The problem of whether or how psychological theories could be developed to transcend this socio-historical relativity need not concern us here. (Berger and Luckmann 1966/1991, pp. 225–226).

When ontological categories are radically different, the conditions for understanding the other's views are precarious. This leads to *equivocation, which may be ressignified* when there is openness to transformation.

Distinct Concepts of Nature

It is possible to identify different concepts of nature when the Amerindians refuse the nature-culture dichotomy. Nature is not an untouched, distanced place. Quite the opposite: it is a cultivated place. However, industrialized products arrive in the communities, confronting the traditional ways of living in the forest: *"It is hard to carry things on in parallel, to manage both [cultures], because today there is no more organic food, it used to be yucca, corn, sweet potatoes, so the husks were useful, they were fertilizers, it was all organic. Today it's cans everywhere; you cannot throw them on the ground because they do not decompose in the forest"*.

Considering that the Amerindians refuse the concept of an untouched nature, the indigenous conservationist discourse is also an effort to maintain their territories and their ways of life. It is worth highlighting once more that the leaders' speeches about territory management and land demarcation do not refer to land as a geometric abstraction, or the surface area of a plot with economical value. The indigenous territory is not defined by the frontiers of Nation-States or private property, although they must presently face these frontiers and fight for land demarcation.

Usually for Western societies nature is the term used to refer to unpopulated lands.

Either exploitation of preservation of Nature share the assumption of an objectified nature, reified as an instance separate from and subjugated by society. Nothing could be more incompatible with Amazonian societies' cosmologies than this type of anthropocentric view. In those cosmologies, the universe is a social whole orchestrated by a complex system of symbolic interchanges between human and non-human subjects. Shamanism is the compass to this system (Albert 2002, p. 257).

Yanomami leader Davi Kopenawa has discussed this topic in many public forums, presenting a common point of view among the indigenous peoples:

We don't use the word "environment". We simply say we want to protect the entire forest. "Environment" is another people's word, it's a white people word. What you call "environment" is what is left of what you destroyed (Albert 2002, p. 259).

The relation with the environment presupposes, to the Amerindians, an indivisible totality: the positions of subject and object are interchangeable. The Amerindian form of subjectivation is known as animism. This designation indicates an ontology in which the social relation is the basis of the relation between the subject and the world. In it, humans and non-humans have subjective qualities, such as intentionality and consciousness. However, different from regular animism, in the Amerindian cosmos, subjectivities conceive themselves as humans and have, analogously, a human corporal shape. If one does not see these subjectivities as humans, it is because they are seeing things from an external position and are therefore mistaken or dissonant in relation to the internal point of view.

Descola (2005) proposed four *ontological routes* as the foundations for the distinct cultural traditions' thoughts and practices. These routes, defined by the anthropologist after extensive study of ethnographic material, coexist in our multiethnic world. Animism is the ontological route in which beings share a similar subjectivity, but have different bodies. This ontology is found in Amazonia, in the north regions of North America, in Siberia and in some parts of Asia and Melanesia. Naturalism, the European ontological route since antiquity, confers subjectivity only to human beings, who share with non-human entities their materiality. In totemism, found mainly among Australian native peoples, humans and non-humans pertain to categories: the beings generated by the same original prototype share physical and moral properties and relate by opposition to other totemic groups. Finally, in analogism, all the elements in the world are distinct from one another and relate through constructed correspondences. This ontological route is found in China, in Renaissance age Europe, in western Africa and among the indigenous peoples of the Andes and of Central America (Fig. 3.1).

The search for a general knowledge involves the researcher's personal-cultural perspective, which determines their theoretical-methodological choices, their beliefs, values, and ethical concerns. These elements are constitutive of knowledge. Scientific truth is produced from a particular point of view, connected to an

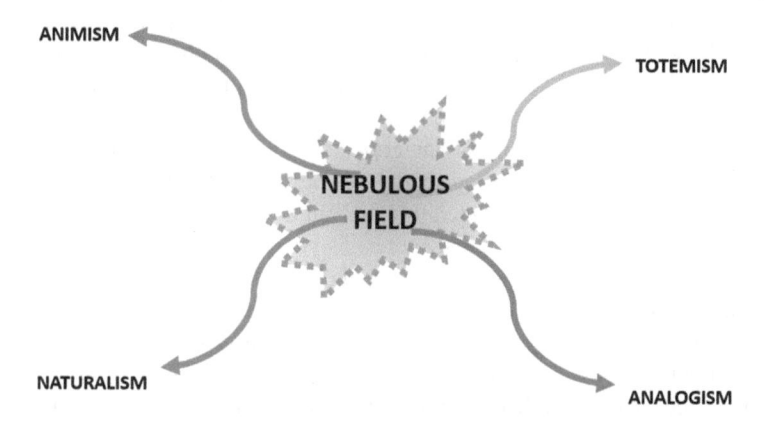

Fig. 3.1 Descola's four ontological routes emerging from a nebulous existential field. (Source: Guimarães 2016, p. xxvii)

individual ontological trajectory in which the person constructs social reality (Berger and Luckmann 1966/1991) mobilizing their personal and collective culture (Valsiner 2012). What each one establishes as their *natural attitude* is related to their sociocultural background. The ritualized practices and mythological narratives from this background offer the basic meanings related to the experience of alterity with people and things in the world.

The ontological routes gain particular relevance in the context of psychology's approach to indigenous peoples, considering Western psychology's ontological birthplace in the naturalist tradition. The naturalist route is not only different, but openly conflictive with some indigenous cosmovisions and practices.

Common sense sees culture as an independent variable, a view that is also present in institutionalized contexts. The reification of cultures as sets of objects produces a naturalized view of cultures as passive realities, subject to the interests of the researcher or consumer. This is coherent with the ontological route of naturalism, in which the world is a collection of objects which subjectively endowed entities, the human beings, can intentionally manipulate.

Subjectivizing rather than objectivizing the other, that is, the view that the other is likewise creating novelty from their own cultural background, has not only epistemological, but existential consequences.

Facing the world and the other as substances endowed with active properties and perspectives of their own implies recognizing the possibilities but also the limits to action. This is because each actor involved in interactions will have the potentials and limitations of their own particular perceptions and imagination, which constitute their points of view. Furthermore, crossing the frontier between distinct ontological routes, which constitute perspectives, may deeply transform a person. Traveling between cultural traditions is affectively demanding. Alternating from one form of creating reality to another demands reconstructing socially shared realities. This requires the person to go through experiences of socialization and affective identification with people in the new tradition, similar to the primary socialization that takes place during early childhood (Berger and Luckmann 1966/1991).

Ontological issues related to how people and cultures construct the world are particularly relevant to indigenous psychology. Given that philosophical issues dialogue with psychological theoretical-methodological propositions, psychological metatheory has underlying philosophical assumptions. Furthermore, I understand from Descola's (2005) ontological categories that different cultural traditions produce unique perspectives, creating reality not only in the sense of relative understandings of a world that is assumed to exist, but as unique existential possibilities shared by a group. The ontological routes, as perspectives generated in different cultural matrixes, are not the points of view of different traditions over a single reality, as in a relativist model (cf. Lima 1996). Instead, they show concomitant constructions over a nebulous background: different forms of existing that coexist and create distinct realities. The notion of dialogical multiplication, in turn, emphasizes nebulosity, the aspect of indetermination that impedes the apprehension of a shared field between the different perspectives in relation.

Realizing there are bodily differences, therefore, does not imply denying the subjectivity of the perceived body. However, for different bodies, equal terms have different objective correlatives. This particular relation to knowledge does not require assuming a transcendental point of view over an impersonal reality. "There is no reality independent from a subject" (Lima 1996, p. 31).

Misunderstandings, therefore, do not relate only to a tension between different points of view or object representations. Since concepts produce equivocation, as they refer to different objects in different perspectives, the experience of the body-subject is determinant in fixing of a point of view. The *reality* of a perspective, thus, is not a relative view over a reality that is negotiable from another perspective, as cultural relativism assumes. Latour's (1991/1994) comparative anthropology states that cultural relativism is based on one of the central partitions of modern societies, the nature-culture dichotomy, which, in turn, is due to the supposed distance man took from nature through the artifice of culture.

Viveiros de Castro (1996) argues that the Amerindian peoples' worldview is different from animism, adressing the need to understand the relation between all beings according to each being's perspective. The attention to a diversity of perspectives is different from the idea of cultural relativism (see also Kawaguchi and Guimarães 2018). In opposition to cultural relativism is the multinaturalist ontology.

(Multi)cultural relativism supposes a diversity of subjective and partial representations, each striving to grasp an external and unified nature, which remains perfectly indifferent to those representations. Amerindian thought proposes the opposite: a representational or phenomenological unity which is purely pronominal or deictic, indifferently applied to a radically objective diversity. One single 'culture', multiple 'natures' – perspectivism is multinaturalist, for a perspective is not a representation (Viveiros de Castro 1998, p. 478).

The mutinaturalist ontology points out the need for a reorganization of the nature-culture duality and its derivates: "[...] universal and particular, objective and subjective, physical and moral, fact and value, granted and constructed, necessity and spontaneity, immanence and transcendence, body and spirit, animality and humanity, among many others" (Viveiros de Castro 2002/2006, p. 348).

In the attempt to comprehend the particularities of indigenous thoughts and practices, and confronting them with the naturalistic tradition of modern psychologies, I observe that the multinaturalistic ontology admits the thoughts and practices of Christian, scientific, and indigenous traditions, without reducing one to the other, nor merging them together. "If Western multiculturalism is relativism as public policy, then Amerindian perspectivist shamanism is multinaturalism as cosmic politics" (Viveiros de Castro 1998, p. 472). The characteristic naturalism of the modern sciences can thus be understood as a case in the broader field of worldviews covered by multinaturalism.

Recursive Temporality

The notion of recursive temporality, at the same time cyclic and irreversible, is present in the idea that the relation with the invader is updated at each new interethnic encounter. The relation with alterity repeats itself, despite each situation being new and irreversible in time. In Gerson's words: "*[...] sometimes we want to fish, but we are afraid. Long ago, I was 13, 14 years old, so many people went fishing, and we were banned by gunmen. We went fishing and it was people running all over, and they were shooting us. And now we are inside our land with our hands tied*".

I have previously discussed this quasi-repeatability in the hierarchical, asymmetrical relations between indigenous peoples and the invaders (cf. Guimarães 2011; Guimarães and Simão 2017). The question that drives this discussion concerns how the autochthonous peoples of the Americas construct knowledge about themselves, others and the surrounding environment, taking this question back to the beginning of colonization (sixteenth century). Europeans were unsure as to those natives' humanity, an issue that, at the time, translated into determining if they had or did not have souls (Lévi-Strauss 1952, 1965/1984, Viveiros de Castro 1996, 2002/2006). The Amerindians, in turn, attempted to verify the supernaturality of the white people through long observations of whether their bodies decomposed or not after death.

Despite their ignorance in relation to one another and of both considering themselves as humans (ethnocentricism), they each created different hypotheses about the other, from which they developed different procedures to create some knowledge about alterity. One of the ways this relation was elaborated is seen, for example, in the first encounters of Amerindians and Europeans, about 500 years ago. Lévi-Strauss (cf. 1952, p. 12) presents an anecdote when discussing this. A few years after the invasion of the Americas, the Spanish enquiry commissions were sent to the Greater Antilles to verify if the Indians had a soul. Meanwhile, the Indians dedicated their time to drowning their white captives, to verify, through lengthy observation, whether their bodies were subject to putrefaction or not (Lévi-Strauss 1952).

To Lévi-Strauss, the anecdote shows that the Amerindians distinguished nature and culture, characterizing themselves as human beings, assuming an ethnocentric attitude typical of all cultures. Viveiros de Castro (2002/2006), differently, affirms the anecdote serves to demonstrate that the Indians do not oppose nature and cultures in the same way the Europeans do. Despite both, Amerindians and Europeans, being ignorant in relation to the other and considering themselves as the legitimate "humans", each culture created different hypotheses from which to build knowledge about the other.

The anecdote, thus, shows that the European culture's modes of subjectivation tended to produce people who assume the objectivity of the other as indisputable data (for sure, the Indians were corporified); however, their subjectivity was questionable (did they or did they not have a soul?). Differently, the indigenous modes of subjectivation lead these people to assume subjectivity as an unquestionable:

surely, the Europeans were "spirits". What remained unknown was whether they were "flesh and blood", like the living.

Since in the Amerindian cosmovision every being potentially has a soul,[1] what characterizes humanity is the construction of a typically human body: at the same time unique and intelligible to the person's cultural collective (cf. Guimarães 2011). Since a person's humanity is determined by a body that may vary in form, a series of symbolic operations are necessary to make this body unique and socially suited.

The anecdote of the Antilles, therefore, characterizes two distinct cultural modes of conceiving reality, which, to a certain extent, blocked the possibility of dialogue, in the dialogical sense (cf. Guimarães 2011). At least to the sixteenth century Europeans, it did not seem legitimate to establish a dialogue with soulless beings. But is this dialogue possible nowadays? Ailton Krenak (journalist, *cacique* in a village in the north of the State of Minas Gerais) says that:

> The facts and the recent history of the last 500 years have shown that the time of the encounter between our cultures is a time that is happening and repeating itself every day. This encounter between the cultures of the Western peoples and the peoples of the American continent did not happen at a fixed date and time, one that we could call 1500 or 1800. We have been dealing with this contact since forever (Krenak 1998, p. 45).

In this excerpt, it is clear that despite chronological time having evidently passed in an irreversible manner since the first arrival of the Europeans to the new continent, something remains from this time in each new encounter with the other's culture (cf. Guimarães 2011). The encounter with alterity, however, makes it possible to update a possible opening to the aspects of the other that exceed the previous understandings about them. In other words, with each new encounter between different people and cultures, those involved face the originality of the people and things they do not entirely know. These encounters and reencounters demand actions that may update, for example, either the oppression the indigenous peoples have suffered over the last centuries or, instead, create new forms of interaction:

> When 1500 is seen as a landmark, people may think they should observe this date and celebrate or debate the event of our encounter as something fixed in time. Our encounters, they happen every day and will continue happening, I am sure, until the third millennium and maybe even beyond. We now have the opportunity to acknowledge this, to acknowledge that there is a script in each encounter. It always leaves the possibility for recognizing the Other, of recognizing, in the cultural richness and diversity of our peoples, the true heritage. The other resources are secondary: the territory, the forests, rivers, the natural resources, our technologies and our ability to promote development together with respect to nature and most of all a freedom-based education (Krenak 1998, pp. 46–47).

Krenak's notion of temporality in this excerpt evokes the Amerindian notion of myth (cf. Guimarães 2011). Lévi-Strauss and Eribon (1990) point out that if we ask an Indian what a myth is, the answer would probably be "it is a story from the time

---

[1] Here, I use the notion of soul [in portuguese: *alma*] to refer to the potential agency of every being. Amerindian cosmovisions name this property diversely, such as the notion of *karawa* among the Wari' (cf. Vilaça 1992); *yuxin*, among the Kaxinawa (cf. Lagrou 2007); *nhe'ë*, among the Mbya (cf. Pissolato 2007), among many others.

when men and animals were not yet different" (p.178). The mythic narrative does not search for historical correspondences in terms of a chronological description of events. The sphere of the myth may be accessed, for example, in the shaman's experience of dream and altered consciousness. The shaman is assumed to be capable of contacting the dedifferentiation of beings from before the beginning of the world, which underlies all events.

Differentiation and dedifferentiation, therefore, coexist as forms of inhabiting existence. The mythical narratives describe the trajectory between these two movements (cf. Guimarães 2011). The myth does not speak of a past nor future moment; it expresses a relational configuration of beings. The myth elaborates the period of differentiation itself, in which the chaos, the existential amalgam, can gain meaning from the separation of elements. However, not all the becoming's from the chaotic amalgam are updated: the "mythical flow continues roaring deafly under the apparent discontinuities between types and species" (Viveiros de Castro 2002/2006, p. 324). Each encounter with alterity updates in a singular manner subjacent processes: "our encounter may start now or a year from now, or in ten years' time, it is happening all the time" (Krenak 1998, p. 48). These remarks show a processual understanding of human encounters, in which the meanings of experiences can be renewed with each opportunity of opening or closing to alterity.

Intercultural Parallelism

The excerpt from Mariano's speech selected for analysis shows that relating to alterity leads necessarily to an integrative synthesis of different points of view, given that a difference between the I and the other remains. But working together preserves, also, a type of parallelism, in which different trajectories of elaborating experience develop without interfering with one another, producing a constant, and necessary, tension: "*It is difficult to carry things in parallel, to manage both [cultures] […]So nowadays we have to deal with indigenous politics, but together, in parallel with you. […] You have to work with the entire situation, you have to work the parallels; the mind has to be in both places at the same time. It is not because we speak Portuguese very well that we say: "I'm not an indigenous person anymore*".

The issues brought forth by Mariano can be connected to James's (1890) considerations on the source of error in psychology: the misleading influence of the language, the confusion between the narrator's point of view, his thoughts and feelings, and the assumption that the thoughts and feelings are intelligible to the narrator as they are to the psychologist. James (1890) calls attention to the fact that the psychological phenomena are only partially accessible to the interlocutor, so that the nebulous space between interlocutors must be taken into account to better understand the psychological phenomenon.

The selected excerpt also presents the issue of sharing values, memories and responsibilities in social relations. As discussed in the first essay of this book, Berger and Luckmann's (1966/1991) phenomenological sociology highlights the issue of the *natural attitude* underlying the creation, maintenance and transformation of social reality. What a person assumes as reality, as well as the assumed reality of structured knowledge systems beyond common sense, results from subjectively created meanings that become objective in the sociocultural field. Objective reality is, furthermore, always subjectively signified through symbolic resources available in the culture. A person's basic understanding of themselves and the world is acquired during early childhood, in a process called primary socialization, through which the child becomes a member of a society that precedes their personal identity formation or their cognitive system's consolidation. Through primary socialization, each person recognizes themselves as a participant in a sociocultural field.

The encounter with other cultures is an opportunity to realize that what we assume as reality may not be the same in other cultural fields, which subjectively and objectively create distinct realities. The contrast between realities, in turn, produces cultural shock and requires adjustments in perspectives to understand the other and their world. The way psychological processes are systematized in the academic culture are incompatible with the way the indigenous peoples understand their subjectivation processes, their thoughts and feelings.

Concerning the diversity of social constructions of reality and their impact in psychology, Berger and Luckmann (1966/1991) state:

> If theories about identity are always embedded in the more comprehensive theories about reality, this must be understood in terms of the logic underlying the latter. For example, a psychology interpreting certain empirical phenomena as possession by demoniacal beings has as its matrix a mythological theory of the cosmos, and it is inappropriate to interpret it in a non-mythological framework. Similarly, a psychology interpreting the same phenomena in terms of electrical disturbances of the brain has as its background an overall scientific theory of reality, both human and non-human, and derives its consistency from the logic underlying this theory. Put simply, psychology always presupposes cosmology (pp. 195–196).

Sociocultural realities coexist, objectivating and subjectivating the world in their own ways. The dialogue between Amerindians and psychologists takes place in a nebulous field in which semiotic elaborations, from both psychologists and Amerindians, do not tend to integrate. Intersubjective sharing tends to inconsistency, even if it is sometimes achieved for a period of time to carry out collective tasks. Both psychologists and Amerindians reach greater consistency when talking to their own community of belonging. The routes for mutual understanding are thus not linear or clear (cf. Rasmussen 2011). The nebulous frontier in interethnic dialogue demands that affective investments be made to permit collective actions, coordinated efforts and coauthorship. This is how I understand Mariano's saying that we must work together and in parallel with psychologists.

From what has been exposed up to now, I understand that the interethnic and intercultural dialogue must focus on the lack of overlap between objects in the interlocutors' speeches. Each cultural field cultivates a relatively independent field of subjective and objective realities that are not necessarily adjustable to other fields' dispositions. Next, I will show that intercultural parallelism inevitably leads to the understanding that the meanings constructed about the other are based on imaginary projections that accommodate the perceived differences in previous, familiar images.

Limited Perceptions and Imagination

When apprehending reality, a person is always articulating perceptions and imagination. Vygotsky's conferences on psychology, held between March and April, 1932, at the Institute of Psychology of Leningrad, show part of the results of abroad research on psychological processes of knowledge construction, organized in the form of an academic course. The fifth conference focused on the notion of imagination and its development during childhood. Vygotski (cf. 1934/2001a, p. 349) proposes that images created during the cognition of reality emerge together with images we recognize as part of the domain of imagination. In the process of increasing abstraction of thought, people create images that cannot be entirely found in reality. This shows the complex relation between realist thought and advanced forms of imagination. Thus, each step the child takes towards a more profound reality releases the child from earlier forms of cognition and demands the conscience's emancipation from some external and aparent aspects of reality, connected to perception. The result of this process is the increment in cognitive complexity and sophistication.

From the interaction between perception and imagination arises a richer and more elaborate apprehension of reality, although these two elements are not always combined. These are psychological processes, which are partly parallel and interdependent in nature. In reality's cognition, however, the imaginative tendencies co-regulate the perceptive process and vice-versa. Reality is, therefore, the result of a psychological construct in which imaginative processes participate, due to the dialogical relation between perception and imagination in cognition.

In 1936, Sartre published a critical study on the notion of imagination in Descartes, Leibniz and Hume, as well as in their followers who, according to Sartre's evaluation, conceived the image as a *thing* and the conscience as "a place inhabited by small simulacra" (Prado Junior and Moutinho 1996). Classical philosophy and psychology had an atomistic understanding of imagination. Imagined elements were seen as inert contents at the basis of sensible contents. Sartre (1936/1989; 1940/1996) sought to describe the phenomenon of imagination as a particular type of conscience and distinguish it from perception: the act of imagination is a magical one, an enchantment that summons the object being conceived in thought, the thing we desire so we may have it.

In Sartre (1936/1989, 1940/1996), perception is phenomenologically seen as the act by which the conscience places itself before an object, in space and time. Imagination, alternatively, is also an *act* through which the intentional conscience presentifies an absence. As a consequence of the mental image's intentionality, every imaginative act involves a type of knowledge. A person that imagines something beyond their current perception must know what they want to represent, even if only intuitively. Thus, to Sartre (1940/1996, p. 84), an image cannot exist without the knowledge that constitutes it. In this sense, knowledge refers to a set of abstract relations that can exist independently from the image, as a possibility derived from the imaginary representation.

In meaning construction, the aspects of experience, imagination, and realist thought overlap and function together. The objects of imagination are constituted as experience is internalized. Imagination extracts its elements from perception and alters them. Distancing oneself from the here and now through imagination gives a certain degree of freedom relative to perception.

When imagination is too distant from the socially shared reality, difficulties arise in communicating the meanings of experience. The closer one is to absolutely new and creative imaginative content, the greater the chance of making communication unfeasible, approaching exceptionality and madness. However, each individual action in culture produces some degree of novelty. The creative aspect intrinsic to providing meaning to reality is present in people's daily lives. Perception and imagination together fine-tune the extent of the continuities and discontinuities in relation to previous experiences.

Morais and Guimarães (2017) consider that the creative process resulting from the activities of perception and imagination can be used as a psychological tool to selectively apprehend the surroundings, giving it meaningful shapes. The everyday objects, including the most simple and common ones, are thus a type of crystallized fantasy (Vygotsky 1990, p. 10). Vygostki uses the same notion of crystallization in relation to human concepts and ideas, which he considers the result of uncountable repeated actions and their effects over the world. The daily life surrounding us has all the necessary premises for creation, and all that exceeds routine, even the smallest parcel of novelty, has its roots in human beings' creative process (Vygotsky 1990, p. 11).

In the imaginative process, personal memories are subject to reformulations that resignify reality and create new arrangements for experience (Morais and Guimarães 2015). The person and the world are transformed together with the perceptive-imaginative process, which, in turn, allows one to produce new meanings and new realities. In this sense, absolutely everything around us is the product of human activity; the world of culture is a product of imagination (Vygotsky 1990, p.10). Still on the same subject, Vygotsky (1990) states that imagination is the means for amplifying a person's experience. If they are apt to imagine what they do not see, they may conceive what they do not personally experience, by means of other's stories and descriptions. The person who imagines is not enclosed in the narrow circle of their own experience. They may distance themselves from their own limits by assimilating, with the help of imagination, other historical or social experiences (Vygotsky 1990, p.20).

Imagination is thus a psychological function that enables people to exceed the limits of their personal experience as it is currently perceived. Valsiner (1998) argued, on the subject of personality development, that constructive internalizations and externalizations make it possible to establish a psychological distance from the immediate surroundings. It gives people relative autonomy in relation to the other's contingencies. This process involves both subjective constructions and the person's attempt to remain socially integrated.

New knowledge and new creations are possible with a certain degree of personal and social expansion, provided by imagination, which is the condition for people's adaptation in the culture. Fiction makes it possible to fix and alter, in a controlled manner, the ever-changing forms that emerge as perceptions succeed one another in the irreversible flow of time. The products of imagination may be manipulated at any time, showing that personal experience of the world is not a given, but results from a process in which people are involved: "human creative action makes them beings turned to the future, who contribute to create and transform the present" (Vygotsky 1990, p. 9).

The activity of transforming the present encounters a crystallized reality that precedes the present actions and which was previously built by others. In this way, imagination, as a creative activity, is directly linked to the diversity of experiences a person has accumulated, because this is the material from which they will fantasize. Thus, the richer a person's experiences, the greater the material for imagination (Vygotsky 1990, p. 17).

Figure 3.2, bellow, shows the articulation of perception and imagination as a field of tensions in which semiotic elaborations take place:

The triad imagination-perception-cognition of reality is articulated to other conceptual triads found in semiotic-cultural constructivism in psychology and in anthropological theory. They present dialogical oppositions that generate a third element, such as in the following examples: (1) *possibilities* (as if) and *real actions* (as is) in life trajectories, from which *symbolic resources* emerge that guide the person towards the future (Valsiner 2007); (2) what *exists* for the person (IS value) and what they *desire* (SHOULD value), which are articulated in their potential for *symbolic action* (Boesch 1991); (3) personal, *intrasubjective elaborations* of experience and *intersubjective social sharing* of the world of life, resulting in *interobjective mediations* (Latour 1996)[2]; and (4) the articulation of what is *really lived* and what is *virtually projected*, in a process that involves the fabrication of the person's body as an *organized set of affections* (Lima 1996). In sum, these triads allow us to understand the cultural construction of meaning that emerges as levels of consciousness between the person and the world. This gap is filled in by the person using their

Perception	Cognition of reality	Imagination
"As is"	Symbolic resources	"As if"
"IS value"	Symbolic actions	"SHOULD value"
Intersubjectivity (I)	Interobjectivity	Intersubjectivity (other)
Real	Body fabrication	Virtual

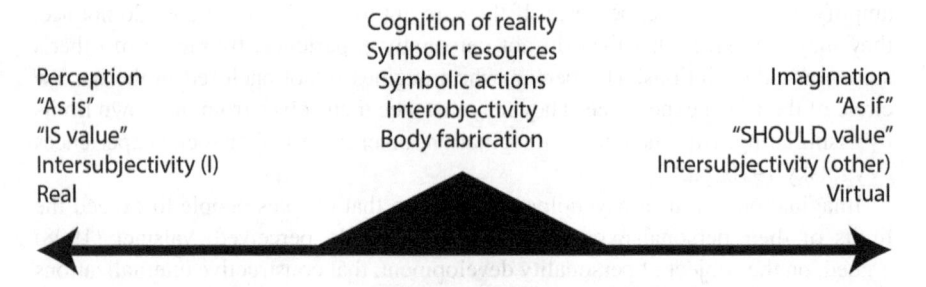

Fig. 3.2 Field of tensions between perception and imagination, articulated in the cognition of reality. (Source: Adapted from Guimarães 2016, p. 363)

---

[2] Latour (1996) discusses the notion of interobjectivity, placing objects as mediators in social relations, constitutive and active parts of the social body (*corpo social*).

sensible body. The values and cosmovisions from their cultural background provide the basis for interpreting new experiences.

Before moving further, I would like to make some considerations about the notion of symbolic resources in the field of semiotic-cultural constructivism in psychology. According to Zittoun et al. (2003), symbolic resources are tools to act on or departing from the physical world, the social world and the psychological reality. These tools are used in the direction of the future and involve actions with varying degrees of reflexivity. These authors understand that the use of symbolic resources in the I-other relations allows people to create their actions' objectives. They are fundamental guidelines of action that offer temporarily stable symbolic framings. The person creates them and uses them to solve tensions generated by the differences between the perceived current situation and the goal of the action, oriented by the desire of a becoming. Symbolic resources can be, for example, the elaboration of limits to an intersubjective relation, the creation of rules, or of scientific, artistic, and cultural texts or objects.

The symbolic resources reorganize the chaos and uncertainties that arise in each person's encounters with the world and the others. Possible actions arise, leading to new problems and new symbolic resources. It is worth mentioning that symbolic resources are used during the interaction with others. Semiotic devices assist the process of integrating the I and the other's perceptions and imagination, changing both interlocutor's views and leading to new experiences and thus adjustments in previous understandings (Zittoun et al. 2003; Zittoun 2006). Symbolic elements are stabilized interaction patterns, converted to resources when someone mobilizes them with a specific objective in mind, in the context of a transition. This process results in a meaningful recontextualization of the resource itself, which can then be employed to handle the remaining problems caused by disruptive experiences and possibly solve them.

The symbolic resources produced and externalized are connected to the person who produced them. Among other characteristics, they work as signatures of their creator. In this way, the other becomes aware, momentarily, of the interlocutor's identity. Each interlocutor's identity is thus negotiated in dialogue. The meanings produced necessarily exceed the producer, creating dissonance in relation to their understanding of the symbolic resource. The person must fight to control what they themselves produced. This exceeding, and disquieting, meaning demands reparatory actions, through the use, modification and creation of new symbolic resources. (Zittoun et al. 2003; Simão 2003).

In the selected excerpts, perception and imagination appear as guidelines in the construction of divergent meanings in the I-other relation. To Mariano, for instance, the perception of a hostile environment that *"messes with the head of the Indian person"* guides his imagination to create strategies for avoiding threats and prejudices: *"This also has to do with people's minds, because people go to the city and they think "I'm a minority, I don't want to say I'm an indigenous person", they will think: "I don't want to say I'm Indian, because if I do I'll be disrespected"*. In the excerpts from Julio César's and Gerson's speeches, the relation between perception and imagination appears as a source of error: *"Then this young man comes and learns our language and says "I'm also an indigenous person, I have my rights", but what about the indigenous feeling?"*, said Julio; *"All Indian children there speak two languages, Krenak and Kaingang. So, we are like this: we are living in a place where many people come and think everything is okay [...]"*, said Gerson.

The selected excerpts show the relation between perception and imagination in the process of elaborating experience. The excerpts also show that when perception and imagination go by unquestioned, they become a source of error. The indigenous images and perceptions do not coincide with the images and perceptions of "visiting outsiders", since the cognitive elaboration of experience is anchored in cultural experiences and concepts. Interethnic situations exacerbate this condition, despite its pertinence to any and all relations. To a certain extent, each interlocutor is willing to be affected by experience and articulate perceptions and imagination in their own particular and divergent manners.

In this respect, dialogue depends on the interlocutors sharing extra-verbal elements, that is, a type of knowledge and worldview from which the utterances depart. I observe, however, from the selected excerpts, that in the interethnic situation extra-verbal sharing is very limited and little evident, creating tensions over basic conditions for dialogical sharing.

Considering the precariousness of the extra-verbal condition between psychologists and indigenous people, Achatz and Guimarães (2018) realized that the interlocutors were performing operations over the nebulous aspects of the relation to enable the formation of the extra-verbal basis necessary for dialogue. The alterity dimension inherent to the I-other-world relations does not need to be overcome, since dialogue is not possible without difference (Simão 2003), but some degree of intersubjective sharing must be established to avoid mistaken understandings. The alterity relation requires dislodging preconceptions and previous schemes of understanding, to include the schemes of understanding of the other. It is nevertheless also important that some resistance to understanding remain so alterity is not lost in the relation, since the new conceptual schemes, although supposedly adjusted to the other, may confine their alterity.

Mutual Affective Transformations

The sensible transformation of the person in a relation is connected to its affective dimension. This aspect is prioritized in the indigenous people's observations, when they show that the cognitive process, marked by perception and imagination, may lead to possibly mistaken elaborations of experience. This concern is present in Julio's speech: *"Because we have many young people in the community, and they can even marry an outsider. Then this young man comes and learns our language and says "I'm also an indigenous person, I have my rights", but what about the indigenous feeling? Does he have the indigenous feeling? The white folk are a different feeling."*

In the same direction, Gerson's speech clearly show his view that perception and imagination may produce equivocation, while affective investment is the path for creating some understanding: *"we are living in a place where many people come and think everything is okay, but in our hearts we know: we know what we've been through and what we need"*.

The trajectories for meaning elaboration, which are guided by the persons manner of socializing, and through rites and myths that supply the first images for the affective organization of the world. In the interethnic encounter, people recruit these images and tend to produce incongruous meanings about the other. The categories that emerge from the cognitive-affective process fail to achieve harmony. New experiences, however, bring the opportunity for reciprocal adjustments of mistaken elaborations, in a process that transforms people and cultures.

People develop their affective schemes through their unique form of organizing the symbolism of cultural expressions (mythical narratives, ritualized experiences, etc.). By adopting social regulations and justifications (mythemes) for life events signified in culture, the person organizes personal aspirations. A person organizes the images available in the myths and rites of cultural life through aesthetic syntheses that, according to Baldwin (1915), create psychological reality.

To Baldwin (1915), reality is constituted by all the contents of consciousness organized or organizable in an aesthetic or artistic manner. Individual conscience is the organ that apprehends and contemplates experience in its totality, organizing it in an aesthetic whole. The aesthetically organized experience, in turn, has the form of a Self. However, the reality formed from these partial points of view is also partial. These views (Baldwin 1915, p. 303) classify reality as presentified, ideal, good, true, or else ways.

Considering that Baldwin (1915) rejects the idea that reality is plural, his theory is reflected here to discuss the multiplicity of socially built realities with particular ontological foundations. In Baldwin's (1915) view, a non-relative reality could exist by means of an aesthetic-affective synthesis. There seems to be a convergence between this view and the verifiability criterion of the consistency of divergent meanings, suggested by the indigenous leaders in the selected excerpts. They call attention to the limits of a cognition distanced from the sensible and fundamentally affective experience. Only the latter guarantees an adequate understanding of the communities' situation.

Finally, while perception and imagination produce mistaken views on reality, the affective apprehension of experience opens the possibility for mutual understanding. Therefore, the continuous elaboration of affective experiences will give the psychologist the tools to control equivocation in the interethnic relation and possibly transduce the experience to communicate it in professional and academic environments. This process also gives rise to collaborative work with indigenous people in their communities.

I have discussed the affective elaboration of experience as a cultivation of the body that dissolves the dichotomy between external and psychic reality, in a continuous and reciprocal dialogue between interiority and exteriority. The work of the Amerindian Network, thus, requires the team to be available not only intellectually, with an open attitude in the mental sense, but physically, with a corporified presence. Reciprocal care with the bodies in a relation produces humanized interactions and may dissipate the obstacles that hinder the relation's continuity. Fear or aggressiveness, for instance, are part of the Brazilian culture's fantasies concerning Indians, which have been disseminated through stereotypes since Americas' first explorers and still today in religious environments, schools and in the scientific production (cf. Jahoda 1999).

Given that the intercultural encounter lacks an antecedent extra-verbal common ground, some sharing may be established as a result of sharing experience in community life. Interaction transforms bodies; in this sense, the foreigner is like a child, who emerges as the product of social relations and must become a member of society. Memory and knowledge are inscribed in the child's or foreigner's body by means of graphic signs, shared nourishment, scents and physical contact, all of which will aesthetically organize the encounters, the rites and values transmitted in the mythical narratives, personal stories, etc. These processes allow interlocutors to share fundamental references for creating new dialogue.

Acknowledgement This work is supported by FAPESP (grant number 18/13145-0).

References

Achatz, R. W. (2016). *Psicologia e povos indígenas: Possibilidades e limites na produção de espaços dialógicos..* (Relatório de Iniciação Científica). São Paulo: Universidade de São Paulo.

Achatz, R. W., & Guimarães, D. S. (2018). An invitation to travel in an interethnic arena: Listening carefully to Amerindian leaders' speeches. *Integrative Psychological and Behavioral Science, 52*(4), 595–613.

Albert, B. (2002). O ouro canibal e a queda do céu: uma crítica xamânica da economia política da natureza. Brasília: Ed. UnB (Série Antropologia). In B. Albert & R. C. Ramos (Eds.), *Pacificando o branco: cosmologias do contato no norte-Amazônico*. São Paulo: UNESP.

Bakhtin, M. M. (1929/2013). *Problemas da poética de Dostoiévski* (P. Bezerra, trad.), 5a. ed., 3a. imp. Rio de Janeiro: Forense Universitária.

Bakhtin, M. M. (1979/2015). *Estética da criação verbal* (P. Bezerra, trad.), 6a. ed., 2a. tiragem. São Paulo: Martins Fontes.

Baldwin, J. M. (1915). *Genetic theory of reality*. New York: The Knickerbocker Press. Avaiable in. https://archive.org/details/genetictheoryofr00baldrich.

Bastien, S. (2007). Observation participante ou participation observante? Usages et justifications de la notion de participation observante en sciences sociales. *Université de Caen Basse-Normandie, 27* (1), 2007, pp. 127–140. ISSN 1715–8705 - http://www.recherche-qualitative.qc.ca/Review.html.

Berger, P. B., & Luckmann, T. (1991). *The social construction of reality: A treatise in the sociology of knowledge*. London: Penguin books. (Original text published in 1966).

Boesch, E. E. (1991). *Symbolic action theory and cultural psychology*. Berlin.

Cornejo, J. (2008). Intersubjectivity as co-phenomenology: From the holism of meaning to the being-in-the-world-with-others. *Integrative Psychological and Behavioral Sciences, 42*, 171–178.

Damaceno, G. C. (2010). Cacique Gerson Cecílio Damaceno. In *Conselho Regional de Psicologia da 6a Região (Ed), Psicologia e povos indígenas* (pp. 73–76). São Paulo, SP: CRPSP.

Descola, P. (2005). *Par-delà nature et culture*. Paris, França: Gallimard.

References

Fernando, M. (2010). *Mariano Fernando. Conselho Regional de Psicologia da 6a Região (Ed), Psicologia e povos indígenas* (pp. 46–49). São Paulo, SP: CRPSP.
Groot, S., Hodgetts, D., Nikora, L. W., & Leggat-Cook, C. (2011). A Maori homeless woman. *Ethnography, 12*(3), 375–397.
Guimarães, D. S. (2011). Amerindian anthropology and cultural psychology: Crossing boundaries and meeting Otherness' worlds. *Culture & Psychology, 12*(2), 139–157.
Guimarães, D. S. (2016). *Amerindian paths: Guiding dialogues with psychology* (p. 366). Charlotte: Information Age Publishing.
Guimarães, D. S. (2018). Affectivation: A cut across the semiotic hierarchy of feelings. In: Cornejo, C.; Marsico, G. & Valsiner, J. (Orgs.). *I Activate You To Affect Me I* (pp. 203–223). Charlotte: Information Age Publishing.
Guimarães, D. S. & Simão, L. M. (2017). Mythological constrains to the construction of subjectified bodies. In: Han, M. (org.) *The Subjectified and Subjectifying Mind* (pp. 3–21). Charlotte: Information Age Publication.
Holquist, M. (2004). Introduction. In M. M. Bakhtin (Ed.), *The Dialogic Imagination* (pp. xv–xxxiii). Austin: University of Texas Press.
Hwang, K.-K. (2015). Cultural system vs. pan-cultural dimensions: Philosophical reflection on approaches for indigenous psychology. *Journal for the Theory of Social Behaviour, 45*(1), 2–25.
Jahoda, G. (1999). *The Images of Savages: Ancient roots of modern prejudice in Western culture*. New York: Routledge (320p.
James, W. (1890). *The principles of psychology*. New York: Holt.
Kawaguchi, D. R., & Guimarães, D. S. (2018). Is everybody human? The relationship between humanity and animality in Western and Amerindian myth narratives. *Culture & Psychology*, 1354067X1877905.
Krenak, A. (1998). O eterno retorno do encontro. In Ricardo, C. A. (Ed.) (2000). *Povos indígenas no Brasil: 1996/2000* (pp. 43–48). São Paulo: Instituto Socioambiental.
Lagrou, E. (2007). *A fluidez da forma: arte, alteridade e agência em uma sociedade amazônica (Kaxinawa, Acre)*. Rio de Janeiro: Topbooks.
Latour, B. (1991/1994). *Jamais Fomos Modernos: Ensaios de Antropologia Simétrica*. Rio de Janeiro: Editora 34.
Latour, B. (1996). On Interobjectivity. *Mind, Culture, and Activity, 3*(4), 228–245.
Leão, M. E. A., & Guimarães, D. S. (in preparation). *Perspectiva Poética da Alteridade: Diálogos entre Rimbaud e Bakhtin*. (Manuscript in preparation. São Paulo: Universidade de São Paulo.
Lévi-Strauss, C. (1952). *Race and history*. Paris: UNESCO.
Lévi-Strauss, C. (1965/1984). *Tristes tropiques*. Paris: Plon.
Lévi-Strauss, C., & Eribon, D. (1990). *De perto e de longe: Reflexões do mais importante antropólogo do nosso tempo*. Rio de Janeiro: Nova Fronteira. Texto original publicado em 1988.
Lima, T. S. (1996). O dois e seu múltiplo: reflexões sobre o perspectivismo em uma cosmologia Tupi. *Mana, 2*(2), 21–47.
Lima, T. S. (1999). Para uma teoria etnográfica da distinção natureza e cultura na cosmologia Juruna. *Revista Brasileira de Ciências Sociais, 14*(40), 43–52.
Marková, I. (2006a). *Dialogicidade e representações sociais: as dinâmicas da mente*. Petrópolis: Vozes. (Originally published in 2003.
Marková, I. (2006b). On 'the inner Alter' in dialogue. *International Journal for Dialogical Science, 1*(1), 125–147.
Morais, H. Z. L., & Guimarães, D. S. (2015). Borders of Poetic Self Construction: Dialogues between Cultural Psychology and Performing Arts. *Psychology & Society, 7*, 28–39.
Morais, H. Z. L. Guimarães, D. S. (2017). Vocational program, creative processes and the constitution of a poetic outlook on reality: A dialogue between theatrical arts and dialogical cultural psychology. In: Semiotic-cultural constructivism workshop. Knowledge and otherness: disquieting experiences in the dynamics of cultural psychology (pp. 130-144). São Paulo: Library Dante Moreira Leite, Institute of Psychology, University of São Paulo.
Moscovici, S. (2003). *Representações sociais: investigações em psicologia social* (p. 404). Petrópolis: Vozes. Texto original publicado em 2000.

Pio, J. C. (2010). Vice-cacique Júlio César Pio. In *Conselho Regional de Psicologia da 6a Região (Ed), Psicologia e povos indígenas* (pp. 83–85). São Paulo: CRPSP.
Pissolato, E. (2007). *A duração da pessoa: Mobilidade, parentesco e Xamanismo Mbya (Guarani).* São Paulo: Editora UNESP.
Prado Junior, B. & Moutinho, L. D. S. (1996). Apresentação Em.: Sartre, J-P. O Imaginário: psicologia fenomenológica da imaginação (pp. 5–7). São Paulo: Ática.
Rasmussen, S. (2011). Encountering being, identity, and otherness: Reconsidering Guimarães's "Amerindian anthropology and cultural psychology" and Amerindian perspectivism, with insights from anthropology of religion, African humanities and collaborative ethnography. *Culture and Psychology, 17*(2), 159–176.
Sartre, J.-P. (1989). *A imaginação* (p. 121). Rio de Janeiro: Bertrand Brasil. (Texto original publicado em 1936.
Sartre, J.-P. (1996). *O Imaginário: psicologia fenomenológica da imaginação* (p. 254). São Paulo: Ática. (Texto original publicado em 1940.
Simão, L. M. (2003). Beside rupture – Disquiet; beyond the other - Alterity. *Culture & Psychology,* 9(4), 449–459.
Simão, L. M. (2010). *Ensaios Dialógicos: compartilhamento e diferença nas relações eu outro.* São Paulo: HUCITEC (286p.
Sztutman, R. (2005). In Universidade de São Paulo (Ed.), *O profeta e o principal: Ação política ameríndia e seus personagens.* Brasil: Tese de doutorado em Antropologia Social.
Teo, T. (2011). Empirical race psychology and the hermeneutics of epistemological violence. *Human Studies, 34*(3), 237–255. Todorov, 1982/2011.
Valsiner, J. (1998). *The guided mind: A sociogenetic approach to personality* (p. 480). Cambridge, MA, Estados Unidos: Harvard University Press.
Valsiner, J. (2007). Human development as migration: Striving toward the unknown. In L. M. Simão & J. Valsiner (Eds.), *Otherness in question: Labyrinths of the self* (pp. 349–378). Charlotte: Information Age Publishing.
Valsiner, J. (2012). *Fundamentos da psicologia cultural: mundos da mente mundos da vida* (p. 356). Porto alegre: Artmed.
Vilaça, A. M. N. (1992). *Comendo como Gente: Formas do Canibalismo Wari'.* Rio de Janeiro: Editora UFRJ.
Viveiros de Castro, E. B. (1996). Os pronomes cosmológicos e o perspectivismo ameríndio. *Mana,* 2(2), 115–144.
Viveiros de Castro, E. B. (1998). Cosmological Deixis and the Amerindian perspectivism. *The Journal of the Royal Anthropological Institute, 4*(3), 469–488.
Viveiros de Castro, E. B. (2004). Perspectival anthropology and the method of controlled equivocation. *Tipití: Journal of the Society for the Anthropology of Lowland South America,* 2(1), 1–22.
Viveiros de Castro, E. B. (2006). *A inconstância da alma selvagem e outros ensaios de antropologia (2ª Ed.)* (p. 2002). São Paulo: Cosac Naify. (Original publicado em.
Vygotski, L. S. (1934/2001a). La imaginación y su desarrollo en la edad infantil. InVygotski, L. S. (2001). *Obras escogidas (Tomo II)* (pp. 423–438). Madrid: A. Machado Libros, S. A.
Vygotsky, L. S. (1990). *La imaginación y el arte en la infancia.* Madrid: Ediciones AKAL S. A.
Wertsch, J. (1993). *Voices of the mind: A sociocultural approach to mediated action.* Cambridge: Harvard University Press.
Zittoun, T. (2006). *Transitions: Development through symbolic resources.* Greenwich: Information Age Publishing.
Zittoun, T., Duveen, G., Gillespe, A., Invision, G., & Psaltis, C. (2003). The use of Developmental Resources in Developmental Transition. *Culture & Psychology,* 9(4), 415–448.

Chapter 4
Third Principle: Dynamics of Involvement and Self-Transformation

Part of the difficulties the Amerindian Network faces in its interethnic dialogues is due to the unfamiliarity concerning indigenous peoples' concepts of person, promoted in the history of interethnic relations that includes the psychological theorization. Then, I start this chapter discussing some indigenous perspectives on the notion of person.

Barrera (2016) introduces the Totzil[1] notion of person, which I adopt here to set a ground for sophisticating the triadic alter-ego-object model of classical dialogism. According to Barrera (2016), to understand the Totzil notion of person, three apparently untranslatable notions must be considered: *takopal*, *chanul* and *ch'ulel* accompanied by the pronoun *vo'on*:

> The Tzotzil pronoun 'I' is 'vo'on.' And now from the person models' (Western and Tzotztl) point of view, we can notice that, although grammatically speaking we can translate one pronoun by the other, I and vo'on do not pertain to the same hermeneutic horizon; that's why the Westerners and the Tzotzils have different attitudes towards life and the world. In accordance with the Tzotzil Person Model, when we pronounce the pronoun vo'on we are not only referring to the organic system delimitated by the epidermis; but in this pronoun we are including the mountains, the caves, the springs, the general environment which is the life niche; and if we look very carefully, life itself is included. That is to say, we must not understand the niche or life like a place where life develops; but as an integral, multidimensional, interactive concept; i.e. there aren't empty niches, in the same manner that there isn't any life without a niche. We are talking about the Tzotzil man's life: the reason why the word takopal is associated with the word k'uxbol is because this last one manifests the life offering (gift) in society (to society). And chanul is the man's mountain bred, untamed part that does not let the community dissociate from its origin and life spring; that's why, in the model, the ch'ulel comes in contact with the other two categories, as if it were the unifying force coming from the wind, the rain, the mountain. (Barrera 2016, p. 21)

The notion of person shows clearly the existence of distinct debate arenas. On one side, the notion of person varies among the different Mayan peoples, of which the Totzil model, presented by Barreira (2016), is a case. On the other side, the

---

[1] The Totzil are a Maian people from the Chiapas region, in southern Mexico.

diverse psychologies developed in academic environments conceive the person in different ways, according to their particular theoretical systems. Dialogical spaces multiply because the object that is being socially represented through the same word is not the same, that is, the hermeneutic horizons of the notion of person do not coincide.

Figure 4.1 shows a gap between the different dialogical spaces as a nebulous and unknown region.

Gow's (1997) analysis of the Piro people's kinship system illustrates another route for reflecting on the construction of the person in Amerindian communities. The anthropologist argues that "kinship is, above all, a subjectivity system, since the basic structures of human conscience imply the conscience of an I [self] among others" (p. 39). Gow (1997) points out, after observing these people manifest kinship, that their network of relational concepts were at the same time unique and comparable to scientific psychology concepts, as the following passage shows:

[…] "mind, intelligence, memory, respect, love". The quality of *nshinikanchi* may be evoked by certain acts from elders, but cannot be taught to children; they need to develop it spontaneously. Its first and most important manifestation is intelligible speech; the use of kinship terms to gain attention and care is the most prominent and powerful aspect of this ability (Gow 1997, p. 45).

And further on:

Why do people feed and take care of little babies? They do so because babies are *kwamonuru*, "cute, sad, pitiful, poor little things". This evokes *getwamonuta*, "to see a person's sadness, pitifullness, helplessness, loveliness", which is an aspect of *nshinikanchi*. *Getwamonuta*, "to see the pain", makes older relatives try to satisfy the baby's desires, which leads to the development of *nshinikanchi* as the child grows (Gow 1997, p. 53).

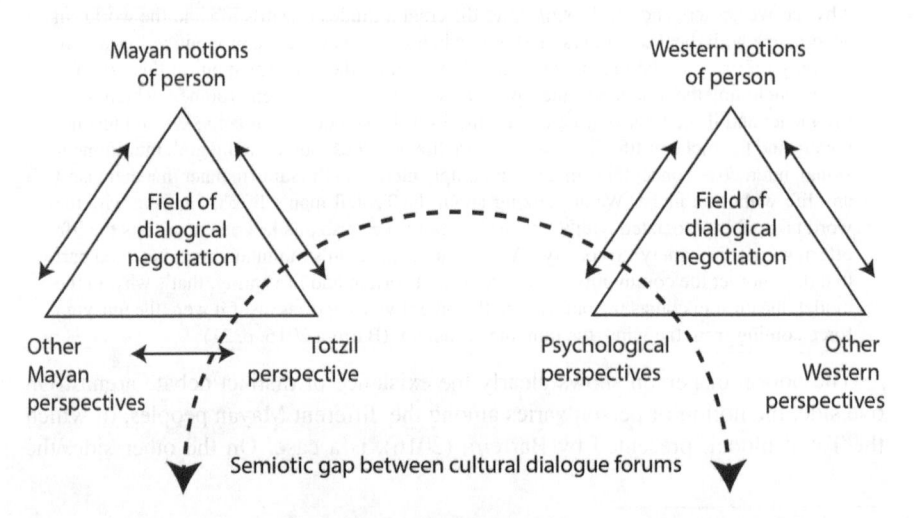

Fig. 4.1 Multiplication of ethnic-cultural dialogue forums, guiding distinct trajectories of semiotic elaboration. .(Source: Guimarães 2016a, p. 314)

The term 'psychology' was created by humanist renaissance thinkers (cf. Krstic 1964) who, recovering the Greek myth of Psyche (ρυχη), joined the name of its main character to the word ending -λογια (–logy), indicating a rational elaboration of some human dimensions referred in the myth, amplifying it. We may suppose that the rational elaboration of the term *nshinikanchi* might lead us to a *nshinikanchi*-logy, a knowledge system founded on the Piro people's cosmology, that could dialogue, through its difference, with the academic psychologies. The indigenous psychology here proposed is founded on the recognition that a mythical basis underlies all knowledge constructions, and that other myths besides the Greek-Roman and Judeo-Christian ones should participate in this process.

Other important illustration to what we are focusing in this chapter comes from Gonçalves' (2016) discussion on how the recently formed Brazilian State continued reproducing colonial ideologies in relation to the natives of the land, restricting these peoples' freedom for self-determination. His study illustrates the tensions surrounding the indigenous peoples' alterity, manifested in the classification terms used to designate them. The terms Tupi and Tapuia were historically used to identify, according to the State's civilizatory interests, noble savages and sordid savages, respectively. From Columbus to Rousseau and until now, the indigenous peoples' identities are confined to dichotomies established in European literature and philosophy. Ideas such as that of the good savage and the bad savage are not terms used by these peoples to designate themselves.

Once more, meaning construction surrounding alterity relations varies according to the cultural field. Ethnic self-affirmation is challenged by heteronomous classifications that come from mistaken images and perceptions.

The inconsistent versions about the multiple identities of the indigenous peoples contribute to their invisibility. To the Amerindians, this invisibility is actively perpetrated by the State and other institutions with similar ideological perspectives (cf. Ideti e Duwe 2010). The indigenous peoples perceive the use of mistaken images as part of the political strategies to depreciate them. This creates hostility among peoples and obstructs constructive dialogue. In opposition to these images, the indigenous communities have developed counter-discourses and practices, in an effort to disseminate other images about themselves, more pertinent in their point of view.

Affective Body: A Territory for Self Cultivation

Guarani and Kaiowá leader Carlito de Oliveira expresses much sorrow regarding the restrictions imposed on indigenous peoples concerning their lands' occupation. These restrictions result from the conflicts generated by colonization. In his understanding, this conflict would not exist if each people found more adequate ways of living with others, since the land, to begin with, does not have an owner:

> When he created this land, the whole world, he didn't say this piece is for the White folk, this one here for the black, this one for the blue, this one for the Indians, this one I don't

know who's getting. He didn't. The land is not just for the Indian, no. This soil here is for everyone. For everyone to live. But on this ground, we live fighting each other.
(Speech from *cacique* Carlito de Oliveira, *Guarani Kaiowa*, in interview for the documentary "The Dark Side of Green" (Baccaert, Navarro and Um 2011)

The following considerations assume the person as a territory for culture to cultivate, as a house or a community's territory, in the metaphorical sense. This requires attention to the "whole world", as *cacique* Carlito de Oliveira emphasized. While doors and frontiers are open, everyone may come into the territory and build things together. People may, alternatively, become territories subject to violent, authoritarian colonization, or disputes between asymmetrical power positions, especially when the person's internalized communitarian perspective does not embrace diversity in dialogical terms (for example, when missionaries reject the indigenous peoples' thoughts and ways of life, and subjectively accommodate alterity in restricted and prejudiced images).

The self is, then, a psychological field for the construction of the person. It encompasses multiple social positions, structured by the person in a unique manner from their experience in a broader sociocultural field that includes other people and the world. The notion of self is, then, be considered the person's symbolic shelter for diversity, a construct that refers to an active field of the person, occupied and cultivated by the culture, with borders that are semi-permeable to dialogue. To a certain point, the person resists the culture's interventions, gaining some autonomy to direct their own paths in the process of transforming themselves and the world.

Understanding the experience of the self requires interactions in which participants are seen as active subjects. The utterances produced can only be understood with further knowledge of each subject's intentionality. Utterances, together with all their semantic anchors, are personifications: "relations between consciences and truths, mutual influences, learning, love, hate, falseness, friendship, respect, reverence, trust, distrust and so forth" (Bakhtin 1979/2015, pp. 138–139). Structured linguistic relations between sentences and styles without the agent of the communicative experience, configure an object-object type of relation, which is not dialogical. If the participants in a relation lose the self-regulatory function, then we have a process of psychological objectification that suppress the possibility of dialogism.

So, if A and B are not subjects in the form of real people but, rather, psychological functions, voices, social objects or systems, for instance, dialogical analysis performs an imaginative leap and considers them *as if* they were people, subjects, active positions with perspectives of their own and purposes. In any case, the dialogical analysis unit is the I-other relation. The model of dialogical interaction presupposes that the elements of the dialogical unit are separate, despite being parts of the same whole. This is an inclusive separation, as discussed by Simão and Valsiner (2007). It shapes a field of tensions that may be known. Dialogism is thus a strategy to understand relations between any communicative systems, not only those involving actual people. The dynamics of the self may be considered, from a dialogical perspective, as a field of social relations articulated by the person.

Social reality becomes a part of the self through the experiences lived by the person throughout their life, in relations with their surroundings. The self stabilizes in the present a historical and teleological organization of active subjects in the world. Personal actions are not determined by the social or natural environment, although the relations with these environments limit the self's activity. This means determinants are not top-down (such as natural, social or mental arrangements that affects on all) nor bottom-up (such as physiological elements associated to the psyche). The self emerges as a semiotic activity from the tensions between these distinct elements.

The tensions in the structuration of the self may be dialogically understood through observation of the self's constitutive parts, which involve intrapersonal and interpersonal aspects. For example: as a participant in a cultural field, the psychologist reflects about their apprehension of feelings and thoughts expressed by someone and assumes the objects of such feelings/thoughts as interdependent dimensions in their comprehension. This descending analytic approach, from the whole of thought to its constitutive elements, must be reverted in an interpretative movement. In this manner, it is possible to understand how micro-transformations in the flow of thought/feeling produce new relations with oneself, with others and with the world. Interpretations, in turn, always take place in a concrete extra-verbal situation.

The dialogical unit includes the situation in which the psychologist is able to identify their own thoughts and feelings in the relation with the thoughts and feelings of others. The relation's narrative reveals import aspects of the meaning and intentionality of the participants' actions. Historicizing the relation helps understand the direction of the flow of thoughts and feelings, thus helping devise more adequate interventions in the present, real world.

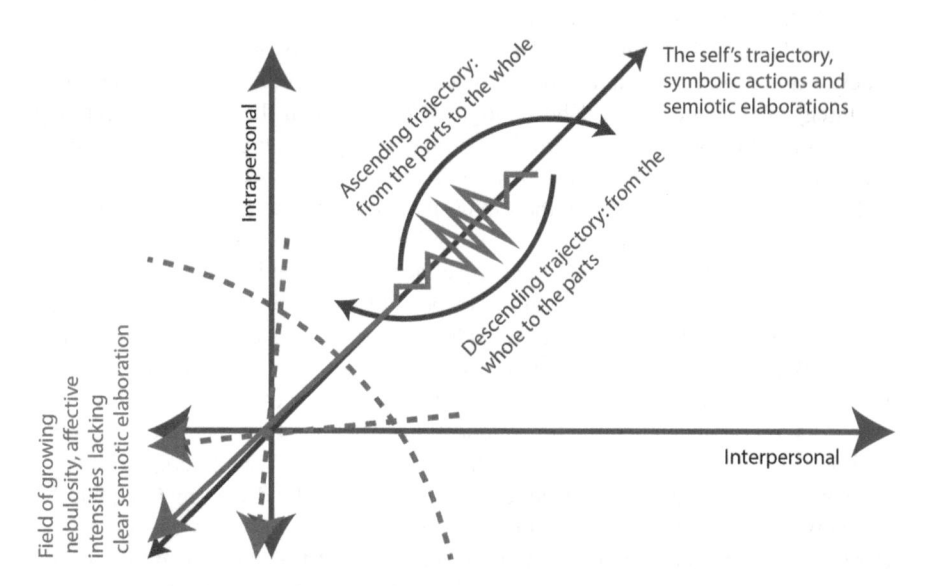

Fig. 4.2 Diagram of ascending and descending processes in the self semiotic activity. (Source: Adapted from Guimarães 2016b, p. 192)

Figure 4.2 shows two dimensions of the self that the dialogical analysis unit contrasts: the *gestalten* that form during the cognitive-affective elaboration of perception (internalization, descending path in the direction of intrapersonal processes: segmentation of the perception by the analytical thought) and the symbolic actions that articulate internal images to communicate or reach some end in the world (externalization, ascending trajectory towards interpersonal processes, recomposition of analyzed segments in a meaningful expression, interpretation of experience).

Dialogical analysis, therefore, starts from the mediated relations between the self and the others in a concrete extra-verbal situation. In the communicative situation, the whole of thought is segmented and re-integrated, in a dual process involving tensions. Our perception works from an initial *Gestalt*, followed by the decomposition of the whole in its interdependent parts. In communication, verbal elements are reorganized in a whole from the elements of experience that were fragmented by the thought process. To understand this dual process, I contrasted the descending, analytical trajectory of internalization of experience to the ascending, interpretative trajectory of externalizing action and communication. I propose this contrast can also be used as a methodological tool to identify relevant tensions in the process of organizing cognitive-affective experiences.

I highlight, furthermore, the role of unshared dimensions in dialogue. Vygotsky (1934a/2001) speaks of "the presence of a hidden purpose, a subtext" (p. 341) in thought and language processes. This assumption suggests the non-coincidence of the descending and ascending trajectories in knowledge construction. This irreconcilable gap requires creative interpretations to fill in for the meanings that have not been explicited. Meanings acquire new forms in this way. Therefore, the unshared dimensions in dialogue provoke a creative immersion in the communicative process. Multiple trajectories for meaning may emerge in this process.

Absolute lack of sharing between the self and its others, when intentional, may function as a protection against hostile invasions. From an ethical point of view, it is a strategy for emancipation. The dialogical restriction in the access to secretive dimensions of the self shows alterity's central role in psychological development; it is essential to sustain creative responsivity in the I-other-world relations.

Dialogue is coauthorship rather than intersubjectivity, precisely because it demands movement from the other, compromised action. Sobral (2014) emphasizes that "The Circle [Bakhtin's] sees the subject not as a puppet in social relations, but as an agent, an organizer of discourses, responsible for their own acts and responsive to others" (p. 24). To Bakhtin (1929/2013), dialogism is the opposite of monologism. Bahktin rejects solipsism, which is a characteristic of the Cartesian subject. With his method of achieving truth, questioning the existence of all things, Descartes (1641/2004) concluded that the first unquestionable certainty is that "when I doubt, I think; if I think, therefore I am". All things conceived that are external to myself can have their existence questioned, can be the illusion of a deceiving God, but the thoughts I have about these things are in me and, therefore, prove my existence. The Cartesian I is thus constituted of its representations of the world, legitimating its existence with its own thoughts (see also Leão and Guimarães, in preparation). The

Cartesian I is thus constituted of its representations of the world, legitimating its existence with its own thoughts.

> [...] monologism is the radical denial of the existence of another isonomous and isonomo-responsive conscience outside itself, [...]. In the monological approach (in its extreme or pure form), the *other* remains only an *object* of conscience, and not another conscience. The other is not expected to respond in a way that may change everything in the universe of my conscience. Monologue is conclusive and deaf to the other's answer, it does not wait for the other nor recognizes in it a *decisive* force. It exists without the other and this is why it reifies, in a way, the entire reality. It intends to be the last word. It closes the represented men and represented world. (Bakhtin 1929/2013, p. 329, author's highlights)

To Bakhtin (1979/2015), conversely, "it may be intuitively convincing and logical that the entire world be inside my head", as solipsism proposes, but "in intuitive terms, it would be absolutely incomprehensible to set the entire world and myself included in someone else's conscience" (p. 36). If I can conceive the world outside myself as an idea in my mind, the other may also imagine the same about the world external to them, which includes me. However, I am certain I truly exist because I think and I cannot admit I am only an idea in someone else's mind. Logic does not sustain the solipsist I. Bakhtin's notion, therefore, challenges the Cartesian notion of self.

To Leão and Guimarães' (in preparation) reading of Bahktin (1979/2015), idealism is a self-experiencing of oneself, not the other; it is being with one's own ideas: "in idealism, experiencing oneself is intuitively convincing, not experiencing the other; realism and materialism are what make experiencing the other convincing" (p.36). However, the I is not a fixed entity that pertains only to itself. The I is mobile, it is a place that may be occupied by the other: "The *I* hides itself in the *other* and *others*, it wants to be only an other for the others, immerse itself inside the world of the others as an other, it wants to get rid of the heavy load of a single *I* (*I-to-itself*) in the world" (Bakhtin 1979/2015, p. 383).

From a dialogical perspective, the self is multivocal, that is, as inhabited by other subjects' voices, which are in constant dialogue (cf. Guimarães 2013). Hermans (2001) opposes the Cartesian *cogito* [I think] to the dialogical notion of the self, stating, first, that "the Cartesian concept of self is traditionally formulated in terms of the expression 'I think'. This expression presupposes the existence of a centralized I, responsible for the steps in reason and thought" (p. 249). He emphasizes, furthermore, that the dialogical self "is social not in the sense that a self-contained individual engages in social interactions with external people, but in the sense that other people occupy a position in a multivocal self" (p. 250).

Figure 4.3, shows the possibility of a person sheltering dialogical tensions between different positions that do not integrate in a field of sharing and interaction. Usually, these experiences are extremely disquieting and disruptive, and demand great effort to elaborate (cf. Guimarães 2013). I conceived this process as the possibility that corporeity may shelter a multiplicity of selves, which could coexist without having to integrate around a dominant position that we would call the center of the person's personality.

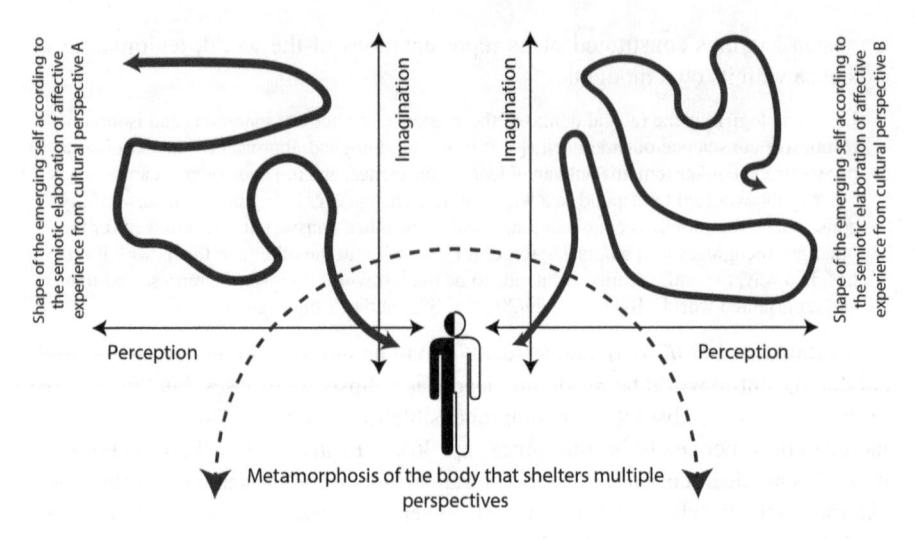

Fig. 4.3 Dialogical multiplication in the self as an anthropophagic phenomenon. (Source: Adapted from Guimarães 2013, p. 234)

The I is intertwined with the other. When they relate, the I losses its original contours and, because of this, is able to create new contours that define it differently from before. The strangeness of the other may inhibit, intimidate, coerce or repress the I. But meeting alterity may also generate growth; new knowledge that one may offer to the other; partnerships that may evolve. In alterity relations that promote disquieting experiences, aspects of the previous self remain unchanged. At the same time, changes take place that produce a subjectivity affected by the interactions, both verbal and non-verbal. The *I* transforms itself but does not merge with the other. Regarding this, Bakhtin (1979/2015) raises an important question:

> What would be gained from my merging with the other, if from *two* we passed to *one*? In which way would the experience be enriched? What would I gain if the other merged with me? He would see and know only what I see and know. He would only produce in himself the impasses in my life; it is good that he remains outside of me, because from this position he can see and know what I, from my position, do not, and can substatially enrich my life's experience (p. 80, italics by the author)

Therefore, the dialogical relation is always an experience of exchange in which the I absorbs what the other has to offer. The self digests the other, swallows it. In this process, the I expands itself, builds itself with the parts of the other it has internalized. New contours arise, different from the ones that existed before, until its previous form ceases to exist entirely and the I becomes someone else, with new worldviews. The I does not merge with the other; it goes through a metamorphosis. Change may, however, come about with violence, when the relation with the other is marked by lack of respect or responsibility. Such circumstances generate more pain and suffering than growth and expansion.

Tuning Bodies

The affective body's activities in the environment are coordinated with others; there is a certain regularity in the different spheres of life. For example, in some families' daily life, the interaction patterns between the family members are co-regulated by mealtimes (breakfast, lunch and dinner). In the academic culture, regulations define class periods, evaluations, coordination of academic production, project elaboration, report production and development, etc. These regulations are connected to specific moments of the day (or the week, month and years) in which these activities take place.

Culture cultivates psychological systems through investments that imply the construction of personal corporeity. These investments involve establishing a social organization at the basis of mutual regulations of activities. Temporality, thus, concerns the personal and cultural ways of living and conferring meaning to the transformations in the course of a life. These transformations may be stabilized through symbolic constructs that the person uses to describe their history in the flow of experiences, thoughts and feelings.

The passing of time implies transformation, but at the same time, the person experiences the eternal return of the present moment. This results from the person's recursive attention to their socially structured environment. Recursive regulation is a property of organic, sub-personal systems that includes coordinating vigil and sleep, hunger, thirst and satisfaction, etc. All these recursive demands, from sub-personal systems and from social tasks, require a rhythmic tuning between the body/person and other surrounding bodies/people. However, the domain of interaction goes beyond human beings (Ingold 2000, p. 199). Our perception of the passing of time is connected to our perception of the entire landscape. This means our attention may be co-regulated, for example, by the rhythms of plants and animals, or further: "the rhythms of human activity resonate not only with other living beings, but also with a whole that shelters the rhythmic phenomena –the cycles of day and night, the seasons of the year, the winds, tides and so on" (Ingold, p. 200). One of the most significant evidences of the reciprocal organization of temporal experiences is found in the scientific definition of a second, which corresponds to the duration of 9.192.631.770 oscillations of cesium-113 atoms. Thus, from the cycles of the sun to those of the cesium atom, the experience of temporality is connected to the recursive resonations of the elements in our environment.

Furthermore, temporality is also experienced in its irreversible and linear character, permanently moving from the past to the future. Valsiner (1994, 2002) has extensively discussed the notion of irreversibility of time, emphasizing the singularity of human development trajectories, in which the present is semiotically stabilized from the emerging flow of experience (Valsiner 2002, p. 50). Semiotic mediation is responsible for the ability to perceive, in an adaptive illusion, the present moment and distinguish it from the past and future projected in the conscience's reflexivity.

Valsiner takes into account Bergson's emphasis on the semiotic mediation of the human consciousness:

> Consciousness separates the flow into units, by way of symbols—and perceives the reality only through the symbol (Bergson 1910, p. 128). [...]. Language performs a dual function: on the one hand, it generates self-reflexive stability in the face of duration (thus eliminating the real "flow" of irreversible personal experience by translating it into symbols reflecting stability). (Valsiner 1994, p. 31)

The recursive and irreversible dimensions of temporality may be integrated by observing the relation between the singularity of developmental trajectories and the cyclic repeatability that is also inherent to human development. The notion of recursiveness is also discussed by Valsiner:

> If the irreversibility of duration is taken seriously, each unity of analysis may be constructed by way of three sequentially distinguishable processual sub-units: emergence, steady state and dissipation. Adjacent units would have temporally overlapping sub-units (e.g., the dissipation phase of one unit is the same as the emergence phase of the next). Furthermore, it may be in principle impossible to determine the exact beginning "point" of an emergence phase (or the end "point" of the dissipation phase). The three-part units can be strictly definable by their middle ("steady state") part, but the relevant material from the perspective of developmental psychology is not in that definable part of the unit of analysis. The "steady state" may merely serve as a basis for detection of a developmental process that has arrived as such "steady state". The focus of analysis needs to be on the fuzzy sub-parts of the unit, and on the transition from one unit (that dissipates) to the next (that emerges). (Valsiner 1994, p. 37)

I Meaningful exprience emerge, stabilize and dissipate along irreversible time. So we have: (1) that phenomena emerge, stabilize and dissipate repeatedly along an irreversible time; (2) that, however, when a cycled is concluded, it does not return to the same starting point as in the previous cycle; (3) that each repeated cycle is marked by a difference that moves the process forward, returning to a new beginning. The prior stage confers historicity to the process of temporality. Additionally, considering (a) Ingold's (2000) reflections about the relation between temporality and reciprocity, when people's actions answer to others and vice-versa, as well as to the distinct elements in the environment; and (b) the fact that one of the main sources for transformation in human development is the search for intersubjective sharing (Guimarães and Simão 2007), therefore: (4) the experience of temporality is promoted by the rhythmic tuning produced by mutual attention between beings in a given environment, where each exerts an influence over the other's recursive processes.

Figure 4.4, is a diagram summarizing the present ideas on the duality between the flow of experience, lived as duration, and the organization of this flow by means of semiotic resources capable of creating the sensation of stability in the dynamic affective experience. When recursive processes interpenetrate each other, they promote movement in their interdependent parts, preventing the current cycle from fully repeating the previous one. The recursive transformations leave behind vestiges that give rise to a narrative, from the past to the future. From this perspective,

Tuning Bodies

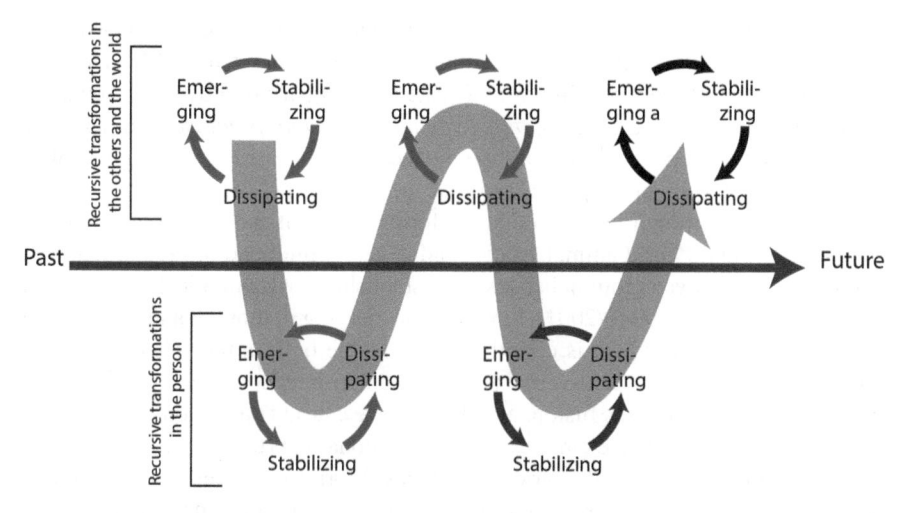

Fig. 4.4 Recursive transformations in the experience of cyclic and irreversible temporality. (Source: Translated from Guimarães 2017, p. 72)

the irreversibility of time is considered the result of the encounters between reciprocal recursive processes, leading to the emergence of different events in the world.

Tuning recursive processes to create shared temporality demands efforts to coordinate the positions of each element in the interaction (artifacts, expressions, melodies, etc.). Each culture, in turn, organizes its own recursive relations of attention between the phenomena that participate in the composition of a shared temporality. That, in turn, creates a certain rhythm that characterizes the forms of giving meaning to the passing of time. Meaningful actions always concern elements of the world with a historicity of their own. Each element in the world is structured by the relations it establishes with its multiple others and should not be assumed as *tabula rasa* for symbolic actions in the present. Cultural productions, such as music, books, paintings, industrialized goods, etc., appear to us, however, as relatively independent from their origin. When these productions emerge, they responded to certain interlocutors who may not be present anymore. They remain as vestiges of a recursive process of reciprocal attention in human relations that happened elsewhere. The same is true for a person's development and their manifestations from moment to moment.

Guimarães and Nash (in preparation) point out that to Vygotski (1934b/2001), phylogenesis and sociogenesis are dialectically connected in the person's ontogenesis. The idea that the dialectic articulation between language and thought is the core determinant of the word's meaning is defended by the Russian psychologist as "the unit of generalization and communication" (p. 23). Concerning the relation between language and ontogenetic development, Vygotsky (1934b/2001) already called attention to the existence of anti-predicative roots at the genesis of verbal development. To Vygotski, the gesture is the visual sign that contains the child's future writing, as the seed contains the future oak tree. Gestures are air-writing, while written signs are often simple gestures that have been fixed (p. 142–143).

The meaning of the word, in turn, "reveals the existence of a dynamic semantic system, represented by the *unit of affective and intellectual processes*" (p. 25). The studies on the phylogenetic roots of thought and word show that in its origins, intelligence and language are separate and that the relation between thought and language varies according to the functions or forms of verbal and intellectual activity. Verbalization in different animal species and in early childhood has the function of expressing subjective emotional states and establishing psychological contact with others. To Vygotski (1934b/2001), however, the merging of thought and language in adults is also partial, which is effective and valuable only in the sphere of verbal thought. Other spheres of non-verbal thought and non-intellectual language are only distantly influenced by this fusion, and do not have causal connections with it.

The most emblematic examples of the emotional-expressive function of language in adult life concern the lyrical and poetical forms of expression, which may be the result of considerable efforts of semiotic elaboration by their creators. The crystallized rhythms in poetic constructions significantly mark people's aesthetical-cultural apprehension of the world they live in, without participating directly in the sphere of verbal thought and concept formation. To understand the making of meaning in experience, it is fundamental to focus on the vertical line of hierarchically organized semiotic affections directed towards cognition, as Werner e Kaplan's (1956) orthogenetic principle suggests, as well as Vygotski's emphasis on the development of scientific concepts (cf. Valsiner 2007, p. 314). However, another line remains horizontal, as Fig. 4.5 shows.

The horizontal line indicates the continuity in the process of rhythmic tuning of affective experiences. Different from concept formation, transformations at this level follow all the levels of generalization and hypergeneralization in the affective regulation of the flow of experience. Different ways of relating to affections through

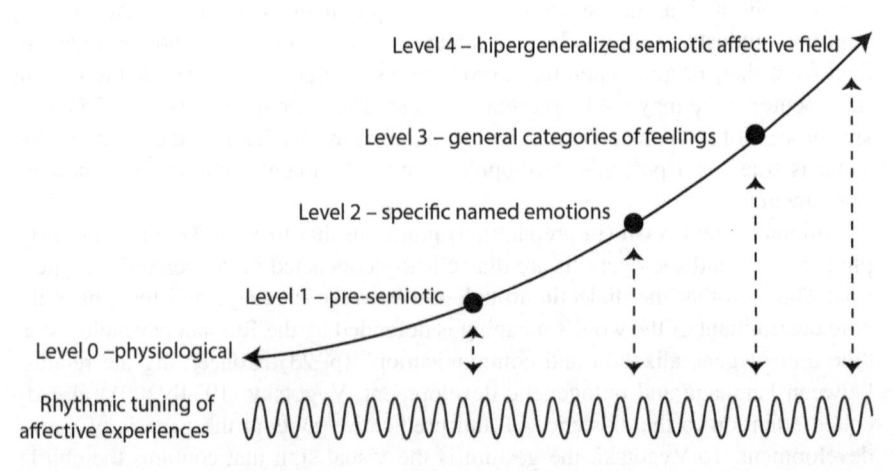

Fig. 4.5 Articulation between the semiotic hierarchy of affects and rhythmic tuning of affective experiences. (Source: Translated from Guimarães 2017, p. 74)

semiotic resources of a given culture also interfere in the person's process of rhythmically tuning the relations with others and the world. At the same time, the way each organism coordinates their subpersonal systems in their relation with the environment guides the possibilities of giving personal meaning to experience. There is a common order to meaning, a consensual understanding characteristic of each culture. Cultural meanings, from the perspective here proposed, are understood as part of the process of *rhythmic tuning/harmonization* in course, or, yet, as "tuning with the other's tuning" (Rommetveit 1992, p. 21).

The experience of temporality is, thus, understood here as the result of regularities that come with transformations in the recursive flow of affective exchanges between different agents. In this regularity, it is possible to identify a rhythm in the cultural relations that participate in meaning construction. The rhythmic nature of the communicative process integrates the symbolic constitution of the expression of feelings (Langer 1953). Since the Greeks, philosophy repeatedly brings up the idea that music is strongly connected to the human kind's interiority (cf. Johansen 2010). I consider that the rhythmic experience in the person's relation with the world, prior to verbal interaction, is at the basis of the heterogeneous process that causes the emergence of multiple meanings of cultural experience.

Guimarães and Nash (in preparation) point out that the term rhythm comes from the Greek *rythmos*. It may be defined, in general terms, as the regular succession of movements, stressed by strong and weak elements. It is a polysemic term. In common sense, there is a tension between the ideas of *flowing continuity* and of *periodically punctuated movement* as definitions of rhythm. Rhythm is conceived, thus, as the ordination of successive strong and weak sounds whose duration may be more or less regular. In this sense, rhythm is part of the musical study of *duration*, being the ordinate division of time one of its pillars. The shorter or longer-lasting units of time and its division in a greater or smaller number of parts is the origin of rhythmic variety: phrases, units, rhythmic successions. There are infinite possible combinations. The strong accent, standing out in relation to the others, represents the point around which each succession, phrase or rhythmic unit must end.

Apart from strict taxonomical approaches to rhythm, which may differ in definitions, the term rhythm usually refers or is directly connected to the ideas of duration, time, and temporality. Therefore, temporality here is not chronology or history. That is, it is not a regular calendar system or a series of events that can be situated in chronological time. Temporality is the sense of the passing of time, of experiences lived in reciprocal activity, in which "the person, performing their tasks, also answers to other's demands" (Ingold 2000, p. 196). Temporality emerges from reciprocal actions, in which those involved, human and non-human, share a chronotope, a rhythm of exchanges that is characteristic of each culture. The members of a culture continuously perceive the other in social relations; they are not hermetically enclosed (Ingold 2000, p. 196), but adjust, moment by moment, their actions to the multiple agents in the environment, whether human or not.

Some rhythms in life, culturally or personally created and experienced, emerge from a reciprocal tuning/harmonization between the I and the other. This tuning is a condition for mutual understanding in dialogue (Rommetveit 1992). This is the way

I understand the existence of resonances in the coordination of daily chores in a given culture, the cycles that move ritualized practices. However, there is also the relation with sub-personal cycles, in which internal rhythms must necessarily be coordinated. The body's cyclic demands, as well as the social tasks that must be done, require a rhythmic tuning/harmonization between the different dimensions involved.

Figure 4.6 is a visual depiction of the different cultural tunings and the noisy region of the encounter between cultures:

The semiotic organization of feelings is cognitive-affectively elaborated by people belonging to a cultural field that allows them to communicate their experiences to one another. The rhythmic experience of the I-other-world relations, in turn, is the precursor of verbal language, and goes along with it. When two people decide to live together, for example, it is necessary that both agree on certain "rules" that may satisfy to some extent individual rhythms. Coordinating rhythms is challenging. Each one will have to find a new rhythm: the couple's rhythm, with new dynamics, regulated by the presence, absence, approach and distance in inter and intrapersonal relations. The rhythm of experience is, thus, the result of redundancies (cf. Valsiner 2007) selected from the reciprocal actions (Ingold 2000), developed from the common experience of co-existing and being influenced by others' transformations.

The rhythmic nature of communicative processes, in certain aesthetically organized arrangements, makes it possible to structure symbolic forms of human feeling. The rhythmic experience of the I-other-world relations, prior to verbal coding, is the basis of processes that lead to cultural actions and works. Culture organizes life rhythms through rituals that relate to those involved; for example, in a family or community, there are usually procedures for having breakfast, preparing lunch or dinner, brushing teeth after meals, playtime with the children, television time – these are rites that encode personal and collective daily life, whether in families, communities or institutions. Thus, cultural practices are tuned in different layers that compose the person-culture relation. Repetition of these practices consolidates

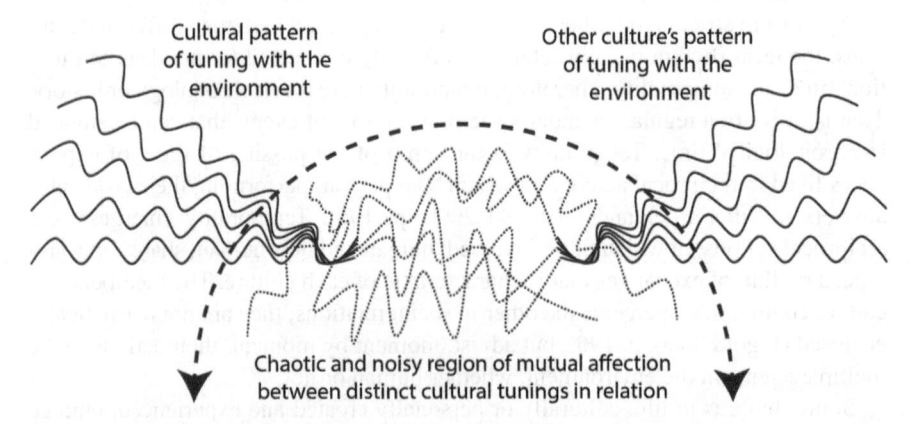

Fig. 4.6 Incompatible rhythms between different cultures. (Source: Adapted from Guimarães 2016a, p. 318)

a stability in experience that may be apprehended in a narrative, as the story of that which was transformed in the recursive process. Critical observation of this process, in turn, stabilizes it in more redundant meanings of the experience.

Resembling the Other

Discussing the tuning process and semiotic elaboration in interethnic relations shows the limits to cognitive appropriation of alterity, calling attention to the relevance of affective experiences articulated by the sensible body. Cognitive-affective feelings are elaborated by people in a cultural field, by means of symbolic resources that make it possible to share the meanings of experience.

I highlight some of the implications of this discussion to the Amerindian Network: (1) psychological practice in the field of interethnic dialogue is always culturally biased and there is no neutrality in objectivating the other's culture; (2) discourse structured according to logical-rational arguments tends to generate mistaken understandings when it is not tuned to the other's perspective; (3) it is necessary to participate regularly in practices that offer the opportunity to tune with the other in order to create shared referents from which dialogue, in the dialogical sense, can be accomplished; (4) the psychologist's translation of perceptions and imagination in relation to the other culture into psychological concepts may lead to an unproductive terminological-conceptual dispute, since it creates a hierarchy between forms of knowledge, instead of balancing them; (5) the Amerindian Network aims at the multiplicity of meaning construction in the different cultural fields, instead of disputing meanings on personal-cultural experiences, assuming them to be correct.

The fruition of aesthetic-affective experiences, condensed in mythic narratives, opens up the understanding of the meanings expressed by people from different cultures. Enjoying being together does not mean, however, merging with the other, being the other or like the other, although the course of actions may lead to this. It is therefore important to keep constant attention to the paths the relation takes. As the relation transforms people, they face disquieting experiences of lack of rule where results are unpredictable, but can and should be controlled, to some extent. The importance of the Amerindian Network's interactions is related to the value of ethnic self-affirmation, as a strategy to handle communities' psychosocial vulnerabilities. In this trajectory, people manifest different trends in their intended actions and projects, which may or may not fit in this horizon, produce pertinent or impertinent equivocation that may be elaborated in the following interethnic encounters.

Guimarães and Simão (2007) propose that one of the main paths for transformation in human development is in the search for intersubjective sharing, which we never fully achieve, however. When a person makes efforts to cover, through symbolic action, the gap between perceived sharing and imagined sharing, this process may lead to novelty. One of the forms of sharing with the other is through imitation. Baldwin (1906b) coined the term "sembling" [to semble, to seem alike by imitation] to explain the selective, fictional and experiential procedure at the genesis of reflexive thought, which consists of a persistent type of imitation of the other, that nonetheless preserves interdependency by exploring the imitation's core properties. As it is impossible to perfectly copy the other, the imitator needs to constantly compare their own actions to those of the other. By imitating, the person learns or imagines the scheme of a set of actions, predicting its successful goal achievement. Valsiner (2008) emphasizes a "permanently unfinished constructive cycle aligned towards the future, in which the established schemes lead to new roles for new objects of exploration, while the latter lead to the establishment of new schemes" (p. 61).

Through reciprocal adjustments in the imitator's actions facing the perceived subject of imitation, controlled imagination leads to knowledge construction and reduces tensions at the crossroads between creative freedom and the efforts to correspond the aimed object in the perceived field (Guimarães and Cravo 2015). People may control or inhibit their intrinsic and spontaneous actional variations, which, unimpeded, would lead them to passively reproduce, to some degree of similarity, what they have perceived from the other. Inhibition, together with internal simulation, permits one to apprehend the other's intentions and the implications of their current actions. Internalizing cognitive-affective schemes for action lets the person imagine their consequences.

When a person acts, they estimate their potential to produce the desired effects in a given situation. Often, the person lacks thorough knowledge of their action potential, but imagination participates in the action plan. Symbolic action, as defined by Boesch (1991), begins with imagining a desired goal – the SHOULD value – concerning something the perceive in the present moment – the IS value. Additionally, memory of past experiences is presentified, evoking models and anticipations, together with the habits inscribed in that person's corporeity. The person's actions in the world transform both the person and their surroundings. From this process, narratives emerge that historicize life trajectories and expectations regarding the future.

Guimarães and Cravo (2015) systematize some of the discussed propositions concerning imitation: (1) imitation can be inhibited and the healthy organism is able to select which gestures they intend to copy; (2) human beings and children in particular can mimic both the means and the ends of an observed action; (3) we often lack full knowledge of our own actions' motives; we simply do certain things due to a passive tendency to copy others, or due to habits formed from previous imitations; (4) the existence of internalized inhibited simulations, which are responsible for empathy, produces both a distance from others and interdependence with them. Thus, mediations between the I and the other are co-regulated, at a physiological level, by the person in different layers of corporal organization.

We conclude that cultural references, which produce thoughts and feelings, are inscribed in people's bodies. The notions of affection and cognition are dialogically related in the construction of the person. Cognition is the person's ability to distinguish feelings over an ambiguous affective background. The notion of cognition is usually used to refer to reflected actions and to decision-making, but affective and subpersonal processes must also be taken into account to understand the prereflexive dimensions of corporeity.

To Baldwin, persisting in I-other relations is the basis of knowledge construction, from childhood to adulthood. He emphasizes the person's sociocultural imbrications. In this process, the search for mutual understanding and sharing of meanings bring up centrifugal movements. These movements take place at the core of the person's actions. They articulate the understanding of the actions' meanings and the person's perceived relative position in the relation with the other. Culture is understood, in these terms, as a collective symbolic field formed by the tuning processes underlying peoples' symbolic actions' (Boesch 1991). From this tuning, a spacetime with objective denotations and subjective connotations emerges, mediated by the meanings that people sustain in their relations.

Culture is simultaneously structure and process (Boesch 1991), both connected to the articulation between stability and transformation in people's relations with the world. Culture channels people's actions, suggesting goals to pursue, creating opportunities for life courses, while at the same time cutting off certain paths, creating barriers and signaling danger zones, so that certain limits are accepted by culture and expressed as tolerance zones and tacit taboos (Boesch 1991). In this process, the person becomes selective with regards to perception, transformation, and integrations of cultural suggestions, using them to structure symbolic action (Simão 2010).

People are constantly acting symbolically while interacting with objects and others. Both people and objects resist the pull towards meaning reorganization in the present (Guimarães and Simão 2017). Thus, the history of their relations is what makes them unique. The relations with the things in the world have a central role in the construction of the self, since objects also mediate the meanings of experience. When relating to objects, people not only create their relations with the world, but also experience the possibilities of acting in this world, structuring their own individually. The symbolic relation sustains the continuity and consistency between past and present. In this manner, through symbolic actions directed to objects, the person performs an integrative activity for their autobiographical consistency; the symbolic object confers continuity and consistency to the experience of temporality, improving the person's perception of the unity and fragmentation of their own existence, constituting the dimension of personal history. Through the symbolic experience with objects, the person may realize their personal memories are reconstructed with others, at the same time that they participate in others' memories. Rites and the narratives that come with them have a central role in the structuring of people's action potential.

Rites are constantly repeated cultural practices. Each culture has specific rites that promote the internalization of valuable ideas for a people's community life. They are the ground for the elaboration of each culture's preconceptions and concepts. This is because the concept is a symbolic elaboration sustained by tons of thousands of repetitions of cultural actions between people and their environment that sediment certain interaction patterns. They are the result of ritualized cultural practices. An example of these practices is the experimental repetition, part of the process of elaboration of scientific concepts. Therefore, knowledge, as cognition, is guided by a given culture's blueprint. That creates the illusion of intersubjectivity, marking in people's bodies a natural attitude founded on the repetition of practices along an infinite duration.

The person, as an embodied entity, tuned to the heterogeneous rhythms of a given cultural setting, articulates the meanings of their affective experiences with aesthetically organized figures, derived from myths (cf. Boesch 1984, 1993). People's symbolic actions transform the images received from their predecessors and current fellow members of the community, thus stabilizing the personal affective experience. The person, therefore, is created from the elaboration of cultural cognitive-affective input. Boesch (1992/2007) called this process the cycle of knowledge, due to its culture-person-culture dynamics. In it, selective perception and the transformation and integration of messages from the cultural field are highly significant. The person is fundamentally multiple. Integration is only obtained through symbolic actions linked to cultural input that is deconstructed and reconstructed throughout life.

The active quality of the process of assimilation of personal *myths* and *fantasms* is what causes the myths' continual transformation along time according to Guimarães and Simão (2017). This process follows the successive experiences in temporal duration that contain the past meanings as more or less crystallized forms, available in the present.

Talking About Affective Experiences

Boesch (1984) suggests that affective scheme's development is related to the aprehension of symbolisms from images present in culture. His theory proposes that human action is structured by symbolic images that emerge from an aesthetic synthesis. In the same line, he defends that affection and cognition are not parallel courses of development, but that affective development produces structures specifically connected to actions. Instead of moral value systems, as Piaget proposed, these structures can be understood as general action regulators that Boesch called 'fantasms'. Fantasms are organized in aesthetical systems. (p. 173)

Thus, the construction of the person occurs together with the development of social narratives. Mythical narratives are one of the main tools for transmitting images produced by culture. Boesch's notion of fantasm, in turn, concerns the personal organization of the socially shared myth, which takes place through an aesthetic synthesis that regulates the person's action potential and establishes barriers and frontiers to the person's relations with their surroundings.

Myths are constantly repeated in each community's social encounters, creating "[...] the patterns of intelligibility that permit the articulation of understandings of the world, society and history, hidden in the borders of conscience" (Lévi-Strauss and Eribon 1988/1990, p. 182). They guide society's symbolic practices, providing values to people's actions, in a specific cultural field. The recursiveness of mythical narratives and of social values and practices guide the ways people feel and think reality; elements of reality are connected to rigid conceptual images, just as musical notes are connected and may be identified from their particular vibration frequency.

Boesch (1991) used Lévi-Strauss's anthropological notion of mythical narratives to understand the narratives' variance as part of a dynamics in which the contrasting images provided by the myth are assimilated and accommodated by each person in a unique fashion. The author emphasizes, in this way, the processual nature of people's structured experience of culture. In Boesch's (1991) view, myths are related to the systems that support a culture's beliefs. The myth is a basis for judgment that underlies all human action and cultural production. It is part of the unquestioned aspects of psychic life. The myth provides all the elementary images that organize experiences and is always present in meaning production:

> The ideational contents of the cultural field are, of course, manifold: from laws, scientific theories, moral beliefs, aesthetic rules, down to prejudice and superstition. It would be presumptuous to try to treat them all. Instead, I want to concentrate on those mostly unreflected frameworks of judgment which somehow appear to constitute our "common sense" and which, as proposed in the section 4.11.2, I call "myths". These, however, as also suggested in the said section, intimately interact with subjective standards of aspiration – the "fantasms" […]. (Boesch 1991, p. 255)

Fantasms relate to the unique manners in which a person appropriates myths, assimilating them to their own previously internalized experiences, notions and narratives, accepting or rejecting parts of the experience of the myth they can access. This is an assimilation and accommodation process, in the Piagetian sense, in which both personal fantasms and myths may be subject to transformation at each new step the person takes deeper into the culture. Myth and fantasm relate dialogically, articulating past and future, collective and individual.

Guimarães and Simão (2017) refer to Boesch's (1991) notions of myth and fantasm to discuss the relation between individual and collective meanings in people's relation with the world they live in. Unique experiences include, necessarily, shared meanings. The person assumes particular versions of the myth's explanation and justification system, which do not require proof or rational deduction. The unquestioned ideas present in the myths provide the images for the elaboration of subjects and attitudes relevant in life. They open opportunities and create obstacles to people's experiences in culture. The mythical stories, in turn, are often condensed into expressions of the type "if…then", known as mythemes, such as "God helps those who help themselves" (Boesch 1991, p. 123), that is, "by word of mouth or behavior models, such attitudes become part of the individual experience. They have a collective origin, but are converted into subjective components of individual reality" (Boesch 1991, p.123).

Guimarães and Simão (2017) also call attention to Boesch's (1991) claim that the notion of fantasm is a broader type of goal than other objectives created by the person. Fantasms are related to hopes, expectations and fears. They are personal connotations attributed to the myth's suggested patterns. Some fantasms, for instance, are connected to the search for happiness, self-realization, obedience, etc. These values may be internalized from a given culture. Boesch (1991) defines fantasemes as "a single topic belonging to a fantasm, normally related to an aphorism of the type don't be afraid to make mistakes", which may be related to the fantasm of self-trust. Last but not least, a fantaseme is what is imagined each time someone relates to a fanstasm, such as the fantaseme "I will not be afraid to make mistakes in my test" (p. 124).

One of the most important relations between these subsystems (the mythical and the fantasmic systems) is that the myths become contents of personal singular experience when they are integrated in the process of structuring the self, modeling personal aspirations in the form of fantasms. In this process, different myths may be segmented and mixed with one another, being transformed in the assimilation process. Having rules for behavior and its justifications, the myths, converted into fantasms, will organize the person's relations with the world they live in, making certain courses of development easier or harder. However, not all myths a person finds along their trajectory will be assimilated: culture is heterogeneous in the way it exposes its repertoire of mythical stories. This produces an unequal assimilation by people, since they structure a fantasmic system capable of encompassing only the myths compatible with the previous structure (Guimarães and Simão 2017).

In the processes described in Boesch's symbolic action theory, "mythical stories are always changing, so it is possible to handle particular aspects from the diversified and successive personal experiences" (Simão 2010, p. 160). This does not mean that the myth's foundations were transformed. Each of the myth's narratives is equivalent to an instance in the "subjacent system of rules of composition" (p.262). To Boesch, as opposed to anthropological structuralism, each expression of the myth cannot be reduced to the meanings of the same structural story. The variations seen each time the narratives are told show a living process of continuous reelaboration of the myths.

Boesch's (1991) notion of myth as a structure subjacent to cultural productions such as narratives, rites, types of knowledge, social and professional practices, etc., is connected to the notion of ideology. Ideology is a polysemic notion that changed throughout history (Chauí 1980). Boesch (1991) associated ideology to the crystallized discourses and social practices a person encounters throughout their lives in the cultural field. During a life trajectory, a person usually meets multiple ideologies in the social field, which they will have to select and articulate, as if each discourse and practice were an image in the person's unique affective organization. Myth and ideology provide contents for the personal elaboration of experience. People incorporate rules of behavior and their justifications through assimilation and accommodation of mythemes – myth segments – in an aesthetic-affective organization.

This perspective does not reduce psychological processes to their rational-cognitive aspects. Boesch's cultural psychology, for instance, emphasizes people's twofold apprehension of the environment, which involves rational-objective aspects and functional-subjective ones (Boesch 1991, 1997). Boesch (1984) emphasizes the role of aesthetic processes for the understanding of affective functioning in psychological systems in general. Morais and Guimarães (2015) note the aesthetic synthesis takes place not only during the production and fruition of works of art: it is a part

Fig. 4.7 Body, imagination and perception in the affective process of the cognition of reality. (Source: Adapted from Morais and Guimarães 2015, p. 34)

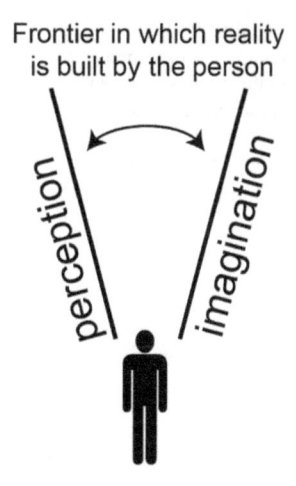

of a constructivist meta-theory concerned with the ontogenesis of psychological processes (Fig. 4.7).

Considering the centrality of the affective body, Morais and Guimarães (2015) studied the relation between the many selves that participate interdependently in the poetic construction of the person, starting with an investigation of the frontiers between perception and imagination that happens in corporeity. The body, as a psychophysiological unit, is marked by the memories of significant experiences and is capable of embracing different identities and realities. Each one of these identities-realities that the affective body shelters brings with it a delimited field of symbolic actions (Boesch 1991). They constitute a dialogical tension between perceptions and imagination that regulate people's relations with the world and with their internalized others. Figure 4.4 is an edited version of Fig. 3.3. It is an attempt to graphically clarify the dynamic relation between corporeity and real experiences of personal perception and imagination in the construction of an aesthetical organization of the world:

Morais and Guimarães (2015) note that the affective body also shelters different realities, as subtexts of the actions a person undertakes in their relation with exteriority. Then the dialogical process that articulates perception and imagination is multiplied in the body. This process creates a field of tensions that involves fragmentation and mirroring inside the person and their multiple expressions of action. The person's internal borders may cause a break from the present stable forms, opening possibilities for personal transformations in the world with others. These ruptures guide the unfolding of new organizational forms of life as aesthetic realities that open to the person and their cultural field. Figure 4.8, represents the frontiers that emerge in the affective body of an actor in a scene, but that could also represent the person in the world with their different social roles. The distance between the actor and the character creates a gap that the actor creatively fills in. By doing so, they create a unique relation with the different internalized others. This is an aesthetically assimilated relation.

Fig. 4.8 Body, imagination and perception in the poetics between actor and character. (Source: Adapted from Morais and Guimarães 2015, p. 35)

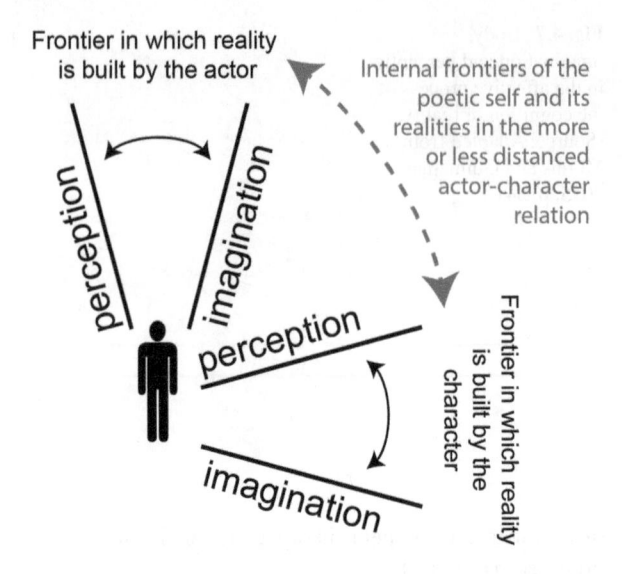

Morais and Guimarães (2015) consider the actor's work, in which the person's internal borders are methodically explored in rehearsals in their corporal dimensions, possibly broadening the limits sedimented in the affective body and, consequently, leading to new forms of expression. The poetic experience, as inherent to the apprehension and construction of realities, emerges in the integration of perception and imagination, in which different sensible and creative experiences are articulated.

The meaning of the other's actions is never unequivocal, since meaning depends on a selective interpretation in a broader symbolic sense, connected to the person's history in a given cultural tradition (cf. Guimarães and Simão 2017). Since each person is immersed in culture in a unique way, each one will interpret the other's actions and discourses in their own manner, although limited to the possibilities of representing alterity present in the specific cultural field. The notions of myth and fantasms, as systems that organize personal meaning in culture, and the notion of corporeity, previously discussed through the notions of imitation, recursiveness, rhythm and ritual, indicate the mediations that myths and fantasms exert over symbolic actions, in their narrative and argumentative genres, expressed in language.

The other's symbolic actions, observed by the person, can serve as models for evaluating the possibilities and limits of their own actions. The meanings of the observed actions can be apprehended in empathic processes that, as previously discussed here, are related to inhibitory processes, in people's innate disposition to imitation. This opens space for intrapersonal simulations of others actions, including the evaluation of the meaning of these actions. The social relation enables the comparison between at least two realities that involve thought, will, expectations and desires. The comparative process, in turn, permits the resignification of the experiences in the course of actions undertaken at each instant.

Steps of Tuning in the Interethnic Relation

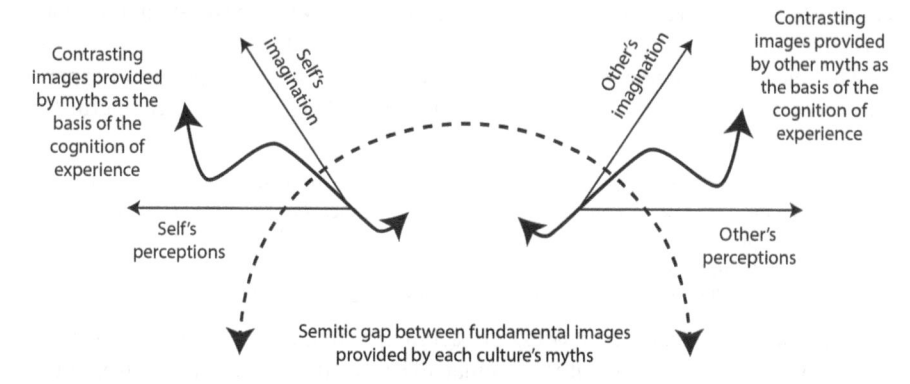

Fig. 4.9 Different spaces of experience elaboration through contrasting images present in the myths of each culture. (Source: Adapted from Guimarães 2016a)

Figure 4.9, systematizes the different trajectories in which the references from each culture's myths provide the images that guide perceptions and imagination concerning oneself and alterity, circumscribing distinct paths of the experience's cognition.

Myths are told in a polyphonic field in which the others' voices, their different versions of the events and of the stories are present (Bakhtin 1986; Holquist 1990). The mythical narratives are expressed by people situated in different positions in the cultural field. Frequently, these positions anonymously compose the draft versions (Rommetveit 1979) of what is possible in terms of interpersonal relations. In all cases, a dialogue with these voices always involves the transformative process of appropriation and validation of the narrated contents. These, in turn, will become a part of the person's affective schemes, as a subtext regulating the modes of acting at each new situation.

Steps of Tuning in the Interethnic Relation

Considering every people and every being as unique, social difference will be the foundation of our reflections about an indigenous psychology. The point here is that the coexistence effort in community life may give rise to some similarity in this context of uniqueness. Social relations are experienced as the dynamics of approaching and distancing between people and groups. This process channels the internalization of alterities, leading to the emergence of novelty. These novelties are expressed in the transformation of bodies that already existed and the emergence of new bodies, originated from social relations. This is the case of the birth of a baby in the formation of kinship. In this way, a baby born as a result of interpersonal bonding will never be a copy of its parents. In a certain way, the child, once born, must become a member of the group "it is a stranger, a guest, yet to be consubstantiated" (Viveiros de Castro 2002/2006, p. 447). Consubstantiality concerns the community's efforts to include the newly arrived.

The relevance of personal interaction is illustrated in an anthropological experience, which shows that, to indigenous people, knowledge is only meaningful for those who participate in social life

> [...] I discovered that much of the collected information from interviews from before watching the ritual were contradicted by the performance (when everything suddenly started to fit in). The same is true for other experiences in fieldwork. More than once I heard the 'elders' complain: "Why does she want to know this if she's not going to live here?" or "Why do you want to know? You don't understand!" (Lagrou 2007, p. 310).

The community leads the process of becoming – that is, the semi-open involvement – oriented towards the future: "human existence depends on the control of the frontiers between phenomena and states of being to produce an equilibrium between fixity and fluidity, stability and transformation" (Lagrou 2007, pp. 29–30). Involvement is understood as a continuous process of articulation between images that may be "incorporated" or "de-corporated" in the I-other relations that lead to the emergence of novelty.

The symbolic use of the body is an intense and significant part of the construction of identities and the circulation of values: "bodies are created by relations and not vice-versa. In other words, bodies are the marks left in the world when relations run their course as they are updated" (Viveiros de Castro 2002/2006, p. 447). Memory and knowledge are inscribed in the body, built from perceptive experiences. The body gains objective meaning from the active subject, who uses paintings, food and sexual restrictions, perforations, etc., to mark their life experiences, individualizing the person.

The notion of body I refer to is not strictly connected to anatomical or physiological dimensions. It is rather a cluster of affections and ways of acting that make up a *habitus*. Viveiros de Castro discusses the relation between body and *habitus* in perspectivism:

> [...] A body morphology is a powerful signifier for these differences in affection. Nevertheless, it may be deceiving: a human figure may be, for example, hiding a jaguar-affection. Therefore, what I am calling the *body* is not a synonym to a distinct physiology or a characteristic anatomy; it is a set of ways or procedures in being that constitute the *habitus*. There is a central plane between the formal subjectivity of souls and the substantial material nature of organisms. This plane is the body as a cluster of affections and capabilities and it is the origin of perspectives. Perspectivism is a bodily *mannerism* and is not related to relativism's spiritual essentialism. The difference between bodies is only apprehensible by others and from an outside view. For the person themselves, each type of being has the same form (the generic human form). Bodies are the way in which alterity is perceived as such (Viveiros de Castro 2002/2006, p. 380).

Setton (2002) argues that the concept of *habitus*, in the sense proposed by Bourdieu, solves the dichotomy between exterior and personal reality, since it indicates the continuous and reciprocal dialogue between the two. In the framework of dialogical multiplication, the *habitus* is formed through the exchanges between different subpersonal agencies within the body, and between them and the world. It is seen in people's narratives about themselves, in the space where narrated and embodied memories encounter each other. However, narratives are not the only support for memory; it is also embodied, and can only be evoked in specific spatial-material symbolic settings.

Figueiredo (1996/2013) relates the notion of housing (the term habitation comes from the Latin term *habitus*) to the Greek notion of *ethos*. This last notion refers to the human ways of dwelling or inhabiting places that create an intelligible world. An ethnic group is, originally, a people who inhabit the world in a similar way, attending to each other and to the environment according to shared action patterns and understandings. Therefore, each culture proposes a distinct way of dwelling that gives sense to experiences—both the personal and socially shared. Figueiredo (1996/2013) states additionally that a serene and confident coexistence with others is a basic condition for enjoying, working, thinking, playing, and exploring the available social and cultural worlds and at the same time transforming them. This is a relevant dimension of human health that is not limited to forced social adjustments or individual convenience.

Differences in the bodies in the social field, in turn, are always perceived from an external view, by somebody else. The skin is an important sign of the evident disjunction between the I and the other. It is one of the main targets of the work of inscribing signs (through paintings or ornaments), together with abstinence practices, nurturing habits and representations of social roles. The internalization of relations people establish with one another is understood as an appropriation of new skins (Lima 2005). This appropriation makes it possible to transit between different ways of being. At the same time, it demands an integrative effort in the field of previously composed images that form a complex relational field.

Ornaments and body paintings objectify, to the subject and to others, the unique organization made from the contact with multiple agencies that the subject finds throughout life. The body, in turn, is heterogeneous, as an arrangement that embodies the social context's plurality. To understand the Amerindian person, Lima (2005) adopts the notion of fractality, created by Wagner (1991) to understand the Melanesians. The fractal person is formed through reciprocal engendering between people. In this way, the person is a divided entity with the common thread of infinite heterogeneous agencies (cf. Strathern 1991). Social life, in turn, consists in giving visibility to internal abilities in a process of representation of action potentials.

Food prescriptions, body paintings and other interventions over the body constitute adequate ways of internalizing and externalizing alterity. The change in the body may come with reclusion. Among the Yawalapiti, who live in the Xingu Indigenous Reservation (State of Mato Grosso), "the being under construction is 'naked". This nudity is characterized by existence in a generic body, such as the baby's (Taylor 1984/1996), not yet unique, since it has no paintings or adornments. Incorporating certain signifying systems through physical markings allows the construction of a shared field of meanings. It involves name-giving and participation in relational dynamics that comprise a given tradition. This is a graphic, physical penetration of society in the body. This process interiorizes social structures (cf. Seeger et al. 1979), but also frees the subject from the impositions of an external political order and from obedience to transcendent laws or divinities.

The social being forges itself through ritualized participation and becomes an entity that complements society, from which it inherited collective values. For example, a person may refuse to follow the social model, standing apart from the group (Seeger et al. 1979). The asymmetry produced when the person repositions themselves relative to the group creates a place of individual distancing that promotes reflections and the ability to guide or change social reality. Therefore, the deviating social roles, due to their undefined, border like characteristic, removed from recognizable social structures, are also those, which produce the shaman, the singer or the community leader. These prominent figures inhabit the border region between different perspectives, each one created from specific corporal similarities.

Willingness to listen to the other, in their difference, is the first step to initiate the interethnic dialogue. However, willingness alone does not guarantee the development of mutual understanding or partnerships. Once the challenge of being open for the other is overcome and the person allows themselves to face the disquieting experience of lack of order and disarrangement of established meanings about the other in the form of prejudice and preconceptions, it is possible to create a temporary basis of shared referents. Once this is established, it is possible to elaborate the ruptures that emerged during the listening process.

The shared affective basis starts being constructed when a common rhythm is found, by regularly listening to the other. The participation in repetitive rhythmic encounters produces expectations in the interlocutors. An initial expectation is that new encounters will come with regularity. When this expectation is confirmed, it leads to the emergence of a basic feeling of trust. Interlocutors will then start to fall into ordered positions in each other's worlds.

In this process, it is critical to assume an attitude in which the interlocutor's discourses and gestures are incorporated through *sembling* (Baldwin 1906a), in collaborative activities: doing things together, acting similarly, participate observing and expressing similarly, even if not identically. Through repetition, certain topics of conversation emerge that may lead to reflections and partnerships. Participation is a condition for psychologists to show communities that they can potentially contribute to finding solutions for demands. In the meanwhile, the psychologist also becomes familiar to the indigenous people. Participating in community life gradually clarifies the intended paths for partnership with the newcomer (the psychologist).

Figure 4.10 is a diagram of the interethnic tuning process, depicted as a series of steps promoted in the Amerindian Network's dialogues. The horizontal wave line indicates the affective tuning process between the interlocutors, which qualitatively accommodates the possibilities of semiotic elaboration of the interethnic experience. The steps shown in the diagram start from the acknowledgement of the coexistence of diverse cultures in a pluriethnic society. The members of society are not always willing to interact with the diversity that surrounds them, but when this happens, it is possible to note a noisy background, a zone of dissonance that may be harmonized to a certain point.

Steps of Tuning in the Interethnic Relation

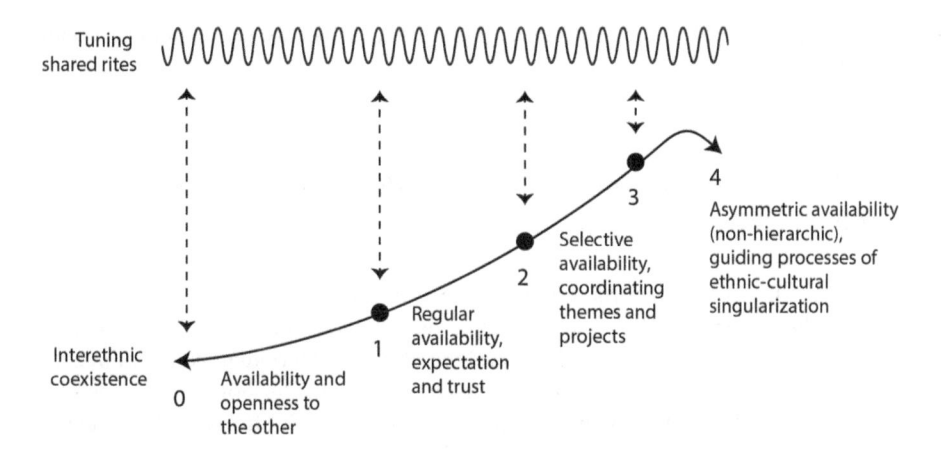

Fig. 4.10 Steps of tuning in the interethnic relation. (Source: Translated from Guimarães 2017, p. 209)

In the diagram's ascending line, representing the search for harmony between different cultural temporalities, I named the first step availability and openness to the other. In the second step, I indicate the regular availability that enables the emergence of expectations and trust in the relation. Each step in this path is moving further in the process of tuning with the other's tune. In the third step, availability becomes selective, since certain subjects are approached from asynchronous starting points from the initial non-directive conversations. Selective availability also creates the conditions for coordinating projects. As familiarity with the psychologist increases, certain difficult subjects, such as the psychosocial vulnerabilities the community faces, start being discussed more consistently.

This process moves towards establishing *a regulated exchange of reciprocal affections and obligations between individuals*, so that each one may, within certain limits, *trust* and count on some particular other's presence (cf. Figueiredo 1996/2013, pp. 73–74). In this way, people may gain confidence to deal with intimate themes and also to share world views.

In Fig. 4.10, the numbered steps denote a progressive development. However, the elaborations are bidirectional: at the same time certain themes are explored and projects evolve, the psychologist's attention must not lose sight of themes that may deviate and point to new selectivity conditions. These alternative conditions may open new paths for collaborative action. The fourth step in the diagram shows an arriving point that I called the asymmetrical non-hierarchic availability. At this stage, the psychologist keeps a certain distance in the relation with their interlocutors, maintaining an alterity zone that sustains the psychologist's possibility to occupy a new position and leave the one in which they have supposedly pre-established purposes for the encounter. The asymmetry happens because the psychologist does not merge with their interlocutor, since the participants in the relation equally contribute to reach the common purposes, reiterated at each new encounter to check for possible equivocations in the always temporary understanding about the other.

The Experience of Undergraduate Students in the Amerindian Support Network

I will now discuss the reports written by some of the University of São Paulo students of the Indigenous Network about their visits to the communities. These reports are part of a preliminary discussion developed by the Amerindian Network's team (Guimarães et al. 2019), in which we aimed to identify the tensions experienced by the students in the relation with indigenous alterity and their efforts to elaborate the affective experience and tune in with the other. The names of the people and communities have been omitted, since the focus is the psychology students' elaboration of their experience.

Guimarães and collaborators (2019) report that the activities of the Indigenous Network are followed by weekly supervisions with the professor. During supervision sessions, we read and discuss texts related to the theoretical-methodological foundations of our work. This moment also involves planning the following visits to the communities, other activities, and evaluating the previous ones. Community visiting days are always scheduled in advance with the local leaders and the Network's partners in the communities. In 2016, when the team did not spend the night at the communities, the professor and the students left the University around 6:30 am, arriving at the communities around 11 am. The team members were then received by the leaders, had lunch and began the conversations. The return was programmed for 3:30 pm. After the visits, the students produced reports for the supervised collective discussion.

Guimarães and collaborators (2019) selected the following excerpt from Student 1, who went on some visits:

> Student 01 (report excerpt from visit on March 17, 2016): When we arrived at the village, we met in a different place from the previous visits. I was amazed at the amount of people that were forming a circle for the scheduled conversation, most of them young. [The village *cacique*] asked us to greet them one by one. After individual greetings, [the *cacique*] explained to us that the young people were there because the elders wished to tell them about the indigenous reality in Brazil [so that] they could have the autonomy to lead their people in the future, inside and outside the *Tekoa*. [...] After our presentations, it was the young Guarani's turn. They said their Guarani and Portuguese names, their ages [...]. I realized they were very shy but interested in the whole event [...]. After all the indigenous people presented themselves, [the *cacique*] started to speak about the terrible conditions the village was in [...] and said that he planned to take a written document [to FUNAI]. [...] We offered to help and [...] started writing a first draft right then and there. It was interesting that, during the draft writing, more and more people showed up, each one remembering some specific problem, making the collective discomfort in relation to the village's conditions evident. In the end, the [team's] initial plan became secondary [...]. (Guimarães and cols. 2019)

Student 1's report shows the team's surprise to find a situation that diverged from their planned activities. Guimarães and collaborators (2019) observed that in supervised discussion, the students realized that the indigenous leaders geared the conversations away from the previous agreements concerning projects and specific activities. With time, the team understood that the community wished to establish bonds on another basis and that certain temporary agreements were not, necessarily, a priority. In other student reports, some ideas seemed, at first, unusual or irrelevant to the work that should be done: playing football, swimming in the river, dancing inside or outside the *Opy* (ceremonial house), go for walks and get to know the places in the indigenous land. These actions sometimes seemed more important to people than the conversations about projects that could or would be done. The few hours spent in the village at each visit left the students with the impression that the work was not getting done from the fact that prepared plans were being consistently rejected in favor of other activities lead us to reflect about temporality and the need to tune the rhythms of the community to that of the University.

In 2016, the Amerindian Network members started to spent the night when visiting the villages. After this, in the beginning of 2017, the visits were restructured in the following manner: the students would leave the university at around 1 pm and arrive at the community around 5 pm, where they would be received by community leader, leave their things in the *Opy* and participate in the *japyxaka,* the moment of public manifestations, from leaders, other indigenous people and visitors. This is also the moment for evaluating the community's priorities, deliberating and planning actions for the next day. Lastly, the team would prepare a collective dinner, set up camping tents and get ready for the night. The next morning, they would have a collective breakfast and then engage in the activities prepared with the community, including conversation circles, workshops, data collection, activities involving text production (documents, reports, publications), audiovisual editing and work on other materials previously defined. After lunch, the professor and students would say goodbye and return to the city.

Guimarães and collaborators (2019) selected the following excerpt from a student who spent the night at the village:

Student 2 (report excerpt from visit on May 26–27, 2017): We arrived at the Tekoa at the night of the 26th. We spent some time in the meeting house, where the men smoked the *petyngua* [pipe]. All of us visitors presented ourselves and agreed with the [*cacique*] to discuss our common projects the next day. We then had dinner at the *cacique*'s house [...] and spent time around the bonfire, hearing Guarani stories. Among these stories, many spoke of animals and the relations between natural beings, which frequently involved predators. They also spoke of their individual views on the Guarani religiosity, which is very important according to them. [...] The next day, after breakfast, we went to the meeting house to talk about the Network's actions and people's proposals. (Guimarães and cols 2019)

The report shows the way the communities usually deal with the team's tasks and actions: there is a great effort to introduce the visitors to the cultural practices that guide tuning processes. This approach is an attempt to adjust the visitors' bodies to a qualified listening concerning difficult issues. Guimarães and collaborators (2019) observed that spending the night in the communities created opportunities for new themes to emerge, since the team was not so worried about the time. They made themselves more available, in a bodily level, to the experience and non-directive exchanges with the other.

Although many of the conversations were pleasant, Guimarães and cols. (2019) noted that the dialogue framework in the communities, especially during the evening *japyxaka*, at times promoted intense affections in the students, which were difficult to elaborate, as the following excerpt shows:

> Student 3 (report about the 2016 visits): The visits to the villages and the constant conversations about the history of the indigenous peoples in Brazil made me question my own origins. I am a white man, my parents are from the state of Bahia and came to São Paulo. But our knowledge about the family tree goes back only to Bahia and the clues as to an European ancestry, either Spanish or Portuguese. To the original peoples, it is as if they carried nature and matter in themselves. They step on their native soil, they see themselves as having the same color as the land. I, the son immigrants, who were themselves grandchildren of immigrants, feel myself as a person full of "foreignness", being a foreigner in one way in the city and a foreigner in another way in the villages. Interacting again with alterity makes me remember this indefinite anguish with no easy answers, which even led me to make an emotionally charged discourse in one of the visits where I spent a night. They invited us to stand up and speak in front of everybody and I was one of the first in our group. I was chocked and contaminated by the professor's speech […] who was the first to go. He talked about his connection to the *Maxakali* and his work's motivations. Maybe I recognized myself in them and maybe I didn't want to anymore. I saw myself once more as a foreigner and this caused anguish. (Guimarães and cols. 2019)

Guimarães and collaborators (2019) discuss that being white, in the village, is, from a certain perspective, to carry in the body an oppressive ancestor. It reminds one of the common origin with the ancestors who invaded and explored the indigenous lands and communities in the past, and who still do so today. However, when the white visitor is treated as a partner or ally – when, for example, the indigenous people feed him, when they have relaxed conversations with him about personal stories and myths, when they play, tell jokes, sing, dance, and let him sleep in the village – a window is opened to experience a reversion of the dehumanized images from both sides, to which people are used. That is, the experiences in the Amerindian Network update the encounter between the white and indigenous people in a different way from the disastrous reality that marks the last 500 years of history. Our activities deconstruct and reconstruct, in the scope of an indigenous-psychological work, the affections evoked by the bodies in relation, so they may appear in a more humanized manner to one another. A reverse psychology also happens during the meetings: the visitor's subjectivity is questioned, demanding at times deep self-reflection about our place in history and in the present world.

When people are available with their bodies and are asked to come forth and speak in a public, their bodies are observed and transformed. The anguish produced in this process is elaborated with time and with the team's support, in the supervision sessions at the university.

> Student 4 (report excerpt from visit on July 07–08, 2017): We arrived at the village after nightfall. I might have been tired from the trip. We took our things to the meeting house.

When we got there, there was an even more radical shift of environment. The smell and the visual aspect of the smoke that filled the entire space of the house, making the shaft of light more visible, the music and the chants in a language I do not know one bit, but that reverberated in me all the same. All these aspects created an atmosphere entirely different from my daily life. I was invaded by the smells, the smoke, the sound, the physical sensation of the sound reverberating in my body, all this struck me and paralyzed me. I became calm. I didn't understand at all what was happening in the meeting house, I thought that maybe it was a healing ritual, I didn't know for sure, I just observed and liked the sensation of calmness, that deceleration of my body, an almost meditative state, provoked not by silence, but by the excess of stimuli (scents, sounds, touch). I noticed some conversation between the group (the Network's team] and some Guarani leaders. I listened a little to what they were saying, but soon realized I didn't want to participate in the conversation, not even pay attention to it. But I knew that was what I was supposed to do, I needed to become familiar with the issues, because it was my first visit. I made an effort and get closer, but I wasn't willing to, I just listened, I didn't feel like speaking and wouldn't even know what to say. At some point, the *cacique* interrupted the conversation, saying he was too involved with the ritual happening behind my back and that he thought it was best that we leave the talk for the next day. I can't deny I was relieved to hear it, because I wasn't physically or mentally capable of engaging in such a serious conversation. I turned my attention again to the ritual, I danced with the women and felt very well, although I didn't know exactly the reason or the meaning of the dance I was participating in. Since I was in a place where everything was new, about which I knew next to nothing, I followed my body. Surprisingly, the next day, we had a very profound conversation, with many inspired speeches, leaving me with the impression that there is a time for everything. (Guimarães and cols. 2019)

This report summarizes several issues discussed in this book. Guimarães and collaborators (2019) note that the students were faced, at a certain moment, with limitations of verbal discourse concerning immersion and understanding of cultural processes. Being involved in certain ritualized experiences with the other significantly affects the body, making it possible to align points of view. The students report that the Amerindian Network's visits produced ambiguous feelings in them concerning alterity. When the experience exceeded their preconceptions and prejudices, they felt simultaneously the desire to approach and a certain fear of the other. The typical theoretical and practical education in psychology doesn't prepare future professionals to handle significant exchanges with indigenous peoples. The skills required to be open to sharing a "common ground" with the other are not there.

Acknowledgement This work is supported by FAPESP (grant number 18/13145-0).

References

Baccaert, A., Navarro, C., & Um, N. (2011). À *Sombra de um Delírio Verde*. Recuperado de http://www.thedarksideofgreen-themovie.com/.

Bakhtin, M. M. (1929/2013). *Problemas da poética de Dostoiévski* (P. Bezerra, trad.), 5a. ed., 3a. imp. Rio de Janeiro: Forense Universitária.

Bakhtin, M. M. (1979/2015). *Estética da criação verbal* (P. Bezerra, trad.), 6a. ed., 2a. tiragem. São Paulo: Martins Fontes.

Bakhtin, M. (1986). *Speech genres & other late essays*. Caryl Emerson e Michael Holquist (Orgs.). Austin: University of Texas Press.

Baldwin, J. M. (1906a). *Mental development in the child and the race* (3rd ed.). New York: Macmillan. Retrieved from http://www.brocku.ca/MeadProject/Baldwin/Baldwin_1906/Baldwin_1906_toc.html.
Baldwin, J. M. (1906b). *Thought and things: A study of the development and meaning of thought, or genetic logic* (Functional logic, or genetic theory of knowledge) (Vol. 1). London: Swan Sonnenschein & Co.
Barrera, J. S. (2016) Tzotzil person model: A guide to understanding indigenous people's behavior and thought. In Guimarães, D. S. (Org.) *Amerindian paths: Guiding dialogues with psychology* (pp. 7–24). Charlotte: Information Age Publishing.
Boesch, E. E. (1984). The development of affective schemata. *Human Development, 27*(3–4), 173–183.
Boesch, E. E. (1991). *Symbolic action theory and cultural psychology*. Berlin: Springer.
Boesch, E. E. (1993). The sound of the violin. *Revue Suisse de Psychologie, 52*(2), 70–81.
Boesch, E. E. (1997). Reasons for a *Symbolic* concept of action. *Culture & Psychology, 3*(3), 423–431.
Boesch, E. E. (2007). Culture – individual – culture: The cycle of knowledge. In W. J. Lonner & S. A. Hayes (Eds.), *Discovering cultural psychology: A profile and selected readinds of Ernest E. Boesch* (pp. 201–212). Charlotte: Information Age Publishing. (Originally published in 1992).
Chauí, M. S. (1980). *O que é ideologia?* São Paulo: `Brasiliense.
Descartes, R. (1641/2004). *Meditações sobre filosofia primeira* (F. Castilho, trad.). Campinas: Unicamp. Disponível In http://charlezine.com.br/wp-content/uploads/2012/04/Medita%C3%A7%C3%B5es-sobre-Filosofia-Primeira-Ren%C3%A9-Descartes.pdf.
Figueiredo, L. C. M. (2013). *Revisitando as psicologias: da epistemologia à ética das práticas e discursos psicológicos* (p. 183). Petrópolis, Vozes. (Trabalho original publicado em 1996).
Gonçalves, B. S. (2016) Neither Tupi nor Tapuia. Free determination and social policies in the historic trajectory of the Brazilian indigenous peoples. In: Guimarães, D. S. (org.) *Amerindian paths: Guiding dialogues with psychology* (pp. 25–44). Charlotte: Information Age Publishing.
Gow, P. (1997). O parentesco como consciência humana: o caso dos Piro. *Mana, 3*(2), 39–65.
Guimarães, D. S. (2013). Self and dialogical multiplication. *Interacções, 9*, 214–242.
Guimarães, D. S. (2015). Temporality as reciprocity of activities: Articulating the cyclical and the irreversible in personal symbolic transformations. In: Simão, L. M., Guimarães, D. S. & Valsiner, J. (orgs.). *Temporality: Culture in the flow of human experience* (pp. 331–358). Charlotte: Information Age Publishing.
Guimarães, D. S. (2016a). *Amerindian paths: Guiding dialogues with psychology* (p. 366). Charlotte: Information Age Publishing.
Guimarães, D. S. (2016b). Descending and ascending trajectories of dialogical analysis: Seventh analytic interpretation on the short story "The guerrillero". *Psicologia USP, 27*(2), 189–200.
Guimarães, D. S. (2017). *Dialogical mutiplication: Essays on cultural psychology* (Tese de Livre-Docência). Instituto de Psicologia, Universidade de São Paulo, São Paulo.
Guimarães, D. S. & Cravo, A. M. (2015). Understanding others without a word: Articulating the shared circuits model with semiotic-cultural constructivist psychology. In: Beckstead, Z. (org.). *Cultural psychology of recursive processes* (pp. 143–160). Charlotte: IAP – Information Age Publishing.
Guimarães, D. S., & Nash, R. (in preparation). *O que nos comunica o ritmo? Reflexões a partir do construtivismo semiótico-cultural em psicologia*. (Manuscript in preparation). São Paulo: Universidade de São Paulo.
Guimarães, D. S. & Simão, L. M. (2007). Intersubjectivity and otherness: A stage for self strivings. In: Simão, L. M. & Valsiner, J. (Orgs.). *Otherness in question: Labyrinths of the self* (pp. 317–347). Greenwich: Information Age Publishing Inc.
Guimarães, D. S. & Simão, L. M. (2017) Mythological constrains to the construction of subjectified bodies. In: Han, M. (Org.) *The subjectified and subjectifying mind* (pp. 3–21). Charlotte: Information Age Publication.

Guimarães, D. S., Lima Neto, D. M., Soares, L. M., Santos, P. D., & Carvalho, T. S. (2019). Temporalidade e corpo numa proposta de formação do psicólogo para o trabalho com povos indígenas. [Temporality and body in proposal for training psychologist in the work with indigenous peoples]. *Psicologia: Ciência e Profissão, 39*. https://doi.org/10.1590/1982-3703003221929.

Hermans, H. J. M. (2001). The dialogical self: Toward a theory of personal and cultural positioning. *Culture & Psychology, 7*(3), 243–281.

Holquist, M. (1990). *Dialogism – Bakhtin and his world*. London/New York: Routledge.

Ideti & Duwe, E. (2010). *Tenonderã - Um olhar para o Futuro* [Documentário on-line]. São Paulo: Recuperado de http://vimeo.com/20263900.

Ingold, T. (2000). *The perception of the environment: Essays on livelihood, dwelling and skill*. Oxon/New York: Routledge.

Johansen, J. D. (2010). Feelings in literature. *Integrative Physiological and Behavioral Science, 44*(3), 185–196.

Krstic, K. (1964). Marko Marulic the author of the term "Psychology". *Acta Instituti Psychologici Universitatis Zagrabiensis, 36*, 7–13.

Lagrou, E. (2007). *A fluidez da forma: Arte, alteridade e agência em uma sociedade amazônica (Kaxinawa, Acre)*. Rio de Janeiro: Topbooks.

Langer, S. K. (1953). *Feeling and form: A theory of art*. New York: Scribner's.

Lévi-Strauss, C., & Eribon, D. (1990). *De perto e de longe: Reflexões do mais importante antropólogo do nosso tempo*. Rio de Janeiro: Nova Fronteira. (Texto original publicado em 1988).

Lima, T. S. (2005). *Um peixe olhou pra mim: o povo Yudjá e a perspectiva*. São Paulo: UNESP.

Morais, H. Z. L., & Guimarães, D. S. (2015). Borders of poetic self construction: Dialogues between cultural psychology and performing arts. *Psychology & Society, 7*, 28–39.

Rommetveit, R. (1979) On negative rationalism in scholarly studies of verbal communication and dynamic residuals in the construction of human intersubjectivity. In: R. Rommetveit; R. Blakar (Orgs.) *Studies of language, thought and verbal communication* (pp. 147–161). London: Academic.

Rommetveit, R. (1992). Outlines of a dialogically based socio-cognitive approach to human cognition and communication. In A. H. Wold (Ed.), *The dialogical alternative: Towards a theory of language and mind* (pp. 19–44). Oslo: Scandinavian University Press.

Seeger, A., Da Matta, R., & Viveiros de Castro, E. B. (1979). A construção da pessoa nas sociedades indígenas brasileiras. *Boletim do Museu Nacional, 32*, 2–19.

Setton, M. d. G. J. (2002). A teoria do habitus em Pierre Bourdieu: Uma leitura contemporânea. *Revista Brasileira de Educação, 20*, 60–70. https://doi.org/10.1590/S1413-24782002000200005.

Simão, L. M. (2010). *Ensaios Dialógicos: Compartilhamento e diferença nas relações eu outro* (p. 286). São Paulo: HUCITEC.

Simão, L. M., & Valsiner, J. (2007). Multiple faces of otherness within the infinite labyrinths of the self. In L. M. Simão & J. Valsiner (Eds.), *Otherness in question: Labyrinths of the self* (pp. 393–406). Charlotte: Information Age Publishing.

Sobral, A. (2014) Ato/atividade e evento. In Brait, B. (Org.), *Bakhtin: Conceitos-chave* (pp.11–36). São Paulo: Contexto.

Strathern, M. (1991). One men and many men. In M. Godelier & M. Strathern (Eds.), *Big men and great men: Personifications of power in Melanesia*. Cambridge: Maison des Sciences de l'Homme and Cambridge University Press.

Taylor, A.-C. (1984/1996). The soul's body and its states: An Amazonian perspective on the nature of being human. *Journal of the Royal Anthropological Institute (N.S.), 2*(2), 201–215.

Valsiner, J. (1994). Irreversibility of time and the construction of historical developmental psychology. *Mind, culture and activity, 1*(1/2), 24–42.

Valsiner, J. (2002). Irreversibility of time and the ontopotentiality of signs. *Estudios de Psicología, 23*(1), 49–59.

Valsiner, J. (2007). Human development as migration: Striving toward the unknown. In L. M. Simão & J. Valsiner (Eds.), *Otherness in question: Labyrinths of the self* (pp. 349–378). Charlotte: Information Age Publishing.

Valsiner, J. (2008). Baldwin's quest: A universal logic of development. In J. Clegg (Ed.), *The observation of human systems: Lessons from the history of anti-reductionist empirical psychology* (pp. 45–82). New Brunswick: Transaction Publishers.

Viveiros de Castro, E. B. (2006). *A inconstância da alma selvagem e outros ensaios de antropologia* (2nd ed.). São Paulo: Cosac Naify. (Original publicado em 2002).

Vygotski, L. S. (1934a). La imaginación y su desarrollo en la edad infantil. In L. S. Vygotski (Ed.), *Obras escogidas (Tomo II)* (pp. 423–438). Madrid: A. Machado Libros, S. A.

Vygotski, L. S. (1934b). Pensamiento y lenguaje. In *Obras escogidas (Tomo II)* (pp. 11–348). Madrid: Aprendizaje Visor.

Wagner, R. (1991). The fractal person. In M. Godelier & M. Strathern (Eds.), *Big men and great men: Personifications of power in Melanesia*. Cambridge: Maison des Sciences de l'Homme and Cambridge University Press.

Werner, H. E., & Kaplan, B. (1956). The developmental approach to cognition: Its relevance to the psychological interpretation of anthropological and ethnolinguistic data. *American Anthropologist, 58*, 866–880.

Chapter 5
Fourth Principle: Towards a General Psychology

The historical-philosophical foundations underlying contemporary psychological theoretical-methodological assumptions is grounded on the articulation of a double pronged point of view about psychology as a modern science: the genesis of novel human sociocultural experiences and the genesis of psychological ideas about these experiences. It is important to understand, historically, how empirical subjects, agents, became equipped with cultural-conceptual tools from which they create knowledge. These empirical subjects use the cultural-conceptual tools available in their tradition (in the sense of Gadamer's *Bildung*). In this way, selected precursory philosophical and scientific reflections are revisited and transformed here.

A combined analysis of historical-cultural and philosophical views is relevant considering that psychological theories and methods cannot be automatically applied to empirical facts or data, as positivist epistemologies assume. A fact only exists within a conceptual framework. Facts are produced or constructed by the researcher, who belongs to a specific scientific community. Given that each research community inhabits a world built from specific meanings, the knowledge they create is embedded in a particular set of interests and assumptions (cf. Figueiredo 1996/2013). Psychology emerges as a modern science in a highly complex historical-cultural context, in which conflicting interests and assumptions generate scientific knowledge. Psychology becomes progressively complex as a self-contradictory field, characterized by both fragmenting and unifying trends (Figueiredo 1989/2009). It brings us back to a discussion started in the first chapter of this book.

Figueiredo (1989/2009) proposes that psychology develops, along the four centuries following the Renaissance, as the result of the rise and fall of the individual. Both movements generated a field of dispersion, where the different forms of psychological knowledge are grounded in different epistemic, ontological and ethical bases.

In the transition from the Middle to the Modern ages, "contemplative reason, unbiasedly oriented towards truth and conceived in the receptive mode of the empirical or rational apprehension of things, progressively gives place to instrumental reason and action" (Figueiredo 1989/2009, p. 13). The rise of the subject is part of transformation in the forms of knowledge construction. In this process, the human being gradually encountered a world open to their curiosity and available to their intervention, in other words: a world that became an object of knowledge.

To great measure, the abovementioned transition into instrumental reason is part of a series of socio-historical transformations produced during the Renaissance: the dismantling of the clear frontiers between feuds and the increasing relations between European societies; the encounter with the diversity of peoples in the recently-explored continents; the disorganization of the clear frontiers in European social hierarchy and in the clear distinction between center and periphery; the increasing permeability between cultures, languages and beliefs. Until then, European life was marked by the circular time of seasons, community rites, and transgenerational continuity in people's social positions. These transformations, while broadening the horizon of possibilities beyond the limited life of the feud, also brought confusion and fear in relation to the mixtures, contaminations and dispersions promoted by the encounter with difference.

The radical transformations in the ways of life of the European man after the Renaissance period led to a series of attempts at reorganizing the world. Some examples are the reforms in the "political, theological, artistic, and scientific spheres and, furthermore, in the customs and forms of civility, among others" (Figueiredo 1992/2007, p. 49. In the scientific debate surrounding the possibilities of knowledge construction, these reforms led to epistemological reflections and procedures for adequate knowledge construction: empiricism, which had a far reach in philosophy of British tradition, and rationalism, adopted in philosophies of French tradition.

Empiricism focused on controlling all the characteristics of the subject that could obstruct the precise access to the truth about the things in the world (cf. Francis Bacon's doctrine of the idols). In contrast to that, rationalism questioned human sensibility: only reason could provide an adequate basis for explaining the phenomena experienced by consciousness (cf. Descartes' Discourse of Method). The method was expected to produce a pure epistemic subject, the source, foundation and guarantee of all certainties. This plenitude required radical autonomy, self transparency, unity and reflexivity. That way, the fully constituted subject should also be fully conscious of itself, coincident with itself and the absolute master of its own consciousness and will. The idea was to produce, through method, "a subject capable of bringing the world before itself (of representing the world), capable of contemplating the world in an unbiased manner, without any interposed mediation. Free, therefore, from any risk of illusion" (Figueiredo 1989/2009, pp. 36–37). Both empiricism and rationalism, as epistemological references, consider the empirical subject as a factor of error.

The reflections in the field of psychology integrate the efforts to conform the empirical subject to the demands of the epistemic subject. Psychological issues emerge in a contradictory position in modern philosophy. Psychology, as a project, reflects this contradiction: to sustain itself as a science, it must have a scientific method, which in turn requires controlling and regulating subjectivity. However, since subjectivity is the object of psychology, this science has to deal precisely with that which escapes control and regulation, that which is purged out of modern science since it doesn't fulfill its purposes.

As a modern science, psychology aims to avoid subjective arguments, at the risk of being disqualified by logic or facts. Knowledge production and validation should, ultimately, result from the increment in the technical mastery over nature and from the subject's supervision, self-control and self correction. These issues gave rise to epistemological and, mainly, methodological concerns, characteristic of our time, and, subsequently, to a project of psychology as the natural science of the subjective (Figueiredo 1989/2009, pp. 18–19).

In the nineteenth century, psychology was still the natural science of the subjective. It is then, however, that epistemological reflections start challenging the limits to natural sciences' method of understanding human phenomena. Dilthey and Wildeband protagonized a part of this debate concerning nineteenth century's scientific method, rejecting positivism and the defense of a single method for all sciences, natural or human. Contrary to methodological monism, Dilthey defended that the scientific method is not only one, but rather methods developed according to each specific type of experience. The experience of natural phenomena is different from the experience of cultural phenomena; the peculiarities of each type of experience should determine the method of scientific investigation (Rezende Junior 2017, pp. 140–141).

Dilthey defended that the natural sciences performed a type of amputation of the experience by removing the subjective element inherent to human experience, dealing only with its objective aspects. To handle the different types of experience, different methods would be needed: while natural phenomena may be understood by establishing causal relations, human, moral and cultural sciences require a historical understanding. Windelband, in a critical dialogue with Dilthey, proposes a neokantian alternative for this methodological impasse. His proposal addresses the difficulties imposed by positivism, which was the dominant epistemology and presented deficiencies in the understanding of the phenomena of interest to the modern sciences.

To Windelband, what distinguishes the different sciences and their respective methods is not experience, but the cognitive objectives of the investigator. These may be establishing general laws or understanding specific events and situations. Windelband (1980) proposes abandoning the division between the natural and the cultural sciences and adopting instead a new division. According to this new classification, sciences devoted to creating general laws would be classified as nomothetic, with an analytical methodology, while those dedicated to understanding events would be classified as idiographic and would have a methodology of their own. The latter would aim to establish the organization and position of the event in the whole of a dynamic process. The sciences would not be defined as nomothetic or idiographic according to the content of the investigation; any object may be studied according to one or another methodology, depending on the cognitive aim of the investigator. That is, it is possible to study physical and biological phenomena from a historical point of view, and to study human social phenomena aiming to establish general laws.

The articulation between nomothetic and idiographic perspectives is a challenge to contemporary cultural psychology, which aims to create general knowledge through the observation, analysis and interpretation of singular experiences.

Psychology is a Self-Contradictory Field

Vygotski, observing psychology's diversity in the early twentieth century, aimed to unify the already highly dispersed field. His first step was to point out each psychological school's deficiencies relative to the project of a general psychology. Vygotski (1927/1991) raises the question of the common factor underlying all psychological phenomena, which makes them psychic facts, from dogs' saliva secretion to the pleasure in tragedy [drama], from the lunacies of a mad man to the rigid calculations of a mathematician. The Russian psychologist points out that to traditional psychology, this common factor is that all such phenomena are psychic and are not physically observable, being accessible only to the perception of those who experience them. To objective physiology, the common factor is that all these phenomena are facts of behavior that have a correlate in activity, reflex, and responses from the organism. Finally, to psychoanalysts, the common factor and the primordial one is the unconscious. Vygotski (1927/1991) concludes that these three answers establish three different meanings to general psychology and designate different study objects: the psychic and its properties; behavior; and the unconscious (p. 266).

Vygotski's conclusion about the diversity of study objects in psychology was that the discipline experienced a problem of dogmatism. Since each approach was impervious to other lines of thought, it was not a case of conflict between lines of thought or disciplinary schools, but distinct sciences. Another form of avoiding tensions in the contact with criticism in psychology is to adopt an eclectic posture. This approach attempts to integrate psychological concepts ignoring that they are connected to theories, and, therefore are not easily translatable or interchangeable. However, any description or reflection about facts is done through words. The word choice implies an underlying theory or system where the words find consistency.

Lastly, Vygotski (1927/1991) identifies an opposition between materialism and idealism at the foundation of the differences between psychological schools. They could be classified according to this: on one side are the approaches associated to reflexology, a science that does not become a psychology, because predominantly ignores the relevance of psychic dimension when explaining human behavior; on the other, those associated to classical psychology and phenomenology, which does not become a true science, because lacks the explicative dimension for most of the human consciousness products. He recognizes the psychoanalytical efforts to integrate the psychic and biological dimensions through the theory of sexuality. He points out, however, that psychoanalysis fails to articulate sociocultural processes related, for instance, to class struggles in its theory. It is worth remembering that Vygotski's writing takes place in a critical historical moment: it was the rise of "historical dialectical materialism" (Marxism) and of the social and cultural events influenced by it.

Vygotski (1927/1991) also considers Gestalt psychology's attempt to integrate materialism and idealism insufficient. In this case, he questions the psychophysiological isomorphism, which reduces the psychic to the physiological, ignoring their differences or that they form a conflicting unity.

Finally, Vygotski (1927/1991) proposes historical dialectical materialism as the structuring principle that could organize the diversity in psychology in a self-contradictory unit, marked by internal tensions that should be solved as the psychological science develops. Psychology's task does not require overcoming or eliminating previous theses, theoretical and methodological concepts, until then dispersed. Rather, it demands the search for principles capable of unifying this diversity in one single unit, on a new basis, encompassing all the previous scientific studies in the field: "this psychology of which we speak does not yet exist, it must be created and not by one school of thought alone" (p. 405).

Vygotski's project of a unified psychology never materialized. Psychology is still a field of dispersion and a self-contradictory unit that is not always dialectically or dialogically articulated. The different schools of thought did not integrate in a recognizable unit, and psychology was not dismembered into distinct sciences. Throughout its history, psychology has always lacked an ultimate epistemological consensus through which the different schools of thought could interact. Criteria vary according to the study object and methodology. The different schools of thought are grounded on different assumptions on the nature of psychological phenomena. The resulting professional practices focus on different psychological issues. This makes sense considering the diversity of ways of life of the contemporary subject, who cannot find a single criterion to create meaning from experience. Since psychology cannot be easily unified and the field continues to disperse, Figueiredo (1996/2013) has recently proposed another criterion for organizing the historical-philosophical foundations of psychological theories and methods.

Figueiredo (1996/2013) mapped the subjectivation modes of modernity, from the late fifteenth century to the late nineteenth century. In this, he aimed to locate and describe the moments of gestation of the psychological space from certain aspects of "experience" that, in one way or another, were excluded from the field of the representation of people's identities. Tracing a genealogy of the psychological space, Figueiredo (1996/2013) starts with the experiences inauguration of the existential field in the Renaissance period. He then discusses the dominant forms of identity construction and self-representation, in the individual, collective and national spheres. Figueiredo (1996/2013) proposes to follow "the progressive consolidation of a private sphere, but also the broadening of public controls" (p. 49).

The person, previously shaped in a closed medieval society, was progressively confronted with the diversity of peoples and things. This diversity refers to the peoples who shared with medieval society a common *ethos*, rooted in the Greek-Roman and Judeo-Christian traditions, but also to radically different peoples, with foreign principles, values, norms of action and sociocultural ideals.

Elaborating these ruptures led to the constitution of the psychological space in the nineteenth century, which Figueiredo (1992/2007) characterized as the "territory of ignorance" (p.147). In this space, three sets of ideas and practices coexisted, sometimes converging and others diverging, guiding the meaning constructions in personal and collective life: liberalism, romanticism and the disciplinary regime. Figueiredo (1992/2007) characterizes the psychological space as the territory of ignorance because "its nature is that of a space of the unknown. The coalition and conflict relations that constitute it survive in somewhat clandestine way (…) The lives lived in this space are fissured. Over them falls the veil of ignorance and oblivion" (p. 148)

Liberalism brought a set of illuminist values and practices. It espoused the ideal of a sovereign "I", "with clearly defined, self-contained, self-controlled and self-known identities, capable of differentiating themselves from one another and of remaining invariant, despite the passing of time and change in conditions" (Figueiredo 1997/2007, p. 147). In this type of individualism, it is possible to produce a clear separation between the private and public spheres. While in public life, "the laws, conventions, decorum and the principle of rationality and functionality" (p. 147) prevail, in private life, the "individual freedom is conceived as a territory free from external interference" (p. 147).

Romanticism carried the "values of impulsive spontaneity, with frail identities, highly affected by the forces of nature, of collectivity and history that make themselves known from the 'inside' and are not imposed by habit or civilized convenience" (p. 147). Acknowledging these forces and their power leads psychology to the "restoration of man's contact with the pre-personal, pre-rational and pre-civilized origins of the "I", with the elements of bestiality, of childhood, etc." (p. 147). Human development is thus seen as "marked by crises, experiences of disintegration, sickness, madness and death", posing a limit to the illuminist ideas of the identitarian unity of the individual.

Lastly, the disciplinary sphere encompasses the "new technologies used to exercise power, both those focused on recognizing and manipulating identities through logical, functional, administrative reason as well as those that target the frail identities, which may be manipulated through calculated evocation of suprapersonal forces" (Figueiredo 1992/2007, pp. 147–148). It comprises the idea of restricting individual behavior to create order in the social field according to the power interests of subordinating individual freedoms. The liberal, romantic and disciplinary ethics are not viable alternatives, since they exclude a significant part of the individual experience. A simple eclectic combination of them would not suffice either (Figueiredo 1996/2013, p. 90–91).

Psychological theories and systems come from a two-fold concern of the empirical sciences, swinging between general laws to specific events. This distinction seems to characterize what Figueiredo (1989/2009) establishes as the scientific and romantic bases of psychology's theories and methods. The author's scientific matrix is subdivided in nomothetic-quantifying, atomist-mechanicist, and functionalist matrixes, the latter being yet subdivided in nativist and environmentalist branches. The psychologies that correspond to these matrixes are, however, all concerned with establishing general laws. The romantic matrixes, conversely, question the possibilities of conforming man to scientific systems. They introduce, in the scope of a critique of philosophy and modern science, the excesses, supposedly present in nature and tradition, which may not be socially regulated or known through instrumental reason.

Figueiredo (1989/2009) points out that the post-romantic matrixes, structuralism and phenomenology, presented alternative methodological and epistemological perspectives. They each aim to avoid the risk of inconsistency and irrationalism, inherited from the excesses of romantism, in approaching the psychological projects. However, in the historical-cultural process that produces the matrixes of psychological thought, Figueiredo identifies a self-contradictory pattern, in which, "from any standpoint in this space, there will always be some part in the shade" (p. 50).

Each psychological matrix occupies a particular spot in the territory of ignorance, the psychological space, as does any identity that takes shape within it. Nevertheless, each psychological theory must be able to establish a connection between the field of phenomena and its own metaphenomena, that is, they must be able to face direct experience, without falling into naïve empirism. They must aim to understand the hidden meanings of the direct experience and the conditions that make it possible. In other words, each psychological theory should, first of all, aim for fundamental alliances and conflicts between liberalism, romanticism and the disciplinary regime. But they should also go beyond, and strive to understand the relations between self representations and self experience, the field of the unknown, which resists knowledge. The particular solution each psychological theory finds in this scope defines its *ethos*, that is, "the place it offers man as we approach the end of the century" (Figueiredo 1996/2013, p. 52).

Figueiredo (1996/2013) proposes a task for the contemporary psychologies, which consists in gradually including new experiences in their conceptual developments. It is also relevant to establish the relations between theory and method construction and the historical-cultural positions that characterize our society.

Reading Figueiredo (1996/2013), I ask myself whether it is possible at all to push psychology beyond the scope of liberalism, romantism, and the disciplinary regime. In Vygotsky's understanding, mentioned before in this text, a new psychology would come from the solution of the social tensions of the industrial bourgeois society. A new man, born from a new society would require a new psychology, with foundations coherent with the new context.

But which type of psychology could be consistent in the contemporary society, where populations with distinct ways of life coexist? I understand that including cultural diversity in psychology demands a new genealogy. This genealogy aims to include issues generated within societies that are distinct from the modern ones. This is only possible from an ethical standpoint that includes new subjects, their words and thought systems, in theory and method construction. I assume this may happen as more psychologists from different cultural backgrounds graduate, participate in the academic life, who will then offer their points of views in the dialogue with the established knowledge from the scientific psychologies.

In our research and experience in university community service with indigenous individuals and communities, I realize that we must understand, besides psychology's contradictions, the subjectivation processes that take place beyond the fissured *ethos* of modern man. In this way, including other peoples and their reflections on psychological theories and practices *broadens, even more, the territory of ignorance that characterizes the psychological space*.

New paths of subjectivation coexist with the fissured *ethos* of modernity and the different traditions worldwide are not late versions of closed, pre-modern societies, destined to fade away or integrate into the modern project. This apparently obvious assertion may open space for new psychological reflections and a complexification of the field. I understand that this is *an important task for the indigenous psychologies*, which is progressively encountering new foundations for psychological thought and practice in distinct traditions and ways of inhabiting and conceiving the world.

The Researcher's Tradition and its Limits for Knowledge Construction

The researcher's cultural position is embedded in the academic environment, marked by the experience in the educational system and the school logic, since most people in academic environments were mainly socialized in schools. The school is responsible for the promotion of a culture "ruled by an epistemic courthouse" (Figueiredo 1996/2013, p. 46), produced in modernity. This culture aimed to create a new man, identified with the epistemic subject, free from any risk of illusion. The school is responsible for reproducing dominant values and at the same time for creating the conditions to overcome these same values through critical thinking.

Despite the current far reach of schooling, to this day, the streets and neighborhood are the "school of life" for many children in large cities worldwide, and oral transmission is still the main practice of many peoples who resist schooling. Currently, large-scale transformations are changing the ways of life of different societies as never before. These are violent changes in different spheres of life: intercultural, economic, family and work relations, among others. Such transformations have altered, even if at a slow pace, the structure of schools and universities, which are forced to adapt in different ways. Considering that the school reproduces social relations, it may also be a source of social transformation: whether adjusting to specific social settings or stimulating peoples consciousness regarding the present context, it may guide the development of its members.

In the 1960's, French philosopher Althusser proposed that the school was the main social institution responsible for reproducing social relations (Moura and Guimarães 2013). Althusser (1969/1980) pointed out the social and material reproduction of exploitative capitalist social relations, focusing on the historically conflictive construction of social institutions. The school, as an ideological apparatus, promotes certain perspectives on human life, starting with the distinction between nature and society. As children acquire skills and knowledge in school, they also learn "the rules of good behavior", "rules of moral, civil and professional conscience", "submission to the status quo" (p. 127) and the "the ability developed by the agents of exploitation and repression to manipulate correctly the dominant ideology" (p. 128).

School's socializing role derives from other, older institutions that historically occupied the role of affectively and intellectually forming youth: family, church, professional organizations, the army and so on. Moura and Guimarães (2013), consider Ariès' (1962) classical work on the history of childhood in Western societies. Until the nineteenth century, childhood involved transgenerational knowledge transmission. Until then, there was no standardized social institution to train children. Specific knowledge and skills were usually transmitted by adults who gave children small chores, which progressively grew in complexity.

Ariès (1962) emphasized the participation of older children in adult life: children socialized with older people in their family or from other homes and learned from personal contact and from performing practical activities under adult instruction. There was no place for school, except in cases of clerical or artistic education. Few technical abilities were taught by people with an expertise. It was only in the nineteenth century that the Nation-States began guiding and financing the educational systems (Patto 1990/2008). This happened at the same time as the dramatic consolidation of social transformations that had been taking place for the last decades: the unification of independent, expansionist nations, which demanded the imposition of common language, habits and ways of life.

The school was progressively seen as humanity's salvation (Moura and Guimarães 2013), with the mission to promote national unification through a merging of people from different social origins, races and beliefs (Patto 1990/2008). This mission was based on two assumptions: first, a firm philosophical stand on the power of scientific reason to organize society. Schooling could propagate knowledge, spreading scientific values throughout social groups, substituting the universal Christian orientation with a new systematic basis for human knowledge. The second is a utopic assumption about school, which saw it as a tool for promoting equal opportunities for all people, overcoming social inequality.

The school was responsible for an inversion in the world population's literacy, which remained, until 1870, mostly illiterate. In the mid nineteenth century, school became (1) a means for achieving prestige and social mobility towards the upper classes; (2) a means to promote technological development, intended to rationalize and speed up industrial production; and (3) for the working class, a false expectation of social ascension, in an increasingly polarized society (Patto 1990/2008).

Ariès (1962) points out that school silenced childhood with an increasingly severe disciplinary system that culminated, in the eighteenth and nineteenth centuries, in the absolute enclosure of the boarding schools. Children lost their freedom to be amongst adults. Punishments formerly reserved to convicts from the lower segments of society started reaching children also. In a paradoxical countermovement, the eighteenth century saw the rise of an obsessive love for children.

Moura and Guimarães (2013) show that discipline was necessary in a society that demanded qualified professionals and adequate attitudes for the new labor settings of factories. The adult should be able to accept "a regular, uninterrupted work rhythm" (Patto 1990/2008, p. 23), that is, the necessary rhythm for industrial development. At the beginning of industrialization, technical specialization was promoted in large companies' technical schools. For the wealthier social classes, the schooling period could promote, besides basic knowledge and discipline, good relations between the youth from the same economical elite, isolating them from other social classes. Furthermore, by institutionalizing childhood, adults saw themselves free from the concerns of fatherhood and motherhood.

Ariès (1962) emphasizes school's highly reproductive role, collaborating in the creation of behavioral and thought patterns in accordance with the new social order. Classical liberalism, defended by seventeenth and eighteenth century philosophers and economists, was the political ideology of the bourgeoisie. The historian points out that both games and schools, initially common to all society, became connected, in the eighteenth century, to a class system. Furthermore, liberal philosophy defended that individual talent should be the criterion for social stratification. This view, together with *nationalism*, made the bourgeoisie class the representative of the national interests (Patto 1990/2008). Social, cultural and personal differences were seen as abstract measures and the economical criterion became central for classifying people: "the concepts of family, of class and, maybe, in other places, the concept of race, appear as manifestations of the same intolerance to diversity, the same insistence in uniformity" (p. 415).

The standardization of childhood left its marks in cultural development. Schooling, higher education and research consequently have a limited reach, struggling with themes related to the diversity of forms of living and expressing oneself, ethnical and cultural plurality, and knowledge beyond the scope of the European traditions.

One of the basic stages of academic-scientific research involves delimiting a research problem through an enunciation that presents and justifies the theme chosen for study. This delimitation is created by articulating meanings from the cultural field, experienced by the researcher. The research problem, as any other enunciation in the dialogical sense of the term, is unique; it is expressed by someone with a particular affective sensibility, purposes and curiosities, in a given historical-cultural context. I understand, however, that if the future researchers are trained within a standardizing perspective, children and youth will have few opportunities for trailing innovative paths in knowledge development. Despite this, we know changes and adaptations are taking place in educational institutions towards different paths from the ones professed by formal education in the late nineteenth century, even if their impact and application is limited.

The Multiplicity of Selves in Contexts of Varying Social Complexity

School's acceptance as the main teaching environment took place in the nineteenth century, when psychology was also consolidated as a modern science. Then, evolutionist views on society, knowledge and human development predominated both in psychology and schooling pedagogy. Ideas from the illuminist philosophy of the previous centuries were introduced, in this period, in the modern social sciences. They claimed the modern human beings had evolved culturally and biologically in relation to their phylogenetic origins, fundamentally due to the development of the brain's intellectual ability:

> Theorists of the eighteenth-century Enlightenment tended to think of human history as the story of man's rise from primitive savagery to modern science and civilization. The idea that human reason would rise and eventually triumph over the brute forces of nature was the centerpiece of their philosophy. Yet they were also committed to the doctrine that all human beings, in all places and times, share a common set of basic intellectual capacities, and in that sense may be considered equal. This was the doctrine of the 'psychic unity of mankind'. Differences in levels of civilization were attributed to the unequal development of these common capacities. It was as though allegedly primitive peoples were at an earlier stage in the pursuit of a core curriculum common to humankind as a whole. In short, for these eighteenth-century thinkers, human beings differed in degree from other creatures with regard to their anatomical form, but nevertheless were distinguished in kind from the rest of the animal kingdom in so far as they had been endowed with minds – that is with the capacities of reason, imagination and language – which could undergo their own historical development within the framework of a constant bodily form (Bock 1980: 169, Ingold 1986: 58).
>
> The immediate impact of Darwin's theory of human evolution, as set out in The Descent of Man, was to subvert this distinction. The scientist and the savage, Darwin insisted, are separated not by the differential development of intellectual capacities common to both, but by a difference of capacity comparable to that which separates the savage from the ape. 'Differences of this kind between the highest men of the highest races and the lowest savages', he wrote, 'are connected by the finest gradations' (Darwin 1874: 99). And these differences were, in turn, a function of the gradual improvement of a bodily organ, the brain (1874: 81–2). Throughout human history, the advance of civilization was supposed to march hand-in-hand with the evolution of the brain – and with it the intellectual and moral faculties – through a process of natural selection in which 'tribes have supplanted other tribes', the victorious groups always including the larger proportion of 'well-endowed men' (1874: 197). This was Spencer's 'survival of the fittest'. The hapless savage, cast in the role of the vanquished in the struggle for existence, was sooner or later destined for extinction. (Ingold 2004, pp. 210–211)

This type of reasoning was used to categorize the different peoples in stages of the civilizatory process. In psychology, it led to the overestimation of the cognitive aspects of human development. Comparing the cognitive ability of learning increasingly abstract operations was the form of classifying people in educational institutions and justifying social inequalities between peoples, cultures, communities and families.

From the notion that the empirical subject was historically subjected to the epistemic subject (cf. Figueiredo 1989/2009, 1996/2013), I proposed the notion of the epistemic self. This notion is an attempt to articulate the constitutive dimensions of the self, previously discussed in this book, to the privileged intellectual development in the school and academic contexts. Figure 5.1, illustrates the notion of the epistemic self, which is instrumental to knowledge construction. This process has affective grounds, founded on the experience of regular and irregular exchanges between the person and their world. Elaborating experience through abstract language starts with narratives, which are communicated and transformed in culture. Myths hold the fundamental beliefs and contrasts from which affections may be elaborated. Logical and rational critique is at the basis of Western philosophies; Greek philosophy emerges from rational thought on myths, which were considered experience narrated in the form of reports. Myths were thus transformed into argumentative discourse. Western philosophy is at the foundation of the modern sciences and relates to their methods for knowledge validation.

School disseminates Western culture and scientific knowledge; it cultivates individuals through ritualized regulation of the body and by ideologically imposing the value of scientific and philosophical knowledge for people's lives. Perceptions and imagination are circumscribed to pre-established references, with a narrow margin for singularization. But school is not only the territory of the *culture ruled by an epistemic courthouse*, characteristic of modernity (cf. Figueiredo 1996/2013). Other aspects of the cultural field participate in disciplining bodies and minds towards the values that constitute the psychological space, as, for example, the liberal values discussed by Althusser (1969/1980) and Patto (1990/2008). School, the main socializing institution in the contemporary world, performs interventions on the minds and bodies of children, youth and adults. It creates a field of tensions between individualization and socialization. Since society and culture are heterogeneous, the school should also comprise heterogeneous paths of meaning construction. In this way, other paths of development for the self could emerge.

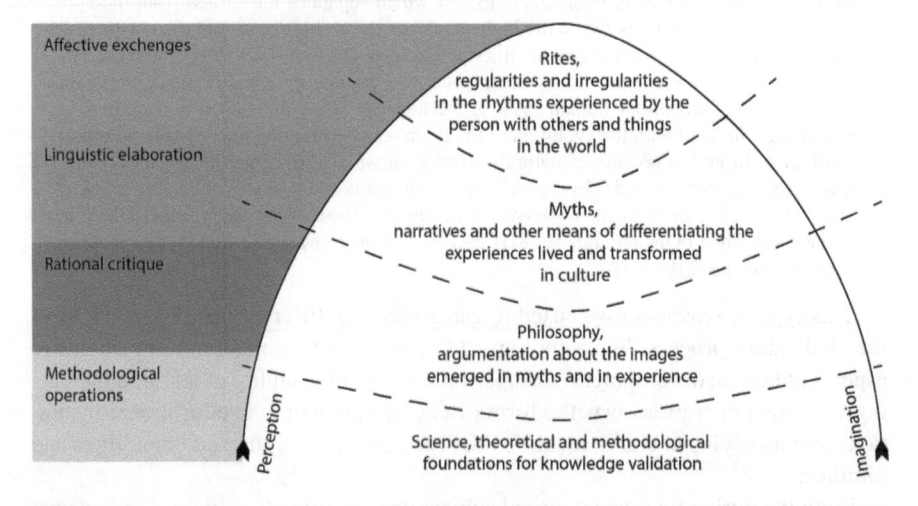

Fig. 5.1 The epistemic self of the empirical subject. (Source: Translated from Guimarães 2017, p. 127)

When cultural heterogeneity is allowed in the school environment, other routes for the cultivation of the self are experimented and articulated to the available socializing fields. This way, they are also legitimized in the collective culture. In several schools, for example, religious education still coexists with secular scientificist understandings of the world. It involves knowing religion, but also experiencing faith. This can be seen, from the point of view of the self's development in culture, as a slightly different route from that of the scientific knowledge. Another route in the heterogeneous school environment involves the discipline and cultivation of the body according to culturally established criteria of efficiency in sports and beauty. Additionally, controlled cultivation of aesthetic criteria can be highly valued in certain school environments, which promote artistic fruition and production. In each route for the self's development, whether the epistemic, religious, artistic or another, the parameters for perception and imagination are altered according to the expectations on the person's action potentials.

Cultivation routes' heteregeneity leads us to think that the person is not monolithically or monologically constituted according to a single predictable pattern. Each person is also internally heterogeneous and their self reflects the unique way in which they were able to articulate, in their life trajectories, aspects from the different cultural routes for development. This internal heterogeneity can be seen as layers of the self, personal zones of experience related to the person's different routes of development.

Figure 5.2 illustrates the assimilation and accommodation of a set of ritualized cultural experiences, from which the layers of the self emerge as distinct routes for development. By articulating mythical themes, the self develops rational-logical critique, the ability to disorganize meanings and create art or, yet, rhetoric skills

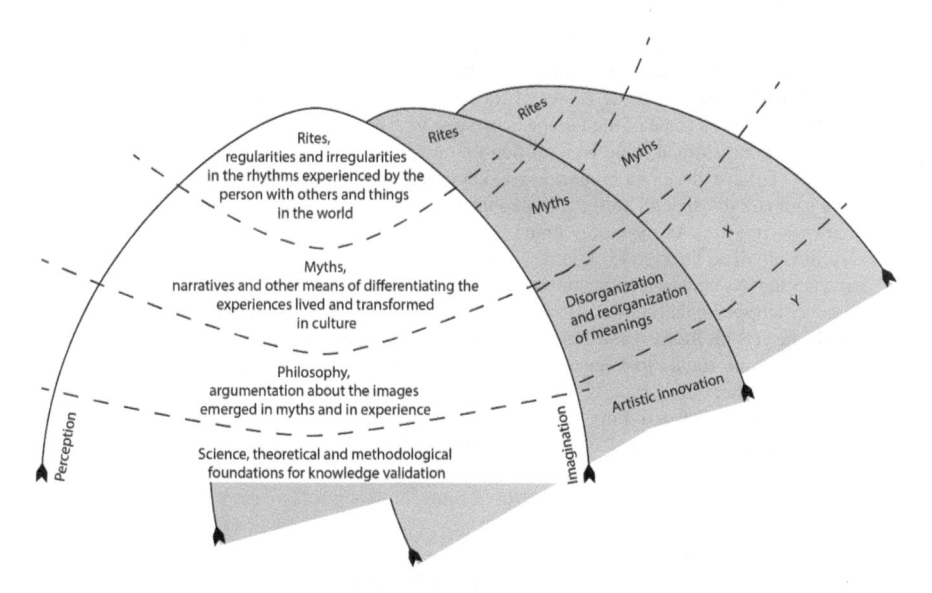

Fig. 5.2 Layers of the self. (Source: Translated from Guimarães 2017, p. 128)

typical of devotional or political discourse, among infinite other possible paths. The present systematization opens the possibility to understand that other trajectories, more or less distinct from the dominant cultural channeling, may emerge and be negotiated in the school environment and in culture in general. These alternatives may rip apart and enrich even further the multifaceted soil of meaning elaboration and development of the self.

I will discuss some considerations from the research project[1] of Marília Antunes Benedito, whose goal was initially to understand indigenous students' thoughts on what it is to be indigenous nowadays. The research aimed to identify the symbolic resources (Zittoun 2006) used by the students to support their ethnic identity in the urban context and how they evaluated the possible differences between their worldviews and those of the elders from their communities. Semi-structured interviews were conducted with five indigenous university students. The interviews were filmed and transcribed for posterior analysis, with the participants' consent, as required by the National Council of Ethics in Research. Part of the results of this study is published (Guimarães and Benedito 2018).

We selected excerpts from the participants' answers that we considered significant for discussing the tensions experienced by the students in relation to the ethnic-cultural ways of life, ideas and values from their communities and life in the urban context, as well as higher education. All the participants resided, at the time of the interview, in urban areas and were enrolled in a university at the state of São Paulo. For ethical reasons, the names, ethnic groups and universities of the participants were omitted, as well as other information that could compromise anonimity. For the present discussion, I will take excerpts from two of the five conducted interviews.

The first selected excerpt is from Participant B, belonging to an ethnic group from the Brazilian Northeast:

> So, actually, it's what I said to you last time. It's like that to me still, before it was very confusing, because, at the same time, the Catholic Church is very present at the village. As I said, there's a church at the center of the village, the center of the village is a catholic church, so the very name of the village is [a name with a catholic reference], isn't it? I think there's even a historical issue which I don't completely master to say why it is called that way, but I believe there's an influence, you know, in the issue of Catholicism and so you can see it's remarkable that all indigenous people worship Catholicism a lot, but they didn't lose their own rituals ... As I said, my grandmother, for example, and my grandfather, they are fervent Catholics. They go to church every Sunday, my grandmother is involved in pastoral care, has always been, even in coming here to the city, but at the same time, my grandfather, he never stopped chanting the songs, when someone comes to talk about the indigenous people, he gets his *maracá* and sings. And when they go there, they participate in the rituals. There are some rituals that are particular of this ethnic group. The *toré* itself, which is common to other ethnic groups, which is a dance, and they do it, they participate. And it's like that, to Catholicism, I think it is a point of some conflict, isn't it? If a priest for example, sees a catholic doing ... participating in the rituals, he will say the person is not a catholic, because they are rituals of those who believe in the Enchanted, aren't they? They don't worship only ... one God, you know? The Holy Trinity, no. They believe there are other deities,

---

[1]The project has been supported by University of Sao Paulo scholarship program (Programa Unificado de Bolsas, 2014–2015).

and so, that the indigenous people ... can make this link, of Catholicism with their own rituals, and that later on I found this very beautiful. So, because even if there was an influence that I think that, there's no way, they resisted in some way, I think maintaining the rituals is a form of resistance. Showing that, in spite they were opened and many characteristics of the ethnic group were lost, the ritual is a powerful thing. […] So, I think it is really important to show that the dominant church is not the only religion, all are and deserve respect, even if they are opposite things. If those indigenous people managed to ... unify these two things and be well, continue worshiping ...what they believe in, I think that is important. (Guimarães and Benedito 2018, p. 579)

The ambiguity of being or not being indignenous, expressed here in a singular way, in the psychological sphere, shows the social condition of the participant's ethnic group, since colonization introduced changes in their ways of life. The efforts to articulate distinct historical-cultural trajectories happen in different levels of the experience of ethnic self-affirmation, and they produce cultural hybrids. Participant B talks, among other themes, of personal interaction as a condition for ethnic acknowledgement and self-affirmation, indicating the internalization of social conflicts regarding this issue. Experiencing prejudice, on the one hand, and ethnic affirmation, on the other, produce tensions that tend to reach a solution in the encounter with a narrative about the historical trajectory of their ethnic group and family, as well as through the aesthetic fruition of their culture of belonging, or strive to belong to. We may identify, furthermore, efforts to integrate and maintain two ontologies: the ontology related to the search for identity rather than contradiction, notably present in Judeo-Christian tradition, and the possibility, from the indigenous tradition, to allow the coexistence of opposites, by means of a religiosity that embraces diversity.

The second selected excerpt is from Participant C, belonging to an ethnic group from the Brazilian Amazon:

Look ...when I'm in my community, they ... don't receive me in a university kind of way. Arriving there I say ... "I'll be like the indigenous people who left here and came back the [same] way." Only the way we work is different, you know? In this case, you arrive with some knowledge ..., you try to clarify it for them, and then they understand, you know? So, they see that we are pursuing something.
[…]
Maintaining and keeping both, because ... It's like, many times [someone] says "oh, today the native is not like in the old days," that time is already gone, isn't it? They already know how it was before. Because many times ... there are [people] who [say] in the interview "oh, but do natives walk around naked inside the village?" People, that's long gone!
[…]
So we say this: since time is, since technology is advancing and we are trying to keep up too, because if we don't keep up who will [do it] for us too, you know? It's complicated. I say this: in general, I think we'll try, to keep up, you know? We see it this way. We're trying to make it happen. Like in my community, I'm ... going, following both. Neither leaving the culture, nor the other side. So, I'm following my rhythm. (Guimarães and Benedito, p. 581)

According to Participant C, ethnic belonging seems to indicate the possibility of freely moving about in community life (Guimarães and Benedito 2018). Borders are more permeable and less perceptible in a familiar situation, enabling the participant to make an interethnic mediation of the 'knowledge' acquired in the academic environment. The efforts from the indigenous people towards participating in the university environment in the urban context also indicate the possibility of welcoming diversity in the forms of knowing the world (Guimarães and Benedito 2018). Interethnic mediation of knowledge impacts people and communities. In this sense, welcoming alterity becomes the condition for strengthening ethnic self-affirmation. It depends on sophisticated skills for handling multiple perspectives, presented in interethnic situations. There is a need to establish coexistence between traditional and academic knowledge. Participant C's conciliatory effort is similar to Participant B's speech concerning their culture's conciliation between Catholic religiosity and the belief in the Enchanted. The ability to promote coexistence, to "keep both", as Participant C says, is possible by maintaining a unique rhythm of attention that enables an autonomously regulated alternation between life in the urban and communitarian contexts.

The indigenous presence in the cities is not recent, given that the first Brazilian urban populations were settled in traditional indigenous territories, in the same place or close to their communities. These cities benefitted from indigenous knowledge and work force. The indigenous peoples were strategically baptized as "blacks of the land" and enslaved, since indigenous slavery was forbidden by the church and the colonial State (cf. Monteiro 1994). The indigenous ways of life were reorganized in colonial villages and they were transformed into rural or urban workers. In this process, promoted by religious missionaries and later by the Brazilian State, their cultural bonds were intentionally concealed.

The miscegenation and whitening of the Brazilian population was, until the second half of the twentieth century, a political project that intentionally and violently obliterated historical memory of the millenary languages and cultural practices of the original peoples. With the Federal Constitution of 1988, indigenous populations' rights were legally acknowledged. However, there is a great distance between this recognition and the effective enforcement of these peoples' rights. In this context, the present indigenous migratory movement towards the cities must be understood as part of a colonial and post-colonial historical process that involves the relations between the Brazilian society and the original peoples. Nonetheless, the meanings the indigenous peoples attribute to their displacements is still largely ignored.

A study conducted with 402 indigenous residents of five Brazilian capitals (Venturi and Bokany 2013) showed that 68% of the interviewed participants claimed having left their communities for economic reasons (search for work, money, better life conditions, access to goods, etc.). Social and family reasons, such as reuniting with family members or marriage were also significantly mentioned, as well as the search for medical care and land conflicts. However, one of the strongest reasons for migration, claimed by 27% of the participants, was the search for education (32% claimed this was one of the best things offered by the city), and access to the university was one of their goals (Venturi and Bokany 2013).

Indigenous leaders and movements understand activism must take their fight inside the State's representative and operational agencies. To do so, they believe it is necessary to dominate Eurocentric forms of knowledge, not only the language, but mathematics, technical-scientific knowledge, social sciences, law, among others. Pursuing academic knowledge is also connected to the need to manage their territories, strengthen the communities' autonomy, legitimate their own views on development and potentiate their possibilities of social intervention inside and out of the communities. (UFRGS 2013, p. 129–130).

Parallel to the images and discourses that stripped the indigenous peoples from their role as historical subjects, the communities are, slowly, passing from a long-lasting invisibility to a protagonist role in intellectual and political movements with strong indigenous participation (Almeida 2012). In spite of this, schooling rates in indigenous populations in urban areas is still extremely low: only 2% of the participants in Venturi and Bokany's (2013) survey had concluded higher education.

Two expectations seem to exist among the indigenous populations concerning higher education: first, the university is seen as the means for acquiring knowledge that is valued by the Eurocentric society to be used for the benefit of their communities. But other positions in the indigenous movement demands higher education guided by intercultural dialogue:

> The post-contact historical movement forced our peoples to systematically adapt to the "knowledge of the whites", but the inverse never happened. Our knowledge is treated as cultural heritage, as if all those who have this knowledge were extinct. They mention the indigenous peoples' contribution to Brazilian culture, but restrict these contributions to a few words from the native languages incorporated in Portuguese. The universities contribute to perpetuating this movement when indigenous issues are only approached in anthropology, history, linguistics, and ethnology classes. Medical school has also much to learn with our peoples' knowledge in the prevention, treatment, and cure of illness. Engineering, agronomy, pedagogy, architecture and so many others could also learn, in a plural exchange. But it is easier to silence and ignore than to learn from the different, who is treated in the Brazilian culture as the inferior (Fernandes 2007, p. 11).

Indigenous peoples also seek to revert the asymmetries in their relation with the Brazilian society by redefining legitimacy criteria for scientific knowledge. Formerly, this fight was directed to confronting the missionaries' religious discourse that aimed to convert the indigenous peoples to Christianity, as we see in some research participants' accounts. Recently, the fight gained a new focus: the supposedly scientific discourse must be appropriated to revert its colonial role and block its destructive influence over the indigenous views.

According to this approach, indigenous student movements have created narratives that guide the relation and dialogue with their universities:

> […] We have to highlight the importance of this meeting [1st National Meeting of Indigenous Students] as a form of giving more visibility to the indigenous students inside the educational institutions. This allows not only non-indigenous students and professors to get to know and recognize the existence and the presence of these students in the academic space but also allows empowering the fronts of support to the demands of the indigenous peoples. Since one of the points agreed on at the end of the meeting was the need for decolonization, the occupation of the academic space (not only with the presence of indigenous students in their courses, but also with the occupation of the physical spaces of the university provided by this meeting) is a very important step. Decolonization also involves decolonizing a fundamentally elitist environment that symbolizes the pretentiously superior and excluding knowledge.

> The universities need to start getting in touch with the Brazilian indigenous peoples and open themselves to the indigenous knowledge and wisdom. That requires them to understand them not only as "popular knowledge", but recognizing the foundations of this knowledge and its validity, even if not proven by the academic science (ENEI 2013, p. 21).

Scientific knowledge is seen as perpetuating colonization and the university as one more space that must be decolonized through greater participation and involvement of the communities in the definition of goals, evaluation and execution of academic activities, review of pedagogical methods and theoretical contents. This way, they aim to create equitative dialogue with the indigenous knowledge (Fernandes 2007).

The multinaturalist ontology, discussed in the second chapter of this book, organizes the indigenous students' relation with knowledge construction towards the coexistence with diversity. This is a factor of cultural shock for the indigenous students, since there is no arena for sharing their knowledge with the naturalist ontology typical of the scientific disciplines in their original system. The church, at the center of one of the participant's community, coexists with ritualized practices from a pre-Columbian matrix. The university students speak of the ways they handle the coexistence of indigenous and scientific knowledge.

Guimarães and Benedito (2018) point out that modern science has historically resisted dialogue, widening the gap between myth and logos (Gadamer 1954/2010a, 1981/2010b). Science relegated certain myths to the condition of folklore, while others remained as fundamental references for scientific development (cf. Stengers 2002). The separation between Amerindian and academic ontologies is a cause of suffering to the indigenous university students. They are in an uncomfortable zone between distinct cosmological matrices, not easily integrable. The university occupies a similar position to the one Christian missionaries did, and still do in some evangelization fronts.

The indigenous people who attend university are also those who graduate in psychology (among other careers) and those who receive psychological care, in communities or in the cities. This population, increasingly present at the universities and in psychological care, brings with it other forms of knowledge, such as Shamanism. These knowledge systems have no space in academic settings except as study objects, analyzed and interpreted from an external position. There is a significant gap between the subjectivation modes of the epistemic subject, cultivated for philosophical, scientific and logical-argumentative knowledge production, and the subjectivation modes guided by Shamanic principles.

Figure 5.3. systematizes this gap, where the interethnic relation with indigenous people is marked by a greater distance than the gap between the layers of the self, previously discussed in the first chapter of this book. This greater distance is given by the specific forms of elaborating the rites and myths from the indigenous people's culture, that is, the elaboration of the affective-cognitive experiences and the images available in each cultural field. In spite of the fact that this distance suggests a gap between two worlds, which Mbya Guarani leader Fernando (2010) evokes when he speaks of the idea of the parallels, I find possibilities to work around it.

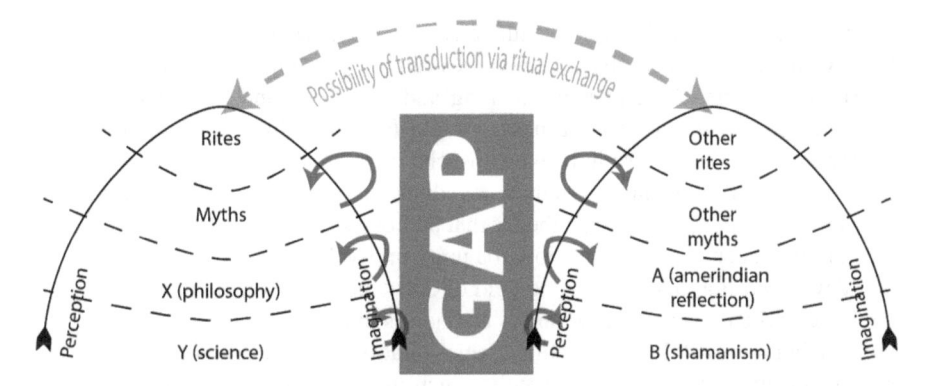

Fig. 5.3 Limits and possibilities to the transduction between the epistemic self and the indigenous person. (Source: Translated from Guimarães 2017, p. 270)

This is done through regular participation in ritualized experiences, which may promote a tuning process with the other, creating an extra-verbal ground for dialogue.

I understand, therefore, that the gap or divisor that characterizes the alterity relation between psychologists and indigenous peoples cannot be understood or overcome by means of logical-argumentative elaborations of the other's perceptions. From the start, the underlying rites, myths, and concepts lead to very distinct affective-cognitive elaborations of experience. Attempting to explain Shamanism through science or vice-versa is a sterile attempt at mutual meaning-making, since these forms of knowledge are grounded in radically diverse cultural experiences. Coordinating and co-regulating actions can be achieved through personal interaction, in which each participant's body acquires the conditions for sensibility in relation to the other's perspective. This interaction demands a bodily willingness to experience different daily rites.

Multiplying Psychologies and the Conditions for an Unstable Dialogue

Teleological projects for a new man and a new society resulting from scientific emancipation failed. Almost one century after Vygotski (1927/1991) promoted psychology's integration, it remains a fragmented field in which old ideas are stereotypically repeated and the tensions and oppositions between the different schools of thought sterilize the creative process expected in scientific development (cf. Valsiner 2012). In contrast, the studies on human creativity are precisely the focus of cultural psychology (cf. Boesch 1997). Psychology, as a science and, therefore, as culture, is faced with cultural diversity. In this encounter, psychology is expected to acknowledge that each culture cultivates in its members a systematized knowledge, notions and methods to highlight events, situations, and processes that have some equivalence with what Eurocentric epistemologies call the psychological processes.

The reflections about meaning-making and the social and natural forces that affect it point to the need for a basic ground for psychological theorization and interaction with the diverse indigenous psychologies. The alternative is rigidly settling on culturally available grounds, avoiding contact with the unthinkable that may arise. It is *better* to adopt a theory that addresses the gap, the differences, than a theory that keeps us in the illusion of a unity in psychology.

I developed Fig. 5.4, to map the field of epistemological disputes between psychologies, when facing the resonances and noises that arise from experiencing phenomena in the world. It is a simplified representation of the tensions involved in the rational critique of images from myths. Such myths influence the formulation of theories and thus guide the understanding of the empirical phenomenon. Myths have the basic function of guiding human intellectual processes. The contrasts they provide must be submitted to rational critique in knowledge construction. When the knowledge produced is accepted as the truth and incorporated into common sense, it is again led to the condition of myth and may be once more resubmitted to critique, in the continual intellectual development.

Figure 5.4 is the result of my work on dialogical multiplication, representing the possibility to theorize schisms in the scope of interethnic and intercultural relations in current psychology. In this systematization, *the relation between the phenomenon and the metaphenomenon* point to ritualistic and mythical dimensions in the culturally grounded process of apprehending experience. Myths, as systems of intelligibility unconsciously assumed in each culture, are at the basis of psychological

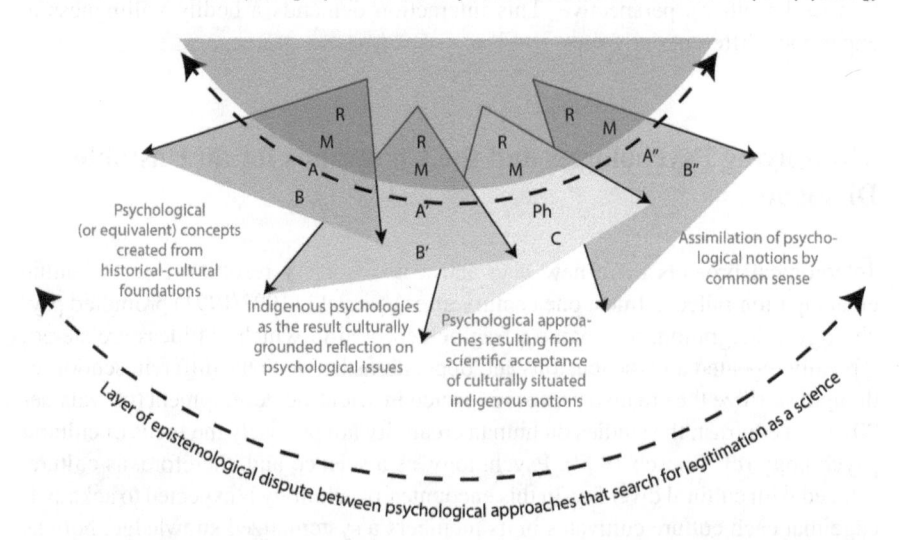

Fig. 5.4 Space for the legitimation of the meaning of cultural experiences in the field of psychology as a science. (Source: Translated from Guimarães 2017, p. 135)

thought, which maintains and propagates reflections from the cultural tradition. The cultures that resist dominant trends sustain the possibility of conceiving and inhabiting the world diversely. They may assimilate and transform the current scientific methods to develop their own indigenous psychologies, thus qualified because they are grounded in local cultural traditions. Indigenous psychologies may, in turn, migrate from their original lands and colonize other spaces, through exchanges between researchers from different backgrounds, who address the nebulous field of psychological issues.

Inclusion and exclusion criteria for knowledge and cultural practices characterize the ethical, ontological, and epistemological concerns that emerge in the notion of dialogical multiplicity. By discussing meaning construction, researchers amplify the territory of ignorance, in an exchange between traditions worldwide. Some meaning constructions may pertain to the field of psychological issues, which leads to a search for proper epistemological foundations, so that the new formulations may reach the academic-scientific field. This trajectory depends, among other things, on people's opportunities and research interests. Generally, the current indigenous knowledge production is not interested in reaching the academic environment and psychology in particular.

I understand indigenous psychology as a field that propagates culturally grounded views. When they reach international debate, these views contribute to the development of local knowledge and practices, or colonize them. This process gives rise to complex ethical issues. I will discuss some of them in the next chapter of this book, focusing on my work in the Amerindian Support Network, at the Institute of Psychology of the University of São Paulo.

The disputes between the fields of knowledge amplify the internal split in psychology, to the point that some areas of study have attempted to constitute an independent science, separate from psychology. These areas are currently part of the basic curriculum in the Brazilian psychology undergraduate program, such as experimental behavior analysis, ethology, psychoanalysis, among others. These diverse psychologies have, however, become a part of the matrices of psychological thought, with their particular methods and criteria for knowledge validation. They multiply their paths for science production and disclosure in the intellectual market. These psychologies may be incorporated by common sense without the critical evaluation that scientific debate requires. They return, therefore, to the condition of myths, as part of the cultural material that communities use to guide their daily practices.

The multiplication of psychologies thus presents challenges to our formulation of a set of principles for an indigenous psychology. In this field of cultural diversity, each tradition creates their own particular knowledge systems to understand the issues that modern psychology defined as pertinent to the field.

Knowledge construction is done by people with a cultural background. It provides the images for the researcher's creative imagination. At the same time, contact with alterity generates questions and disquieting feelings that relate to the researcher's life trajectory. The disquieting experience concerning the lack of order leads to new reflections in the attempt to accommodate what exceeds the familiar images. In this sense, intercultural and interethnic relations are prolific; the other culture establishes a frontier with their radically different forms of coordinating actions and conferring meaning to them. The notion of dialogical multiplicity, in turn, makes it possible to map the different layers that together determine meaning-making. These layers span from the pre-personal level, in which the organism regulates recursive exchanges with the environment and with others by copying or simulating actions, to the most abstract levels, in which perceptions and imagination lead to the construction of complex theoretical and conceptual systems.

Indigenous psychologies exist in the framework of semiotic-cultural constructivism in psychology. This field provides the ethical foundations that guide my reflection and practice, given the importance it confers to the other's perspective. From this theoretical framework, I attempted to produce theoretical innovations, for instance, addressing the specificities of interethnic dialogue, but also to create possible generalizations to other contexts of disquieting experiences—such as the possibility of considering each human being as a foreigner from the other's point of view.

In this path, some epistemological principles had to be established in order to make knowledge construction possible, and legitimate, in a situation of ethnic diversity. First, knowledge construction depends on the preliminary constitution of an ethically constructed ground for coauthorship and innovation. The selected topics for investigation emerge from the newly-formed ethical arena for mutual exchange. Next, the researchers (and their interlocutors) must be willing to delve into the ethnic-cultural perspectives involved in the dialogues concerning the selected topics for investigation, transforming possible preliminary, preconceived psychological conceptions and practices. The psychologist must be careful not to impose their cultural values, theories and methodologies, without reflecting about their ethnic-cultural belonging and about the implications of their assertions to the people they address in the investigative or professional work. This type of approach is necessary, despite not easily achieved, to enable the hermeneutic experience of questioning current forms of knowledge. Only then, new knowledge may be developed at this interethnic border.

Acknowledgement This work is supported by FAPESP (grant number 18/13145-0).

References

Almeida, M. R. C. (2012). Os índios na história do Brasil no século XIX: da invisibilidade ao protagonismo. *Revista História Hoje, 1*(2), 21–40.
Althusser, L. (1969/1980). Ideologia e aparelhos ideológicos do estado. São Paulo: Editorial Presença and Martins Fontes. (Originalmente publicado em 1969).
Áries, P. (1962). *Centuries of childhood: A social history of family life*. New York: Alfred A. Knopf.
Boesch, E. E. (1997). Reasons for a *Symbolic* concept of action. *Culture & Psychology, 3*(3), 423–431.
Encontro Nacional dos Estudantes Indígenas. (2013). *Documento final do I Encontro Nacional dos Estudantes Indígenas*. São Carlos: UFSCAR.

Fernandes. (2007). Ensino superior para indígenas: desafios e perspectivas. Trabalho apresentado no *Seminário Formação Jurídica e Povos Indígenas Desafios para uma educação superior*, ocorrido entre os dias 21 e 23 de março, em Belém, Pará.
Fernando, M. (2010). Mariano Fernando. Conselho Regional de Psicologia da 6a Região (Ed), Psicologia e povos indígenas. (pp. 46–49). São Paulo: CRPSP.
Figueiredo, L. C. M. (2007). *A invenção do psicológico: quatro séculos de subjetivação 1500–1900* (p. 184). São Paulo: Escuta. (Trabalho original publicado em 1992).
Figueiredo, L. C. M. (2009). *Matrizes do pensamento psicológico* (p. 208). Petropólis: Vozes. (Trabalho original publicado em 1989).
Figueiredo, L. C. M. (2013). *Revisitando as psicologias: da epistemologia à ética das práticas e discursos psicológicos* (p. 183). Petropólis: Vozes. (Trabalho original publicado em 1996).
Gadamer, H.-G. (2010a). Mito e Razão. In H.-G. Gadamer (Ed.), *Hermenêutica da Obra de Arte*. São Paulo: Martins Fontes. (Texto original publicado em 1954.
Gadamer, H.-G. (2010b). Mito e Logos. In H.-G. Gadamer (Ed.), *Hermenêutica da Obra de Arte* (pp. 65–68). São Paulo: Martins Fontes. (Texto original publicado em 1981).
Guimarães, D. S. (2017). *Dialogical mutiplication: essays on cultural psychology* (Tese de Livre-Docência). Instituto de Psicologia, Universidade de São Paulo, São Paulo.
Guimarães, D. S. & Benedito, M. A. (2018) The Construction of the person in the interethnic situation: Dialogues with indigenous university students. In: A. Rosa; J. Valsiner. (Orgs.). *The cambridge handbook of sociocultural psychology* (pp. 575–596). (1sted.). Cambridge: Cambridge University Press.
Ingold, T. (2004). Beyond biology and culture. The meaning of evolution in a relational world. *Social Anthropology, 12*(2), 209–221.
Monteiro, J. M. (1994). *Negros da terra: índios e bandeirantes nas origens de São Paulo*. São Paulo: Companhia das Letras.
Moura, M. L. & Guimarães, D. S. (2013) Commentary. Social reproduction and its transformations: Relationships in educational institutions. In: Y. Omi; L. P. Rodriguez; M. C. Peralta-Gomez. (Org.). *Lives and relationships: Culture in transitions between social roles* (pp. 19–94). (1sted.). Charlotte: Information Age Pub Inc.
Patto, M. H. S. (2008). *A Produção Do Fracasso Escolar [The production of scholar failure]*. São Paulo: Casa do Psicólogo. (Texto original publicado em 1990).
Rezende Junior, J. (2017). O Problema da Experiência na Disputa sobre o Método Científico: Dilthey, Windelband E Rickert. *Conjectura: Filosofia e Educação, 22*(1), 136–160.
Stengers, I. (2002). *A invenção das ciências modernas*. São Paulo: Editora 34. (Texto original publicado em 1993).
UFRGS (Universidade Federal do Rio Grande do Sul). (2013). *Estudantes indígenas no ensino superior: Uma abordagem a partir da experiência na UFRGS*. Porto Alegre: Editora da UFRGS.
Valsiner, J. (2012). *Fundamentos da psicologia cultural: Mundos da mente mundos da vida* (p. 356). Porto Alegre: Artmed.
Venturi, G., & Bokany, V.. Orgs.)(2013). *Indígenas no Brasil: Demandas dos povos e percepções do opinião pública*. São Paulo: Editora Fundação Perseu Abramo.
Vygotski, L. S. (1927/1991). El Significado Histórico de la crisis em Psicología [The historical meaning of the crisis in psychology: A methodological investigation (van der Veer, R. Translator)]. Em Vygotsky (1991) *Obras escogidas I: problemas teóricos y metodológicos de la Psicología* (pp. 257–407). Madrid: A. Machado Libros, S. A.
Windelband, W. (1980). Rectorial address, Strasbourg, 1894. *History and Theory, 19*(2), 169–185.
Zittoun, T. (2006). *Transitions: Development through symbolic resources*. Greenwich: Information Age Publishing.

Chapter 6
The Infinite Process of Dialogical Multiplication: Considerations for Psychological Research and Professional Practice

I introduced this book with the words of Timóteo da Silva Verá Tupã Popygua, a Mbya Guarani *Xeramõi*, claiming that knowledge is like a necklace: it is aesthetically structured by each of its pieces. I hope the pieces put together in the present text is able to compose a whole that can be used in the ongoing project of constructing the indigenous psychologies. This necklace can thus be tested in new endeavors. The themes discussed here certainly demand further consideration, but I understand they are fundamental dimensions of psychological research and professional practice, in the scope of the indigenous psychologies under construction. From where I stand, the path of construction for the indigenous psychologies seems infinite, and each new step founds a new beginning.

The notion of dialogical multiplication has been proposed, throughout the book, as a construct that enables the psychologist and the researcher interested in the indigenous psychologies to consider and intervene on the multiple meanings that emerge from the disquieting experience with alterity. From semiotic-cultural constructivism in psychology, I discussed dialogical and alterity philosophies, Americanist anthropology, and experiences in the work with indigenous people and communities to present a set of principles with impact on research methodology and psychosocial intervention practices.

To conclude this text, I will summarize some turning points argued to be significant for future elaborations in the scope of the indigenous psychologies.

One of these points refers to the relation between myth and logos, seen (1) in the construction of philosophical and scientific knowledge (Gadamer 1954/2010a, 1981/2010b); (2) at the basis of human thought, providing patterns of intelligibility (cf. Lévi-Strauss Eribon 1988/1990); and (3) in subjectivation processes, guiding cognitive-affective elaborations of experiences with others, in a culturally structured world (cf. Boesch 1991). Another relevant point concerns the self's development, understood as a corporal sensibility that comprises a unique experience of others and of the things in the world; it is a useful construct to understand the transformation of stable meanings in culture. This notion of the self includes a dynamic relation between differentiations and de-differentiations, which lead to novelty in the course of personal lives and history.

Relations are marked by the risk of equivocation, which are inevitable to some extent. This dissonance between the meanings created from distinct points of view demands efforts of reparation and control so that discord does not result in the destruction of the relation. In this respect, I found correspondences between the notions of controlled equivocation, discussed by Viveiros de Castro (2004), and controlled imagination, discussed from Baldwin's (cf. 1906) notion of *sembling*. The distance and opacity between the I and the other, the impossibility to fully understand their actions and desires, demands continuous efforts to elaborate the meanings of experience. The underlying lack of order that enables absolute reciprocal adjustment may cause varying degrees of disquieting feelings (cf. Simão 2015).

It is, therefore, a psychologist's responsibility to supervise the exchange spaces. Whatever is expressed in the dialogue may multiply in the direction of forming an *ethos*, where several standpoints coexist, with no exclusion or forced silencing, and the psychologist must contribute to ensure that. In the timeline of exchanges that take place within the dialogue's positions, dominance, precedence and temporary purposes must evidently be established. This takes place so that, or until each emergent expression manages to be acknowledged, strengthened or even to achieve consistency as it transforms itself along the path determined by relations in the timeline. Each participating standpoint's consistency in the dialogical context is important so that, once they are established, new expressions may be incorporated as fertile ground to expand human creativity. In this perspective, the psychologist's role is to cultivate diversity and caringly monitor its growth towards reciprocity among participants.

Born out of the interdisciplinary relations between psychology, philosophy and anthropology, the notion of dialogical multiplication has been further developed along the many and rich encounters I had with indigenous individuals, inside and outside their communities, through our joint activities and academic extension projects. Novel ideas were interwoven within the intercultural and inter-ethnic community relations and added to that construct. In this sense, all this work is just a starting point from which different projects may be developed with the people and communities involved up to now. Moreover, other conceptual offshoots may emerge, including interlocutors not addressed in the present study.

Considering potential fields of inquiry based on ideas advanced here, I consider three dimensions as specifically relevant for future research: first, the notion of dialogical multiplication. It refers to the perspective that at the core of the psychological space is the concern with universal theories and systems. There is a basic conflict at the core, though: psychology is formed as a modern science from historical-cultural tensions underlying the subjectivation of man. The whole process shares a basic *ethos* founded in European cultural traditions. The modern psychological field, then, sits over the bedrock of a sedimented Greco-Roman and Judeo-Christian heritage, recursively reproduced and updated in contemporary times. Psychology's disciplinary issues stem from that. They evolve, adding contributions still based on that unchallenged and mostly unquestioned foundation. That is not all, though.

Psychology also emerges through the cultural cracks resulting from the encounter between European colonizers and the diversity of things and peoples around the world. No wonder that anthropological issues are so deeply ingrained in psychology.

Even though psychology hasn't always kept either an effective or reflective proximity with cultural diversity, it could never ignore the importance of anthropology's concerns. This is particularly true about the frequent references to cultural diversity in constituting legitimizing claims on its theories and practice, regardless of the adopted theoretical approach. Each cultural tradition active in this disciplinary dynamic has its own history, its own worldview and issues guided by specific principles and values. One of meta-theoretical tasks that lay before indigenous psychologies, then, would be to provide the conceptual tools to identify and acknowledge the multiple voices that constitute the psychologist's space. This is needed beyond liberal, romantic or disciplinary concerns that characterize modern man's subjectivation.

Indigenous psychologies, as conceived here, broaden the "territory of ignorance". Figueiredo (1992/2007, p. 146) suggested this concept to describe the set of ideas and practices in the type of society that gave birth to psychology. It seems appropriate to include other cultures as constitutive parts of the indigenous psychologies, in this perspective. The notion of dialogical multiplication could render itself as an important tool to construct psychological genealogies that can include a wider variety of existential experiences, both disorderly and disquieting. They must, however, assimilate their different ordering systems to protect their meaning and viability. My goal is to contribute in the constitution and maintenance of an *ethos* capable of hosting diversity in a contemporary world so deeply stained by polarization, oppression, silencing of others and smothering of alterity. Dialogical multiplication, from a semiotic-cultural constructivist perspective in psychology, may be a tool in that direction.

As a second dimension for future research, I suggest that the notion of dialogical multiplication establishes guidelines for the psychologist into culturally rooted subjectivation processes. That happens because dialogical multiplication involves the construction of a new *ethos*, one characterized by the ethical drive to embrace all that exceeds the universalizing project of modern science's epistemological structure and ontological foundations. In its affective-cognitive dimensions, the *self* is constituted by recognizing the active person's historicity. That dimension is defined by their participation in the complex set of actions both symbolically ritualized and created through the images available in the cultural field's myths. Their experiences within the cultural field make up their perceptive and imaginative framework from which different paths may follow. On the one hand, we may have the "monoculture" type path determined by the modern project of disciplining bodies and minds to conform to the ideals of a purified subject. This is the subject that can represent the world in a clear and distinct manner, in absolute coherence between the social and the knowledge order with no inconsistencies nor contradictions. On the other hand, cultures, in their diversity, have developed different forms of cultivating the person. Some of them may be closer to the "agroforest" type path in which different options, each with their unique trajectories and mutually nurturing, may coexist, even if not always harmoniously. We assume that "the ethical individual may build their home with relative independence" (Figueiredo 1996/2013, p. 74). The challenge, now, is how this individual may become responsible for the preservation of the other. This involves qualitative and semiotic-cultural aspects of this individual's "home", considering their specific affective-cognitive conditions. In this respect, it seems important to continue the Indigenous Network's activities, further developing the inquiry lines concerning responsible psychological intervention in the field of intercultural and interethnic relations. This project looks even more promising by incorporating new indigenous approaches to the cultivation of the person (not only Amerindian).

In a third opportunity for future research, the notion of the cultivation of the *self* suggests levels of cultural experience that can only take place in the timeline of personal interaction. In other words, in community life. Along this book, I tried to explain why the cultivation of the *self* takes place during an experience that cannot be properly represented in any discourse about it. We need to understand the semiotic-cultural processes imbricated in ritual participation, beyond discourse. That is, the locus of corporeity in the construction of the senses, senses that guide the body's transformations while being with the other. It is important to understand the role of the body in repairing and controlling equivocal meanings about the other and their world; in the transduction of the senses expressed by the other as a meaningful dimension for psychological reflection and practice; the co-participation of other bodies, both subjective and objective, that constitute the ecological environment where meaning construction takes place; among so many other possible issues that emerge from the way people produce and reproduce meaning in their experiences with the world and the others. Dialogical multiplication can contribute to "de-delude psychology" (Figueiredo 1996/2013, p. 53). In the present context, this means acknowledging the split between the experiences of cultivated persons from different cultural fields, embrace these differences and deconstruct certain meanings. Deconstruction concerns the meanings that emerge from a cultural locus. It is the result of embracing them and giving them the means to mobilize alterity perspectives.

To move on together and side by side is the invitation I leave as I close this book's narrative. I hope the indigenous psychologists devotes their serene and confident efforts to continually search for ways to foster the emergence of meanings expressed in experience. I hope he keeps seeking, from growing experience, the cultural conditions to make this possible. At the same time, I invite the indigenous psychologist to contribute in the cultivation of affective-cognitive resources that lead to a home to diversity within themselves and their interlocutors.

Acknowledgement This work is supported by FAPESP (grant number 18/13145-0).

References

Baldwin, J. M. (1906). Thought and things: A study of the development and meaning of thought, or genetic logic. In *Functional logic, or genetic theory of knowledge* (Vol. 1). London: Swan Sonnenschein & Co.
Boesch, E. E. (1991). *Symbolic action theory and cultural psychology*. Germany: Berlin.
Figueiredo, L. C. M. (2007a). *A invenção do psicológico: quatro séculos de subjetivação 1500–1900* (p. 184). São Paulo, Escuta: (Trabalho original publicado em 1992).
Figueiredo, L. C. M. (2013). *Revisitando as psicologias: da epistemologia à ética das práticas e discursos psicológicos* (p. 183). Petrópolis: Vozes. (Trabalho original publicado em 1996).
Gadamer, H.-G. (2010a). Mito e Razão. In H.-G. Gadamer (Ed.), *Hermenêutica da Obra de Arte*. São Paulo: Martins Fontes. (Texto original publicado em 1954).
Gadamer, H.-G. (2010b). Mito e Logos. In H.-G. Gadamer (Ed.), *Hermenêutica da Obra de Arte* (pp. 65–68). São Paulo: Martins Fontes. (Texto original publicado em 1981).
Lévi-Strauss, C., & Eribon, D. (1990). *De perto e de longe: Reflexões do mais importante antropólogo do nosso tempo*. Rio de Janeiro: Nova Fronteira. (Texto original publicado em 1988).
Simão. (2015). The contemporary perspective of semiotic cultural constructivism: For an hermeneutical reflexivity in psychology. In Marsico, Ruggieri and Salvatore (Orgs.) (Ed.), *Reflexivity and psychology* (pp. 65–85). Charlotte: Information Age Publishing.
Viveiros de Castro, E. B. (2004). Perspectival anthropology and the method of controlled equivocation. *Tipití: Journal of the Society for the Anthropology of Lowland South America, 2*(1), 1–22.

Commentary 1
Developing Psychology From the Diversity of Living Conditions

Mogens Jensen

A basic premise for cultural psychology is to see the development of human and of culture as two sides of the same or to put it differently as so intermingled that one cannot be understood without incorporating the other. In these processes humans are active in creating meaning in their experiences and these processes are facilitated, influenced and constraint by the culture in which the specific person grew up and the one in which s/he is living presently – that is her/his personal history (Valsiner et al. 2016).

These premises raises some apparent problems or challenges. A science of psychology will always seek to reach some kind of general knowledge on it's subject but when each specific human is constrained by her/his personal history and her/his culture how can we then establish a science that encompass the great variety that inevitably result from these processes? We aim for a science that can handle the specific and unique individual and simultaneously establish a general knowledge. These questions become crucial when you turn to indigenous psychology but in return exactly indigenous psychology can contribute with important evidence that clarify these questions. Since my field is social and social pedagogical work in Denmark I will analyse experiences and empirical data from this field but argue that the same considerations can be applied on experiences and empirical data from research in indigenous psychologies. Because I grew up in Denmark and is educated here my approach to psychology as a science is also influenced by this background and could or should be revised by a juxtapositioning with indigenous psychologies. I return to this question at the end of the chapter.

In this chapter I will elaborate on how psychology can support social and social pedagogical work and how it should be elaborated with this aim and on the other hand how the context/field of social and social pedagogical work with it's diversity of conditions for human development can contribute to the development of psychology as a science. When you engage in social work as a psychologist in Denmark with a middleclass background and an education from a university you meet people with a different background at work. To apply psychology this needs to encompass and handle this challenge. I try to establish a framework within which these challenges can be met and understood in both an ethical and suitable way. At the end I will consider how this in parallel with indigenous psychology can contribute to the development of psychology as a science.

Inspiration From Biology

The late biologist Jacob von Uexküll (2010) developed an understanding of how living creatures experience their environment. Through evolution each species' abilities and sensory system have developed especially to perceive the aspects of environment that is relevant for this species. A fly needs different information than I do on the room I am sitting in. I do not have to worry about spiders since these are not dangerous for me living in Denmark. We do not have spiders poisonous for humans. I cannot fly behind the bookshelves or sit on the ceiling so the room offers different possibilities for the fly than for me. We have developed through evolution with different sensory systems that fit different needs and different ecological niches. As a result we practically live in very different contexts – we perceive things other species do not perceive and vice versa. Different species live in different contexts even though they inhabit the very same environment.

There is however a very important difference between most animals and humans. When humans are born they are unfinished. So are some animals but they then finish their development in the way their genetic inheritance determine within narrow variations. Their genetic inheritance ensure they achieve the competences they need in life as long as the environment supply with needs for surviving. Humans on the contrary can finish their development in very varied ways and this takes place in relation to the specific environment in which they develop. The competences they develop depend on the environment in which they grow up and is therefore suitable for exactly this environment.

A new born human can be described by two characteristics:

- The infant is helpless and therefore in need of care
- The infant needs to learn many of the competences necessary in life

The need for care is biologically prepared for by attention towards faces and human interaction – first as reflexes and later as deliberate effort (Harwood et al. 2008). Early on infants rely on other human beings by adjusting their own behaviour in attempts to establish or maintain contact and by this secure the care they need. We are oriented towards social interaction. As a cultural being we learn from others the needed competences as these have been developed in the culture in which we grow up. Infants have a tendency to imitate the behaviour of others (Tomasello 1999) and by this they learn the needed skills. As an infant imitation is done more as a playful activity but imitation in a way presupposes that there is an intention in exercising the behaviour. They do not imitate reflex actions but those experienced as purposeful. Somehow the infant is oriented towards others as intentional beings, and from the beginning participate in interaction with others as it is conceptualised in theories of dialogicality (Marková 2016). Instead of a genetic determined repertoire of skills humans are supplied with the necessary skills in and by the culture in which they grow up.

From developmental psychology, we have reports on children showing different perceptual competences depending on the everyday life in the environment where they grow up so even at a very basic perceptual level differences develop (Cole 1996).

This continues through life so if you are biologist specialised in plants you do not just perceive "green plants on the field" but immediately recognise it as turnips. Your perceptual system has been adjusted (Gibson 1983) to distinguish between plants and does so without special effort.

This human flexibility is possible because of the great developmental plasticity of mainly the brain but also the rest of the body. The brain is at birth prepared for this developmental process with superfluous cells and connections to a degree where decay has started even before birth (Johnson 1997).

When the function of the brain is understood in line with the premises of cultural psychology as described above it is conceptualised as a dynamic system where several perceptions, interpretations or ideas are processed in parallel and finally one becomes dominant and reach awareness (Juarrero 2002). This resembles processes in nature where a lot of possible projects are initiated and by selection only a few but sufficient survive because they show their capacity in the specific environment at that time. Seen in a developmental perspective this organisation imply that the brain like the rest of the body becomes adjusted in relation to it's use. If life in a specific environment demands specific skills then the brain part of these skills is exercised and expanded while other possibilities fade away. This process is especially dominant during childhood (Johnson 1997). In line with the description from von Uexküll mentioned above this selection is based on the perceived context of the specific person.

Seen as part of evolution these characteristics of human development become a great advantage and has enabled humans to have a dominating position all over the planet. Where animals to a much greater degree need to change their genes in order to adjust to different environment we can do this in one or a few generations by bringing up children in this new environment so they learn what they need to fit in. The context a species experiences and can handle is mostly genetically determined whereas humans develop a similar personal context through the process of growing up in a specific environment. This is illustrated in Fig. 1.

A human lives in an environment but only part of this is actually perceived and this selection results in what I conceptualise as a **personal context**. This is established and developed through life and in this process, the environment of course influences the personal context – arrow b. Conditions, possibilities and challenges in the environment enhance or hinder the construction of different aspects of the personal context. The process is mutual so the person also influences the environment – arrow a. There is however, an additional process because even though you live in and experience through a personal context this personal context does not

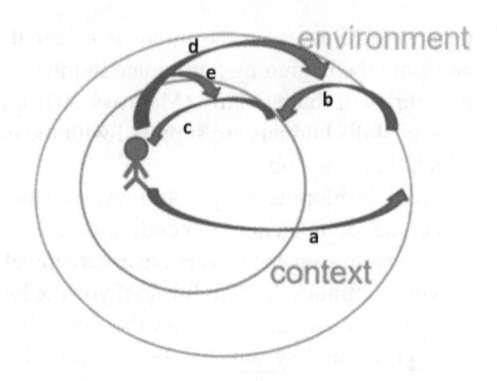

Fig. 1 Analytical diagram of dynamics in development of self

necessarily influence your personal development in a certain definite way – arrow c. In infancy you are not aware of these processes and you are formed more directly but even infants quickly learn to distinguish between persons and as example they learn more openly from persons who take care of them as parents do than from people whom they do not know. Later on we become better at reflections and gradually we can decide to a greater degree how our personal context is allowed to influence us – arrow e. Even though people around me tell me I cannot graduate at the university I can decide that I will not let this influence my self understanding and struggle to manage anyway. Finally it should be added that we can decide to enrich and expand our personal context by studying specific phenomenon like taking an education – arrow d.

As mentioned infants are more open to just imitate what they meet but through the interaction with others they gradually meet other's perspectives and learn to negotiate the interaction. This competence of interaction develops into an ability to reflect and consider different perspectives on a topic and in relation to Fig. 1 this result in a certain amount of agency concerning one's own development as shown by arrow d and e. These considerations will of course rest on one's experiences until now and even though we develop our reflection and can revise our understanding of earlier experiences it will still be founded and developed on what we learned in infancy although in a diluted and elaborated version. Our personal context is constructed and developed through our personal history and an understanding of why it has become like this demands a biographical study of the specific person.

As mentioned a core presupposition in cultural psychology is the understanding of humans as actively relating to their experiences where they create a interpretation and meaning of their experiences. When a person experience something, s/he will create meaning **in relation to** their personal context and act in relation to the values and attitudes this includes. This also imply that some experiences are judged to be unimportant and no resources are spent on relating to these.

Since all stimuli are interpreted on the background of the individual's personal history including consequences of this such as specialised attention towards specific phenomenon you cannot generalise on consequences of a specific stimuli. Stimuli will always be interpreted in relation to one's own personal context. This can of course include the knowledge that others might experience things differently but this is again an aspect of one's own personal context then.

> Case 1: I once taught at a course for pedagogues on developmental psychology. During the break two pedagogues came to me with a question: they worked with mentally disabled persons and among these a 42 years old man who lived in his own small apartment where they came by every day a couple of hours to help him organise the day. Their problem was the following: as part of his daily duties, he should take the garbage from the kitchen and bring it down to a container outside the house. When he came back they praised him for this and sometimes he got angry at this so what should they do? I asked if they could just stop praising him but they answered that their guidelines stated they should praise him whenever he did what he should to reinforce his good behaviour.

This case shows how any stimuli is interpreted in relation to a personal background. The behaviouristic instruction they had got did not work since it did not take into consideration that the man could interpret the reinforcement differently. If you are praised for doing something very simple it will often be understood as a comment that you are not that clever. When I mention this example while teaching I often add that if I brought down the garbage at home and my wife praised me explicitly at return, then I would interpret it very differently. In a normal dialogue part of the background that is important for a correct interpretation of what is said is unspoken. It is under-determined (Przyborski and Slunecko 2009) and mediated through the situation, personal knowledge of each other or simply just presumed.

This shows a very important point if you are interested in influencing people's development as we are in social work: if you affect people by the same stimuli then you cannot predict the influence on their personal development without a thorough knowledge on the specific person and her/his background. The result depends on the way they interpret the stimuli and besides they can for different reasons decide not to let you influence them (Jensen 2018a, b; Fitzpatrick 2011). You have to know a minimum of their personal context to intervene effectively.

If several people grow up in the same (sub-) culture you can describe 'rules of thumb' because their personal contexts will be similar to a greater degree but there will still be some variety even within the same (sub-) culture which is not an abnormality but common variability (Valsiner 2014).

This way of understanding the relation between person and environment has consequences both for communication between two persons from different (sub-) cultures (Guimarães and Jensen 2018) and for my field: social and social pedagogical work where you want to influence a person's development. In both cases you have to consider a 'first person perspective' as it is called in critical psychology (Scraube 2013), where you take the specific person and her/his background into account in an attempt to understand their way of experiencing and acting.

> Case 2: A Norwegian psychologist Per Lorentzen (Lorentzen 1996) got a daughter who because of genetic disorders was born deaf and blind. When she was still an infant he noticed that in different activities she touched the back of her neck when the activity finished. Reflecting on this he realised that if you are both deaf and blind then the primary sense is the tactile sense. If you then consider the daily routines of infants a recurring event is meals. Whenever a meal is finished you untie the napkin around the neck of the infant and this his daughter experienced as a tactile impression at the back of her neck. The clever girl

had transferred this to other activities as a sign for 'finished'. He could then confirm he perceived her sign by touching her neck and then give the socially accepted sign for 'finished' in tactile sign-language and by this develop her communication competence, just like we do in normal language development (without noticing).

When people grow up on conditions and constraints very different from our own they experience their world differently. Per Lorentzen's daughter experienced mainly by tactile sense so her personal context was very different from Per Lorentzen's. In order to establish communication you have to interact in order to gather information and examples to interpret and in this interaction you have to imagine how your partner experience. We will never be able to experience in totality how it is to be born deaf and blind but humans actually have the potential to come close if we make an effort. An important point is here the interaction where we try to understand the other's actions by imagining the way they experience the interaction through consideration of their actions. Sometimes it will take a lot of interaction and imagination before we catch their intentions. We have to experience several different episodes. Figure 1 illustrates aspects of this dynamic by the distinction between environment and personal context. As I understand Guimarães' concept of "dialogical multiplication" (Guimarães 2013; 2016) this concerns the difficulty of establishing a dialogue between people from different cultures.

Social Representations

The theory of social representation (Marková 2003a, b; Moscovisci 2001) offers an attempt to conceptually bridge the specific personal development of an individual and her/his personal context with the influence and development of the culture in which the individual grow up. Social representations can be defined like this:

"A social representation is the ensemble of thoughts and feelings being expressed in verbal and overt behaviour of actors which constitutes an object for a social group" (Wagner et al. 1999)

A crucial premise here is the dynamic aspect of the representation (Marková 2003b). A social representation is not a fixed entity but rather a phenomenon people use to handle part of their experiences in collaboration. When a group of people face a common phenomenon they need to signify it in order to facilitate communication and by this share experiences and learn in collaboration. In the development of a social representation they delimit and characterise the phenomenon. When they use the label they choose, they start objectifying the phenomenon and confirm an experience of it as part of reality. The dynamic aspect stresses that the social representation changes along the way if members of the group get different experiences and/or if their needs change which will result in gradual changes in the representation.

When we develop psychological concepts and theories the same dynamic aspects have to be considered. They are created in a culture and at a time for some purpose and we have to take this into account when we read and apply them (see also Guimarães 2017; 2018).

When a child is born in a certain environment many social representations will already be in use among the people who inhabit this environment and the child will appropriate these in the way it understands them. This can be slightly different from the common understanding in the culture but sufficiently close for the social representation to function in communication with fellow human beings. This "loose linkage" in the meaning of a social representation is sufficient because everyday communication encompass many possibilities for checking and correcting misunderstandings. Once a child appropriates a social representation the phenomenon becomes part of the personal context of the child and it influences the way the child onwards in life will perceive, experience and create meaning of future experiences. Gradually as the child grows older it will be able to reflect on experiences and especially when language becomes elaborated these reflections can enable the child to both form it's own representations or own versions of common representations and to decide how these social representations should influence personal development, attitudes and standpoints. These are aspects of individual agency illustrated in Fig. 1.

I would like to stress that reflection does not take place only after language is appropriated nor only mediated by language. Schön (1983) describe how professional practitioners reflect in action to solve problems. They do not have a plan at the beginning but along the way they reflect on observations, try out different possibilities and observe the consequences of these and by these reflections along with the actions they solve the problem. It seems to me that even in Schön's examples practitioners sometimes reflect through actions. In general a trial-and-error approach to solving problems is seen as primitive but a qualified way of trying out solutions and observing the consequences can be a very advanced strategy. Since psychology as a science is mediated so overwhelmingly by verbal language we have a tendency to underestimate non-verbal aspects of human life. In studies of practitioners some even call for a different understanding of knowledge – or knowing as they prefer – than the one traditionally accepted in psychology where practical problem solving is the starting point rather than reflection and logical thinking (Molander 2015).

When we do not understand other people's behaviour we are challenged to create an understanding of their personal context. In social and social pedagogical work in Denmark psychologists are often employed exactly for delivering new understandings of persons in care or of episodes and situations where social workers and social pedagogues cannot manage to establish a proper understanding and develop an intervention by themselves. To supply with this we have to consider at least three points:

1. How the person experience the problem or the episode in question. In order to do this we have to know of their personal context since this is the background or frame within which they create their understanding.
2. What the aim of their actions are? What are they trying to achieve or avoid by acting as they do? So we have to interpret their wishes and attitudes as part of their personal context.

3. Finally we have to investigate their repertoire of possible actions from which they chose the actualised one. If they do not have any other option for acting to achieve their goal we might need to teach them other ways of coping.

All of this stresses the need for a "first person perspective" as mentioned above.

Case 3: I was asked as a psychologist to observe a 16 year old girl born deaf and only with very limited sight – so called tunnel vision where she only had sight in a small field. Besides she was mentally disabled. She managed a little sign-language when you caught her limited sight-field. The pedagogues complained that she sometimes without any reason or warning could attack them and turn them over at the floor.

I arrived at the place where the girl lived a little before lunchtime. The girl was sitting in a sofa playing with some toys and at the table her primary pedagogue and a substitute pedagogue were drinking coffee. A little later the primary pedagogue went to the office to do some accounts on shopping the day before. After a while the girl got up and came to the table presumably searching. Neither I nor the substitute managed sign-language so she clearly found us useless and got more agitated. Then the primary pedagogue returned and she sought him. He got a little confused and told her to calm down. As she kept on being agitated he said it was lunchtime and went to the kitchen where he gave her a pile of plates. I assume he tried to distract her. She looked confused, went to the table and placed them there and then returned to the primary pedagogue. He gave her a platter of food which she then placed at the table. She went back to the kitchen, grab hold of the primary pedagogue and turned him to the floor. Both the substitute and the primary pedagogue got hold of her and held her until she calmed down. "There you see – no reason whatsoever" the primary pedagogue exclaimed.

This short account of the episode is of course framed to illustrate my conclusion and when we experience in real life they are mostly more confusing. It is quite common for severely disabled people to have a higher level of insecurity and many of them are in some way aware of their dependence on other people. The girl in case 3 knows quite well that she cannot manage her world by herself so she needs somebody whom she knows and trusts to be able to manage. Because of her limited sight she apparently did not see the primary pedagogue leaving the room so suddenly she was left with two other persons she did not know and who even did not manage sign-language. So she got anxious. When the primary pedagogue returned she needed comforting but he did not understand this. In his view there was nothing to be worried about. When she after several attempts did not receive any comforting she knew by experience that if you throw another person to the floor then they will come and hold you tightly – "give you a hug". This is clearly described in attachment theory as a dynamic in the interaction between a child and a parent. Because of the different personal context of the girl with her different experiences it's appearance becomes different but the process, the dynamic of personal interaction is the same. If we want to support her and her development we have to find out how she experiences the situation (1), we have to interpret what she is trying to achieve (2), and finally we must consider to teach her another way of achieving this (3).

In social and social pedagogical work with people from a very different background and who develop on very different conditions and constraints you have the opportunity to clarify what are specific local constraints and what are general psychological patterns. What is general are the processes through which we develop, learn and act. If we turn to general conditions then we have to sort out what the essence of the episode is. In case 3 the general conditions are dependency on other people, trust as depending on knowledge of each other established through a common history of interactions, the challenge of communicating with other persons who's personal context is very different from yours (they saw her actions as having no reason and no sign to warn you in advance) etc. (For an analysis of the challenge of communication see Guimarães and Jensen 2018)

I mentioned the dynamic aspect of social representations above where they emerge from the everyday life of people in relation to the specific conditions and constraints they meet. To me it is crucial to maintain the dynamic characteristic of the concept of social representation rather than focus on structural characteristics.

Summing up the Analysis

a. When we study human psychology the environment of everyday life should be considered as this influence the specific person but equally we should consider the specific personal history as this appears in varieties of ways of acting and understanding.

Human grow up in an environment that includes certain conditions, constraints and challenges. From this and from experiences during upbringing the individual form a personal context. All experiences are then interpreted on the background of the personal context. As we grow older our reflective competence develops and we can start to deliberately change the personal context our upbringing supplied. We cannot understand another person without considering this dynamic including her/his personal history and abilities.

b. In cultural psychology there is a widespread focus on semiotics but we should be careful not to focus solely on verbal signs in language. Part of our practical life is quite as dominated by actions and observing result of actions. These can be conceptualised with semiotic theory too I assume, but this practical side has yet to be developed even more.

In general the great variability of humans is apparent and I have tried to establish a frame where human development is closely connected to everyday life. It will be important for psychology to study aspects of development in close connection to these everyday activities. The process of sign-use is important for humans but even sign-use should be studied in connection with everyday life. Processes of sign-use might be general but why should "internal structures of signs" or "internal structures in social representations" be universal? Rather they will mirror different life-conditions and show quite as big a variation as these.

c. Social representations are dynamic and develop in relation to the needs and the environment of the people who apply them. They will vary in relation to different (sub-) cultures.

Even though you appropriate and develop social representations in a specific culture you still develop your own version of them that is more or less similar to those of others. In everyday life this loose linkage is not a problem since interaction include several opportunities for adjusting to a common understanding. Similarities in social representations will appear because of commonalities in living conditions and in the processes of establishing them but since this originate in the everyday life attention for variations should be prioritised. Exactly these variations should be studied since they are informative concerning the dynamic processes. Parallel to case-studies (Flyvbjerg 2001; Yin 1994) examples from very different cultures can be beneficial for informing on both the general processes and the connection to the specific environment. To be more precise examples on (sub-) cultures emerged from humans living on different conditions in everyday life should be in focus.

Differences between (sub-) cultures result in different constitutions of human beings but process of creating social representations and of creating a personal context are common and these processes can be studied as general for all humans. This is where a scientific approach is possible. It should take into account both different cultures and the variations these create and simultaneously incorporate both the influence of culture on human development, the agency of the individual person and the variation we experience in psychology.

In order to clarify aspects of psychology I have elaborated on experiences from my research in social and social pedagogical work where I meet people who have grown up and live on very different conditions from what I do. Exactly the same beneficial process can take place if we study people in other (sub-) cultures to see how they develop and function. This could be in indigenous psychologies.

What Is General in Psychology As a Science?

In this chapter I have tried to conceptualise some general aspects in psychology that enable us to develop a common science of psychology that incorporate the interaction between culture and individual development and the plasticity that result in such a variability among human beings and among cultures.

I have argued that humans across cultures have some common conditions and constraints in life that creates possibilities for understanding each other even though we grow up in very different cultures. This understanding will never be complete but through interaction we establish common experiences and when we create meaning out of these we gain a least a partly insight in the other's personal context. This is what happens in case 2 when Per Lorentzen is able to interpret the home-made sign of his daughter signalling 'finished'.

Some of the common conditions and constraints I have mentioned are:

- A need of care to survive infancy;
- A need to grow up in a culture to ensure care and learning of needed skills;
- A need for relating to other humans;
- Influence from the culture where we grow up on the construction of our personal context.

I have also argued for some common processes in handling these challenges that human beings share. With ideas from biology and from theories of the cultural aspect of human development as a species, I have analysed aspects of these processes:

- Creation of personal context;
- Social representations;
- Communication.

In some cases these processes appear in a strange way as when the girl in case 3 appeal for a hug to calm herself down by throwing the social pedagogue to the floor. This is an extreme example of the challenge of understanding other humans who have a very different personal context. To establish a mutual understanding we should be able to see the "general in the specific" (Davydov 1990) – we should consider how the personal context is when you have very different conditions in everyday life and while growing up, and from these considerations interpret the meaning of the interaction. I mentioned three steps in this as considering her perception and understanding of the situation, her aim when acting as she does and finally her repertoire of action possibilities. In many cases the creation of such an interpretation and insight demands a process where you try out preliminary understandings to see if they function. You reflect by acting in relation to the world to learn more and correct along the way.

A premise for this approach is that the purpose of a science of psychology is to find general patterns across different cultures with different life conditions. This has to be done in a way where we incorporate the variability of humans, the interconnection of culture and personal development and the possibility as an individual to remain some level of agency in one's own life.

Inspiration From the Sciences of Literature and History

In the analysis above, I have tried to consider psychology in a way where we become able to approach each human being as unique even though we in science search for general aspects and processes. If we briefly look at theories on literature they are used to handle each text as unique.

In literature you have different genres such as poems, advertisements, novels, research articles etc. When you assess such texts you have to do this in relation to the contexts that they are aimed for. It makes no sense to evaluate them on the same general premises. You can use a text aimed for one context in another and sometimes this can be very inspiring and productive as when you use lines from a poem to pin down the point in a research article but there are different traditions within the different genres and not applying to them can create communication problems. This could be seen as metaphor for people growing up in different cultures. Here you likewise have to assess their behaviour and psychological development in relation to their everyday environment. Understanding a single unique person demands that you assess this individual's personal context.

If you consider theory on the process of reading a text, some fruitful suggestions appear. An author writes a text in relation to her/his personal context so one way of studying the text is to assess this personal context and seek for connections and meanings in the text originating in this. Ricoeur (1991) among others stress that once the text is published it also becomes fixated and from now on it is beyond the control of the author – it becomes autonomous. Readers can interpret the text on different conditions – within their own personal context – and multiple meanings of the text are now possible. Ricoeur even stress that you cannot decide "the right" meaning of a text because the meaning emerge in the interplay between the text and the reader. A text written years ago in one context can achieve a new meaning when read in another time and context. Likewise an action by a person becomes autonomous once it is carried out. Just like an author the agent might have had one meaning or intention by the act but others perceiving the act can interpret it differently. A Danish saying states "Done deed cannot be changed". It has become autonomous. This raises difficult philosophical questions concerning responsibility but this is beyond the aim of this chapter. Nevertheless, you can as a person experience that your acts become interpreted within a different frame or context and in this connection achieve a meaning that you never had in mind when you acted. Especially when you interact with people from a background very different from yours this risk is growing since they interpret your acts from their personal context. To establish mutual understanding demands some effort from both sides.

The same considerations have taken place in the science of history. Earlier on research of history searched for 'the truth' of what happened and how this came about. For the last decades arguments in line with literature science has stated that the way we understand an episode in history can never be settled (Simonsen 2003). We continue to understand the episode in relation to our present context and when this changes we might reach a new understanding of the episode. The task for science can be seen as developing concepts and theory "just in time" (Juul Jensen 1999) – that is to develop concepts and theory that fit both the phenomenon and the present time. In fifty years new concepts and theories might be needed and more appropriate.

In the science of literature they have made a huge effort on analysing, describing and understanding the processes through which we read texts. When you deal with unique phenomenon we have to focus in science on the processes through which we create an understanding of the phenomenon. This goes for texts as well as for humans in psychology. We can categorise in genre – or cultures, behaviours etc. in psychology – but we should keep in mind that this only result in "rules of thump" and should be open to variations that challenge our categories. Here the study of 'alterity' (Kadianaki and Gillespie 2015) or 'otherness' (Simão 2003, Guimarães and Simão 2007) is especially relevant since this open the opportunity to study both what is general in the specific and simultaneously the processes of how this general aspect is influenced and formed in local conditions.

There is however a crucial difference between texts and humans. Humans keep developing and changing through life. Where an action can be described as fixated a human keeps changing and in principle nothing is fixated.

Dialogue With Indigenous Psychologies

I am not working with indigenous psychology but within the field of social and social pedagogical work. I have tried to illustrate how meeting people with different backgrounds helps develop a psychology where we focus both on general aspects and still allow for the special appearance of local conditions and constraints that result in unique individuals. A dialogue between different psychologies seems to me to be a potentially productive way forward because of these special opportunities. This dialogue has to be between equal partners since none of us has 'an eternal truth' (Molander 2015) of psychology as a science – it does not exist – (see also Guimarães 2018) and openness towards the other allows for discovery of aspects of one's own understanding that are unseen because they have become self-evident parts of our personal context.

Critical Reflections Looking Back at the Chapter

When I look back at this chapter it appears to me that it includes some presumptions that are part of my personal context as researcher in Denmark and that might not be accepted in other environments. I have build a great part of my argument on evolution theory and this ontology is questioned by some people. Likewise I have just as it is often done in occidental psychology omitted spiritual aspects of human life. I have tried to incorporate an understanding where culture and the individual person are intermingled to a degree where it does not make sense to study them apart. Nevertheless, I also tried to preserve individual agency and this will be challenged and nuanced in some cultures I guess.

Also in these aspects I look forward to the continued dialogue with indigenous psychologies and I am sure it will contribute to the elaboration of a "Danish" psychology too.

References

Bruner, J. (1990). *Acts of meaning* Cambridge: Harvard University Press
Cole, M. (1996). *Cultural psychology. A once and future discipline.* Cambridge: Belknap Press of Harvard University Press.
Davydov, V. V. (1990) Types of generalization in instruction: Logical and psychological problems in the structuring of school curricula Vol.2. In *Soviet studies in mathematics education*, Reston: National Council of Teachers of Mathematics.
Fitzpatrick, C. (2011). What is the difference between 'Desistance' and 'Resilience'? Exploring the relationship between two key concepts. *Youth Justice, 11*(3), 221–234.
Flyvbjerg, B. (2001). *Making social science matter.* Cambridge: Cambridge University Press.
Gibson, J. (1983). *The senses considered as perceptual systems.* Westport: Greenwood Press.
Guimarães, D. S. (2013). Self and dialogical multiplication. *Interacções, 9*, 214–242

Guimarães, D. S. (2016). Psychology in the paths of Amerindian people. Final considerations. In D. S. Guimarães (Ed.), *Amerindian paths. Guiding dialogues with psychology*. Charlotte: Information age Publishing.

Guimarães, D. S. (2017). Amerindian psychology. Cultural basis for general knowledge construction. In B. Wagoner, I. Brescó de Luna & S.H. Awad (Eds.), *The psychology of imagination* (pp. 221–238).

Guimarães, D. S. (2018). Towards a cultural revision of psychological concepts. *Culture and Psychology 0*(0), 1–11.

Guimarães, D. S. & Jensen, M. (2018). Expanding dialogical analysis across (sub-) cultural background. *Culture and Psychology, 24* (4), 403–417.

Guimarães, D. S. & Simão, L. M. (2007) Intersubjectivity and otherness: A stage for self strivings ch.13. In L. M. Simão & J. Valsiner. *Otherness in question*. Charlotte: Information Age Publishing.

Harwood, R., Miller, S. A. & Vasta, R. (2008). *Child psychology. Development in a changing society* (5th ed.). Wiley.

Jensen, M. (2018a). Fellowship as social-pedagogical treatment. *Scottish Journal of Residential Child Care, 17*(3), 1–21.

Jensen, M. (2018b) Desired ambiguities and dealing with ambivalences in the context of social work Chapter 12. In E. Abbey & I. Alberts (Eds.), *Cultural psychology of transgenerational family relations: Investigating ambivalences*. Information Age Press.

Johnson, M. H. (1997). *Developmental cognitive neuroscience*. Malden: Blackwells Publishers Ltd.

Juarrero, A. (2002). *Dynamics in Action*. Cambridge: The MIT Press.

Juul Jensen, U. (1999). Categories in activity theory: Marx' philosophy just-in-time. In S. Chaiklin, M. Hedegaard & U. Juul Jensen (Eds.), *Activity theory and Social Practice*. Aarhus: Aarhus University Press.

Kadianaki, I. & Gillespie, A. (2015) Alterity and the transformation of social representations: A sociocultural account. *Integrative Psychology and Behavioral Science, 49*(1), 73–88

Lorenzen, P. (1996). *Example given at a course on development of communication when congenital deafblind at Nordic Centre of Deafblind*. Dronninglund.

Lorentzen, P. (2009). *Kommunikasjon med uvanlige barn [Communication with unusual children]* Oslo: Universitetsforlaget

Marková, I. (2003a). *Dialogicality and social representations*. Cambridge: Cambridge University Press.

Marková, I. (2003b). Representations of the social: Bridging theoretical traditions. *Journal of Community Applied Social Psychology, 13,* 413–416.

Marková, I. (2016). *The dialogical mind*. Cambridge: Cambridge University Press.

Molander, B. (2015). *The practice of knowing and knowing in practices*. Frankfurt am Main: Peter Lang Edition.

Moscovici, S. (2001). *Social representations*. New York: New York University Press.

Przyborski, A. & Slunecko, T. (2009). Against reification! Praxeological methodology and it's benefits Chapter 7. In J. Valsiner, P. C. M. Molenaar, M. C. D. P. Lyra & N. Chaudhary (Eds.), *Dynamic process methodology in the social and developmental sciences*. Dordrecht: Springer.

Ricoeur, P. (1991). *From text to action*. London: Northwestern University Press.

Schraube, E. (2013). First-person perspective and sociomaterial decentering: Studying technology from the standpoint of the subject. *Subjectivity, 6.1,* 12–32.

Schön, D. (1983). *The reflective practitioner*. London: Temple Smith.

Simão, L. (2003). Beside rupture-disquiet: Beyond the other-alterity. *Culture & Psychology, 9*(4), 449–459.

Simonsen, D. G. (2003). *Tidens tegn [Time's sign]*. Copenhagen: Museum Tusculanums Forlag.

Tomasello, M. (1999). *The cultural origins of human cognition*. Cambridge: Harvard University Press.

Valsiner, J. (2014). *An invitation to cultural psychology*. London: Sage.

Valsiner, J., Marsico, G., Chaudhary, N., Sato, T. & Dazzani, V. (2016). *Psychology as the science of human being. The Yohohama Manifesto* Springer International Publishing.

Von Uexküll, J. (2010). *A foray into the worlds of animals and humans.* Minneapolis: University of Minnesota Press.

Wagner, W., Duveen, G., Farr, R., Jovchelovitch, S., Lorenzi-Cioldi, F., Marková, I. & Rose, D. (1999). Theory and method of social representations. *Asian Journal of Social Psychology, 2,* 95–125.

Yin, R. (1994). *Case study research* (2nd ed.). London: Sage Publications.

Commentary 2
Pōwhiri: Rituals of Encounter, Recognition and Engagement: A Commentary on 'Dialogical Multiplication: Principles for an Indigenous Psychology'

Shiloh Groot, Pita King, Linda Waimarie Nikora, Kara Areta Beckford, and Darrin Hodgetts

We would like to begin by congratulating Professor Danilo Silva Guimarães for producing a seminal text on Dialogical Multiplicity. Professor Guimarães has produced a book that offers insight into the spaces in between our different communities and psychologies. In doing so, he shifts our attention to look beyond simplistic notions of 'culture shock' and into spaces of encounter and dialogue. This book sets out the overarching principles for indigenous psychologies, which are timely for those of us engaged in re-pluralizing the discipline of psychology (King and Hodgetts 2017).

Our task here is to offer a commentary in response to Professor Guimarães work and in doing so contribute to ongoing conversations between diverse cultural and indigenous knowledges regarding the nature and orientation of psychology as a contemporary social science (Groot et al. 2018). In this commentary we reflect on a ritual of encounter indigenous to Aotearoa New Zealand, the pōwhiri. It is through such rituals of encounter that Māori (indigenous peoples of Aotearoa New Zealand) establish ways of conversing, listening, witnessing and creating spaces for intergroup encounters that form the foundation of an ongoing dialectics of engagement. If we are to truly re-pluralize psychology to better reflect the diversity of humanity, then we must engage in deep dialogue regarding the nature and focus of our discipline and what it means to be human. As Professor Guimarães contends, central here is the notion of ethos and custom and how we might engage each other as indigenous peoples on our own terms and not just as the mere subject-objects of Eurocentric traditions in psychology.

People take shape through their interactions with others that are in turn moulded by the histories and traditions of the groups with whom they belong. In other words, what it means to be a person is shaped within socio-historical contexts (Hodgetts et al. 2010; 2020). As people engage in various cultural practices and adapt our traditions, we reproduce the very cultural systems that have shaped our lives dialectically. We emerge within groups; they are part of us, and we are very much a part of them. It is from them that we exist and derive a personal ethos. In this context, culture is not simply seen as an abstract set of concepts or variables to be manipulated in an effort to map causal relationships. Culture is an abstraction that is materially and psychologically vibrant and realised within the conduct of everyday life. As such, culture constitutes a field of human action, meaning-making, and self-production (Guimarães 2018; Nikora et al. 2007). They are neither static nor unchanging, but rather living entities that are continually being renewed and reshaped to meet the needs of our ever-evolving peoples.

Foundational to this discussion is how cultures not only produce people, but also foreground the psychologies they inhabit or enact. For Māori, being a person means existing through relational entanglements, which are navigated in accordance to our core cultural values (King et al. 2017). This involves embracing our shared humanity and responding to the cultural expectations and obligations that texture the places in which we reside as well as the metaphysical worlds that are at play in our lives. Everything and everyone is related and interdependent in our world. We have a primary duty of care for others, particularly those with whom we are related and/or reside (Nikora et al. 2017).

All Māori can lay claim to multiple descent lines through maternal and paternal lines that echo back to cosmological origins and ripple outwards across generations in particular places. Kinship networks provide spaces for selves to rest, renew and become energized towards collective action. When one part of the network is for some reason stressed and burdened, the network reconfigures as we attempt to meet our duties of care. Our state of interconnected being within which friendship and professional networks are also interwoven can be difficult for people operating from other cultural psychologies to unravel and fathom (King et al. 2017; Rua et al. 2017).

As with all indigenous peoples, Māori retain a unique and distinctive worldview. Indigenous psychologies in Aotearoa New Zealand recognise that Māori have complex and highly developed understandings of ourselves. This approach to psychology also posits that there is more than one legitimate approach for understanding the social world and the place of different people within it (Groot et al. 2012). Despite working in disciplinary environments often textured with issues of cultural violence and de-legitimation, Māori psychology has a strong presence not only in Aotearoa New Zealand but also internationally and continues to expand. Many Māori psychologists continue to fight for the centralising of cultural nuance and approaches in the development of locally-relevant theories, methods and practices (Nikora et al. 2006; Nikora et al. 2007; 2014; 2017; Hodgetts et al. 2010; Hodgetts et al. 2018; Groot et al. 2018).

In asserting an ethos for Māori psychology, it is important to note that our orientation does not exist, or develop, in isolation from other cultural traditions and psychologies today. Like other indigenous traditions, our psychology has been brought into conversation with the hegemonic traditions from North America and Europe. However, this is only one small element of the dialectical relationships through which our psychology is evolving. We are also in dialogue with other indigenous traditions from our Pacific and Asian neighbours as well as colleagues from further afield who are also articulating their own indigenous approaches (Li et al. 2017).

This chapter constitutes a conversation between the psychology reflected in the work of Professor Guimarães and our own.

In the following three sections we attend to how dialogical multiplicity can be understood and engaged in from a Māori perspective through a discussion of pōwhiri. It is important to note that pōwhiri is a cultural practice that is dynamic, responsive and has always been with us, as we have navigated our lives and futures. We provide exemplars of the Māori cosmological and psychological elements embedded within the encounter space of pōwhiri. We begin with the pōwhiri when they are at their most poignant and spiritual, enacted against a backdrop of mourning procedures laden with ancestral and tribal symbolism. This enables us to foreground the ethos and values foundational to this ritual. We then reflect on the ritual itself as commonly practiced within culturally distinct spaces, such as marae (Māori cultural epicentre). From there we consider the use of such encounter spaces for intercultural dialogue between our own and other indigenous psychologies, whereby networks of resistance, reciprocal care, and meaningful collaboration can take form. By focusing on such rituals of encounter we can better understand how indigenous scholars might open up spaces for collaboration and cooperation that can also support positive outcomes across a range of contexts.

An Invocation in a Time of Need

In drawing on Māori cultural concepts within this chapter to explore social practices for establishing intercultural dialogue, we recognise the plurality of the practice of pōwhiri and the dilemmas of attempting to tether such a dynamic ritual of intergroup engagement to a fixed definition (*cf.*, Mika 2015). What we provide is a simplified introduction to pōwhiri that is imperfect, and which cannot capture all that it entails. Like many practices inherent to Te Ao Māori (the Māori world), pōwhiri are not static, but rather reflect the evolving nature of our ways of being and encountering one another. As Pacific way finders and voyagers, Māori history has always been one of movement and adaption to shifting contexts and encounters (Groot et al. 2011). We will situate the social practice of pōwhiri within the moving social, cultural, economic, and spatial contexts within which Māori have come to dwell in response to colonial displacement and our encounters with diverse groups of peoples (Drury 2007; Stewart et al. 2015; Nikora et al. 2017; Walsh-Tapiata et al. 2018).

Although the shape and conventions associated with pōwhiri can be and are performed in almost any setting, they are at their most moving and spiritual when enacted against a backdrop of ancestral and tribal symbolism (*c.f.* Walker 1992; Nikora et al. 2012). As such, we will situate the practice of pōwhiri within the context of tangi (customary Māori death and mourning death rituals). This will enable us to foreground the ethos and values foundational to these cultural practices that provide a framework for engaging other indigenous knowledges and psychologies.

Tangi refers to a range of procedural mourning rituals, their beginning marked by the return of the deceased and the immediately bereaved to their marae (Māori cultural epicentre). It is understood that once the deceased arrives at the marae, the death must be shared with a broader grieving community, not just close family members (Nikora et al. 2012; Nikora et al. 2017). For Maori, the institution of tangi provides a customary way to respond to death. It is an enculturated pattern learned through repeat engagements beginning in childhood (Nikora 2007). At times of death, custom is a lifeline. It affords security, comfort and reassurance that all will be made right.

It is useful here to turn our attention to the marae, as a physical and spiritual location that remains central to Māori community life (Walker 1992). It is here that the social practice of pōwhiri as integral to tangi have been historically located. Maori are a tribal people with each tribe comprised of allied sub-tribal groups (hapū) that through genealogy and customary practices function to draw extensive networks of extended families (whānau) together as a political and caring community (Walker 1992; Nikora et al. 2012). The cultural heart of hapū is the marae, a community meeting place, often with elaborately carved buildings that symbolize the identity of those families that constitute the hapū (Walker 1992; Nikora vet al. 2012). The marae-complex itself can be understood as a Māori spatial formation for everyday living that is based on systems of kinship and which takes form through a collection of physical structures (Te Awekotuku 1996). It typically consists of a whare tūpuna (house of ancestors or the meeting house) with the marae ātea (courtyard) located in front of the house of ancestors, and a wharekai (dining hall) as well as an ablution block.

Although the marae is often thought of in such spatial terms, Te Awekotuku (1996) offers a more fluid and dynamic understanding of the marae: "For it is a Māori belief that wherever Māori people gather for Māori purposes and with the appropriate Māori protocol, a marae is formed at that time, unless it is contested" (p. 35). The marae, then, can be understood as both a place *and* as a network of culturally patterned relationships, reflecting the interconnectedness of physical locations and human action, and how such spaces are produced and reproduced in everyday life (*c.f.* Lefebvre 1974/1991; Tilley 1994). As Nikora, Masters-Awatere and Te Awekotuku (2012) note; "It is to these tribal lands and this culturally imbued environment and landscape, layered with spirit and memory, that Maori have traditionally returned to mourn and inter their dead" (p. 401). Pōwhiri are the shared template that we operate from in such times of need. In the next section we will outline the pōwhiri process against a background of grief and mourning imbued with ancestral and tribal meaning. This will allow us to convey the ethos that informs dialogical multiplicity from a Māori perspective.

Pōwhiri: Being Invited

Every time Māori 'encounter' rituals are performed the world is recreated. Encounter rituals such as pōwhiri; those patterned behaviours performed upon meeting, greeting and welcoming people, embrace and re-enact the very essence of the Māori cosmological universe (Marsden 2003; Rewi 2010; Nikora et al. 2012; Nikora et al. 2017). Such rituals speak to our lives shared together in the past and present - and the potential for ongoing dialogue in our futures. The intent of the pōwhiri is to ensure accountability to the universe, to transform visitors and to integrate tangata whenua (hosts) and maunhiri (visitors) so they can share in the purpose of the intended gathering (McCullum 2011). The role of manuhiri in this context is to provide assurance, they present a lifeline in a time of grief and shared devastation.

As groups of manuhiri (visitors) arrive at the gates of the marae to pay their respects, the kai karanga (the first voice) starts the proceedings by piercing the air with her invocation. She invokes and calls forth the rivers, mountains, ancestors, and our attention and emotion on a single held breath. The shape of her invocation is known as the karanga, which contain the first words exchanged between the two groups, with each group honouring the other by replying and in doing so paying careful homage to those they represent who have gone before. Pōwhiri are not held at random, the purpose of tangi is to care for the dead and the presence of the living is invoked to bear witness.

The karanga is not just an invocation from one person to another but a spiritual call that carries the mana of each group. Mana refers to an extraordinary power, essence or presence that applies to the energies within and beyond the natural world. There are as many degrees of mana as there are experiences of it, and life reaches its fullness when mana comes into the world (Royal 2019). There would be no pōwhiri without the karanga; "The mark of the karanga person is to be able to engender the emotion, is to break the stone heart of the warrior" (Temara 2011).

The karanga is typically performed by women who are viewed as possessing natural or intuitive abilities to connect others to Te Ao Wairua (the spirit world), this opens a safe pathway for people to cross into the scared space of the marae atea. It requires magnificent mental and emotional preparation (McCullen 2011). As such, the karanga births a space of transformation that is generated by women who bring to the fore their personal ihi (authority, charisma, awe-inspiring psychic power), which encompasses the physical, spiritual and psychological elements of their very being (McCullen 2011). Experiencing the cry of the kaikaranga (the invoker) can feel like a discernible cold chill racing through your spine, lifting the hairs on the back of your neck. This is because karanga is a manifestation of wehi or the effect that one person's power has on another (McCullen 2011). Now the formalities of dialogue can begin.

At this stage of the pōwhiri for incoming manuhiri (visitors), the orators have a platform from which to rise. Speakers for each group are chosen who will carefully consider the foundations of the conversation that has brought them all together. The speakers establish relatedness. In the marae context, when groups of extended whanau gather, everyone has a place, a purpose and a responsibility. Hui means to gather, and there are many reasons Maori might come together (Salmond 1976). One obvious reason within the context of tangi, is to consider the issues impacting families and to make decisions on how they can support one another (Love 2000). As Love (2000) notes, hui gather together people who matter, who can provide guidance and resources, who can show leadership and a pathway forward. Through the process of hui, people seek inclusion, actively listen, express views and ideally reach an agreed upon outcome (Nikora et al. 2012). However, this is not enduring, there will always be uncertainty as the conversation does not simply end here, responsibility toward one another is ongoing and accountability is forever. But if everyone is happy, then in that moment the world has been successfully recreated and following the ritual cleansing of the deceased's house and feasting, the process is completed. The family is released back to the mundanity of everyday life (Nikora et al. 2012). In the following section we move beyond culturally distinct spaces to consider how such encounter rituals allow for intercultural dialogue between our own and other indigenous psychologies.

Marae Atea: Spaces of Encounter

The marae atea (the courtyard in front of the ancestral house) is not only a two-dimensional space. Marae Atea stretch beyond and above its physicality to become multi-dimensional and cosmic. The word 'atea' denotes not merely a threshold but a space of infinite potential (McCallum 2011). The atea can be viewed as a microcosmic reimagining of Papatūānuku and Ranginui. Papatūānuku (the land) is a powerful feminine life-force who bestows many blessings upon her children. From a Māori world view, the land gives birth to all things, including humankind, and provides the physical, emotional and spiritual basis for all life. Ranginui (the great heavens) was joined with Papatūānuku in a lover's embrace before their children, who lived between them in the deep wetness of infinite darkness, separated them and brought our world forth. McCallum (2011) poses that the liminal space created in the separation of these entities can be understood as the first marae atea, a space of human interaction and encounter. The melting down of the boundaries between the physical and metaphysical - time and space - in the sacred space of the marae atea allows for encounters to be adapted beyond the physical boundaries of the marae. Thus, the underpinning ethos forged within this space can be disseminated outside of the marae in many ways and can invoke members not physically present.

Although somewhat limited in its translation of spirit or spirituality, the concept of 'wairua' has been identified as an intrinsic part of the Māori psyche (Barnes et al. 2017). Wairua (spirit) is central as is mauri (life force), the two combined and embodied allow for life. As Hohepa Kereopa describes (Hohepa Kereopa cited in Moon, 2004, p. 92), all animate things have mauri and wairua. Mauri enlivens and animates providing energy and vitality, and, more importantly, a place for wairua to reside and flourish. As mauri dissipates though the dying process, life wanes and eventually ceases; the way opening for wairua to journey beyond flesh and into an afterlife. As Nikora and colleagues (2017) have discussed, in the Māori after-life, judgement is not an aspect of death or spiritual journeying.

The role of wairua and spirituality is integral to indigenous knowledge sharing and building networks of survivance between Māori and other peoples. Spirituality is the connective thread that links us as indigenous peoples across tribes, flesh, nations, colonial borders, histories, diasporas, and oceans – it is the restorative force that reunites us. Pōwhiri grabs at those engaged in it from the inside and they are able to experience its spiritual force in ways made manifest only to them. In embracing our own spirituality through such rituals of encounter Māori also open a space for other indigenous groups to engage with their own spiritual processes and ways of being. This is important because spirituality is integral to Indigenous knowledge exchange and efforts to connect with one another and share. It is a core element in how we and other Indigenous peoples understand ourselves and each other as healthy relational beings. These overlapping cultural values are brought to the fore during pōwhiri no matter where the encounter ritual occurs. This is because when Māori seek to encounter and know others, we consider all these dimensions.

The resulting shared ethos that underpins the practices we have outlined in this chapter have survived because of their ability to be adapted within a range of new spaces where Māori dwell and interact with others (King et al. 2018; Marsden 2003; Te Awekotuku 1996). These now include schools of psychology in our universities and social service providers, where Māori have experienced increased participation in recent years. In many ways, marae-like structures, in the relational sense, are formed on a daily basis within colonial institutions when Māori meet for Māori purposes following Māori protocols. Through these culturally patterned encounters, a shared ethos can be established that enhances the collaborative efforts of Māori with other indigenous peoples and knowledges.

Establishing a Shared Ethos

As is reflected in the continued enactment of cultural practices such as pōwhiri and the underlying values and concepts inherent to these, Māori psychology maintains a position of strength. What we have offered here is evidence of our desire and will to engage with other indigenous psychologies and in doing so to share our ways of being, engaging and collaborating. Similarly, Māori psychology is adaptive and evolving as we populate new spaces, encounters and relationships. What Māori psychology does offer is a unique way of thinking and engaging with each other; one which implicitly desires and creates space for dialogue.

In this chapter, we have focused on a particular ritual of encounter and dialogue as a pathway for managing the uncertainties that often occur when groups come together to explore the nature of their relationships, to resolve tensions and to decide whether to cooperate. As such, there are many possible outcomes that could emerge from an encounter. This is because as opposed to a multiplicity of characters within a unified world, there is a plurality of consciousnesses located in different worlds (Mika 2015; McCullum 2011). Within the context of pōwhiri, both tangata whenua (hosts) and manuhiri (visitors) alike are not only drawn into a shared space for encounter, but enter a liminal state, which encourages emotional and ontological shifts, the outcomes of which are cloaked in uncertainty for participants (McCullum 2011).

By focusing on the process of pōwhiri we are able to raise some of the complexities of Māori engagements with other groups and how we enter into intercultural dialogue. However, it remains to be seen what the outcomes of our connections might be moving forward together. Relevant here is Friere's (1970) understanding of dialogical action, which involves co-operation, unity for liberation, organisation and cultural syntheses whereby the 'oppressed' deconstruct legitimising self-narratives, discover the oppressor and themselves including their ability to change reality and challenge unequal power relations. These challenges to liberation for indigenous peoples are better faced when we are armed with our own cultural-spiritual knowledge of being. Moreover, in recognising each other as fully realised human beings we make way for a deep sense of connectedness in the liberation struggle and beyond. The inherent potential to connect, and through connection expand our efforts, lends itself to knowledge sharing between and across time, space and cultures. Being available for one other has been an important guideline in our emerging work with other Indigenous groups, including Amerindian peoples. It is through our collaborations that we can develop shared knowledges and strategies for action.

Indigenous psychology in Aotearoa New Zealand is anchored by, and emerges from, a worldview that values balance, continuity, unity, purpose and interconnection (Nikora 2007). It is not widely written about, yet it is understood and assumed by Māori, and acted upon and expected (Nikora et.al. 2017). We need psychologies that speak to diverse contexts (Watkin and Shulman 2008). Central to the approach we have outlined in this chapter are efforts to build solidarity and dialogues for change within and between different socially positioned indigenous communities. Such moves from centre to margin, from colonising to indigenising research, demand and contribute to the democratization of psychological knowledge (Land 2015; Watkins and Shulman 2008).

References

Barnes, H. M., Gunn, T. R., Barnes, A. M., Muriwai, E., Wetherell, M., & McCreanor, T. (2017). Feeling and spirit: developing an indigenous wairua approach to research. *Qualitative Research, 17*(3), 313–325.
Canales, M. K. (2004). Taking care of self: healthcare decision making of American Indian women. *Health Care for Women International, 25*, 411 e435.
Cram, F., Smith, L., & Johnstone, W. (2003). Mapping the themes of Māori talk about health. *New Zealand Medical Journal, 116*(1170), 1 e7.
Durie, M. (2001). *Mauri Ora: The dynamics of Māori health*. Auckland: Oxford University Press.
Durie, M. H. (1985). A Māori perspective of health. *Social Science and Medicine, 20*, 483–486.
Durie, M. (1999). Marae and implications for a modern Māori psychology: Elsdon best memorial medal address polynesian society annual general meeting. *The Journal of the Polynesian Society, 108*(4), 351–366. Retrieved from http://www.jstor.org.ezproxy.auckland.ac.nz/stable/20706887
Drury, N. (2007). A Pōwhiri Poutama approach to therapy. *New Zealand Journal of Counselling, 27*(1), 9–20.
Freire, P. (1970). *Pedagogy of the oppressed*. London: Penguin Books.

Guimarães, D. (2018). Towards a cultural revision of psychological concepts. *Culture & Psychology, 25*(2), 135–145.

Hill, P., & Smith, G. (2010). Coming to terms with spirituality and religion in the workplace. In: R. A. Giacalone & C. L. Jurkiewicz (Eds.), *Handbook of workplace spirituality and organizational performance* (pp. 171–185). Routledge: Abingdon.

Hussain, D. (2011). Spirituality, religion, and health: reflections and issues. *Europe's Journal of Psychology. 7*(1), 187–197.

Lee, C. C., & Armstrong, K. L. (1995). Indigenous models of mental health intervention. In J. G. Ponterotto, J. M. Casas, L. A. Suzuki, & C. M. Alexander (Eds.), *Handbook of multicultural counseling*. Thousand Oaks: Sage Publications.

Li, W., Hodgetts, D., & Koong, F. (Eds.) (2019). *Asia-pacific perspectives on intercultural psychology*. Palgrave: London.

Izquierdo, C. (2005). When "health" is not enough: Societal, individual and biomedical assessments of wellbeing among the Matsigenka of the Peruvian Amazon. *Social Science & Medicine, 61*, 767 e783.

Mark, G. T and Lyons, A, C. (2010). Māori healers' views on wellbeing: The importance of mind, body, spirit, family and land. *70*(11), 1756–1764.

Marsden, M (1992) God, man and universe: A Māori view. In: K. Michael (Ed.), *Te Ao Huirhuri: Aspects of Māoritanga* (pp. 117–137). Reed Books: New Zealand.

McCallum, R. (2011). Māori performance: Marae liminal space and transformation. *Australasian Drama Studies*, (59), 88–103,205. Retrieved from http://ezproxy.auckland.ac.nz/login?url=https://search-proquest-com.ezproxy.auckland.ac.nz/docview/1290646676?accountid=8424.

McClintock, K., Mellsop, G., Moeke-Maxwell, T., & Merry, S. (2012). Pōwhiri process in mental health research. *International Journal of Social Psychiatry, 58*(1), 96–97.

Mika, C. T. H. (2015). "Thereness": Implications of Heidegger's "presence" for Māori. *11*(1), 3–13.

Nikora, L. W., Masters-Awatere, B. & Te Awekotuku, N. (2012). Final arrangements following death: Maori indigenous decision making and tangi. *Journal of Community & Applied Social Psychology, 22*, 400–413.

Nikora, L. W., Awekotuku, N., & Tamanui, V. (2017). Home and the Spirit in the Maori World. In U. L. Vaai & U. Nabobo-Baba (Eds.), *The relational self – Decolonising personhood in the Pacific* (pp. 153–162). Suva: The University of the South Pacific and the Pacific Theological College.

Ratima, M. (2008). Making space for Kaupapa Māori within the academy. MAI Review 1.

Richmond, C. A. M., & Ross, N. A. (2009). The determinants of First Nation and Inuit health: a critical population health approach. *Health & Place, 15*, 403 e411.

Robbins, R., PhD., & Hong, J. Y., PhD. (2013). Building bridges between spirituality and psychology: An indigenous healer's teachings about befriending the self. *Journal of Transpersonal Psychology, 45*(2), 172–197. Retrieved from http://ezproxy.auckland.ac.nz/login?url=https://search-proquest-com.ezproxy.auckland.ac.nz/docview/1519077647?accountid=8424

Stewart, G., Karaitiana, K. and Mika, C. (2015). 'Infinitely welcome: Education pōwhiri and ethnic performativity', *Mai Journal, 4*(2): 91–103.

Tangihaere, T. M., & Twiname, L. (2011). Providing space for indigenous knowledge. *Journal of Management Education, 35*(1), 102–118.

Te Ahukaramū Charles Royal, 'Te Ao Mārama – the natural world – Mana, tapu and mauri', Te Ara – the Encyclopedia of New Zealand, http://www.TeAra.govt.nz/en/te-ao-marama-the-natural-world/page-5. Accessed 10 July 2019.

Walsh-Tapiata, W., Simmons, H., Meo-Sewabu, L., & Umugwaneza, A. (2018). Pōwhiri: A safe space of cultural encounter to assist transnational social workers in the profession in Aotearoa New Zealand. In A. Bartley & L. Beddoe (Eds.), Transnational social work: Opportunities and challenges of a global profession (pp. 155–170). Bristol/Chicago: Bristol University Press.

Wilson, K. (2003). Therapeutic landscapes and first nations peoples: An exploration of culture, health and place. *Health & Place, 9*, 83e93.

Index

A
Affective body, *see* Self cultivation
Affective experiences
   aesthetic synthesis, 88
   anthropological structuralism, 90
   Boesch's cultural psychology, 90
   Boesch's symbolic action theory, 90
   broader symbolic sense, 92
   cognition of reality, 91
   dialogical process, 91
   identities-realities, 91
   ideology, 90
   imagination and perception, 92
   intrapersonal simulations, 92
   mythical narratives, 89
   myths, 88–90
   poetic experience, 92
   psychophysiological unit, 91
   social narratives, 88
   social relation, 92
   social roles, 91
   spaces of experience elaboration, 93
   symbolic actions, 92
   transformative process, 93
Affective-cognitive conditions, 132
Affective-cognitive dimensions, 131
Amerindian Support Network, 2, 20, 37
   community, 98, 99
   cultural processes, 101
   deconstruct and reconstruct, 100
   indigenous lands and communities, 100
   Indigenous Network, 98
   psychology students' elaboration, 98
   team's support, 100, 101
   theoretical and practical education, 101

B
Behaviouristic instruction, 139

C
Center of Indigenous Education and Culture (CECI), 30
Cultural psychology, 135, 143
Cultural tradition
   cognitive-affective tuning process, 48
   cross-cultural psychology, 47
   dialogical relations, 49, 50
   direction of knowledge construction, 47
   discursive communication to complex constructions, 49
   extra-linguistic factors, 48
   extra-verbal situation, 48, 49
   intercultural experiences, 47
   intercultural parallelism, 60, 61
   limited perceptions and imagination
      activity of transforming, 64
      classical philosophy and psychology, 62
      complex relation, 62
      construction of divergent meanings, 65
      degrees of reflexivity, 65
      dialogical oppositions, 64
      extra-verbal condition, 66
      extra-verbal elements, 66
      historical/social experiences, 63
      interethnic situations, 66
      perception and imagination, 62
      psychological function, 63
      psychological processes, 62
      semiotic-cultural constructivism, 64, 65
      symbolic elements, 65

Cultural tradition (*cont.*)
  symbolic resources, 65
  type of knowledge, 62
  visiting outsiders, 66
 linguistic processes, 48
 logical and concrete-semiotic relations, 50
 mutual affective transformations, 66–68
 nature
  active properties and perspectives, 56
  characteristic naturalism, 57
  constitutive of knowledge, 55
  diversity of perspectives, 57
  intentionality and consciousness, 55
  notion of dialogical multiplication, 56
  public forums, 54
  researcher's personal-cultural perspective, 55
 observant participation, 47, 50
 perspectives
  certain psychological theories and practices, 53, 54
  interethnic dialogue, 53
  interethnic field, 53
  interethnic relation, 53
  ontological categories, 54
 polyphony, 49
 psychological knowledge construction, 47
 recursive temporality, 58–60
 special attention to indigenous speeches, 47
 structural particularities, 49
 theoretical-methodological dialogism, 48
 theoretical-methodological grounds, 48
Cyclopes, 26

D
Decolonization, 121
De-delude psychology, 132
Dialogical multiplication, 8, 131, 140
 equivocation, 130
 interdisciplinary relations, 130
 myth and logos, 129
Dialogism, 8, 48, 71
Disquieting experience, 8, 9, 17, 18, 23
Dynamics of involvement and self-transformation
 academic psychologies, 73
 diverse psychologies, 72
 inconsistent versions, 73
 interethnic dialogues, 71
 psychological theorization, 71
 scientific psychology concepts, 72
 self-determination, 73
 triadic alter-ego-object model, 71

E
Ecological epistemology
 academic community, 3
 bodily transformations, 6
 course of life, 2
 cultural activities, 3
 cultural innovations, 7
 cultural psychology, 7–10
 dialogical multiplication, 7
 ethnic-cultural nature, 2
 feed-forward approach, 4
 institutional level, 3
 interdisciplinary border, 7–10
 interethnic dialogue, 3
 knowledge construction, 5
 philosophical concepts and scientific categories, 4
 scientific knowledge and method, 4
 self-ethnic affirmation, 2, 3
 semiotic-cultural constructivism, 5
 subjectivizing/objectivizing, 6
 technical-scientific knowledge, 5
 unconventional methodology, 4
 university extension project, 3
Empirical self, 105, 106
Epistemic self, 116, 123
Extra-verbal situation, 48, 49, 51, 75, 76

H
Hermeneutics, 28
Historical-cultural context, 114
Human flexibility, 137

I
Indigenous psychology, 27, 131, 147, 158
Interethnic relation
 anthropological experience, 94
 asymmetry, 97
 community, 94
 ethnic group, 95
 form of prejudice and preconceptions, 96
 horizontal wave line, 96
 initial non-directive conversations, 97
 interlocutor's discourses and gestures, 96
 internalization of relations, 95
 I-other relations, 94
 name-giving and participation, 95
 progressive development, 97
 selective availability, 97
 social difference, 93
 social field, 95

Index

social model, 96
social relations, 93
social roles, 96
steps of tuning, 97

K
Knowledge construction, 106, 112–114

O
Observant participation, 47, 50

P
Personal context, 137–139
Phenomenological sociology, 8
Philosophy of alterity
  audiovisual recordings, 29
  communicative skills, 15
  concrete and conceptual resistance
    academic community and public, 29
    demand, 29
    differentiation and dedifferentiation, 26–28
    diversity of indigenous, 14
  education
    CECIs, 30
    classical educational model, 32
    cognitive-affective involvement, 35
    community, 30, 33, 34
    construction, 30, 31
    customs and collective actions, 36
    development of responsibility and respect, 33
    elaboration of experience, 35
    ethnic-cultural perspective, 33
    facing colonial and post-colonial marginalization, 36
    human mind and body-standardizing package, 32
    intercultural and interethnic equity condition, 31
    knowledge exchanges, 32, 33
    multiple sociocultural spaces and contexts, 34
    negotiations, government institutions, 36
    social division, 34
    teaching-learning relation, 31
    traditional and scientific knowledge, 31
    umbrella-shaped pedagogical structure, 33
  ethical issues
    adaptation process, 24
    cultural shock, 20, 21
    cultural tunes, 24
    demands constructing and reconstructing views, 22
    essential anarchy of multiplicity, 21
    interethnic dialogue, 25
    interethnic relation, 25
    interpersonal exchanges, 25
    justice and rights, 20
    match-and-mismatch relation, 21
    mutual learning, 23
    ordinary social situations, 22
    point-of-view battlefield, 22
    semiotic walls (SW), 24, 25
    sense of responsibility, 22
    social field, 22
    social multiplicity, 21
    social relations, 21
    susceptibility and subjectivity, 21
    translating indigenous languages, 25
    violence, 23
  partnership construction and collaborative projects, 29
  psychological issues
    cognitive development, 20
    communication/cultural manifestations, 17
    complex sociocultural circumstances, 16
    cultural shock, 15
    diversification and complexity, 15
    ethnic and cultural diversity, 15
    human societies and cultures, 19
    intense emotional responses, 16
    intercontinental nautical explorations, 16
    match-and-mismatch, 18
    mermaids and cyclops, 18
    population and familiar languages, 16
    psychologist's cultural and epistemological positions, 20
    social and material environment, 20
    sociocultural and psychological determinants, 19
    unease, confusion and dispersion, 15
  publication, 29
  travelling, interethnic arena
    adequate environment for communication, 42
    cosmological foundations, 40
    CRPSP meetings, 36
    differentiated healthcare and education, 38
    differentiation and dedifferentiation, 38
    form of listening results, 37
    forms of sensibility, 37
    general academic community, 36

Philosophy of alterity (*cont.*)
  indigenous communities, 37
  indigenous speeches, 37
  leaders' speeches, 37, 39
  non-indigenous audience, 37
  non-indigenous healthcare and
    education professionals, 40
  notion of spirituality, 41
  opportunities, 39
  partnership construction, 38
  personal and collective experiences, 41
  personal and social experience, 37
  problematic attitudes, 37
  problem-solving attitude, 37
  project's formal submission, 42
  psychological intervention projects, 42
  psychologists and indigenous leaders,
    37, 38
  psychosocial vulnerabilities, 37
  semantic rectifications, 40
  spirituality, 41, 42
  surrounding society and mistrust
    rearises, 38
  valuable and intimate, 41
  victimization, 40
Pōwhiri, 151, 153, 158
Psychology
  concepts and theories, 140
  cultural-conceptual tools, 105
  cultural phenomena, 107
  disciplinary issues, 130
  field of dispersion, 105
  historical-cultural and philosophical
    views, 105
  historical-philosophical foundations, 105
  human sociocultural experiences, 105
  knowledge construction, 112–114
  knowledge production and validation, 107
  multiplying psychologies and conditions,
    123–126
  radical transformations, 106
  researcher's tradition, 112–114
  self-contradictory field, 105
  socio-historical transformations, 106
  subjectivity, 106

R
Regional Council of Psychology of São Paulo
  (CRPSP), 29
Resembling the other
  aesthetic-affective experiences, 85
  basis of knowledge construction, 87
  cognitive-affective feelings, 85

cycle of knowledge, 88
heterogeneous rhythms, 88
interethnic encounters, 85
internalizing cognitive-affective
  schemes, 86
intrinsic and spontaneous actional
  variations, 86
process of assimilation, 88
symbolic action, 86
symbolic relation, 87
transformation, human development, 85
tuning process and semiotic elaboration, 85

S
Self-contradictory field
  contemporary psychologies, 111
  diversity of study objects, 108
  field of dispersion, 109
  fundamental alliances and conflicts, 111
  historical-cultural process, 111
  historical dialectical materialism, 109
  human consciousness products, 108
  human development, 110
  materialism and idealism, 108
  objective physiology, 108
  psychophysiological isomorphism, 109
  risk of inconsistency and irrationalism, 111
  social field, 110
  territory of ignorance, 110
  theories and systems, 110
  theory and method construction, 111
  thought and matrixes, 109
  university community service, 112
Self-critique movement, 28
Self cultivation
  academic culture, 79
  alterity relations, 78
  cognitive-affective elaboration, 76
  communicative processes, 84
  cultural practices, 84
  cultural productions, 81
  cultural relations, 83
  dialogical interaction, 74
  dialogical multiplication, 78
  dialogical relation, 78
  dialogical unit, 75
  duality, 80
  emotional-expressive function, 82
  experience of temporality, 83
  feelings/thoughts, 75
  field of sharing and interaction, 77
  irreversible and linear character, 79
  language and ontogenetic development, 81

non-verbal thought and non-intellectual language, 82
organizing cognitive-affective experiences, 76
psychological development, 76
recursive and irreversible dimensions, 80
recursive transformations, 80, 81
semiotic mediation, 80
semiotic organization of feelings, 84
social reality, 74
structured linguistic relations, 74
temporality, 83
thought and language processes, 76
transformations, 79, 82
verbal and intellectual activity, 82
visual depiction, 84
Semiotic-cultural constructivism, 7
Semiotic resistance, 18, 24
Shamanism, 54, 122, 123
Social and social pedagogical work, 141, 142
Social complexity
  academic environment, 119–120
  assimilation and accommodation, 117
  cognitive ability, 115
  coordinating and co-regulating actions, 123
  cultural heterogeneity, 117
  epistemic self, 116, 123
  ethnic group, 118, 119
  forms of knowledge, 122
  historical-cultural trajectories, 119
  indigenous, 120–123
  intellectual and political movements, 121
  intercultural dialogue, 121
  interethnic mediation, 120
  interethnic relation, 122
  internal heterogeneity, 117
  layers, self, 117
  logical and rational critique, 116
  logical-argumentative elaborations, 123
  psychological space, 116
  school and academic contexts, 116
  scientific development, 122
  scientific knowledge, 116, 122
  semi-structured interviews, 118
  society and culture, 116
  society, knowledge and human development, 115
  symbolic resources, 118
  teaching environment, 115
Social constructivism, 9
Social representations, 140, 143
Socio-historic psychology, 28
Spirituality, 156

T
Temporality, 52
Theoretical and methodological innovation, 4, 7
Tradition, 105, 106, 109, 112, 125
Trial-and-error approach, 141

W
Wairua and spirituality, 156
Western, Educated, Industrialized, Rich and Democratic (WEIRD) societies, 47